CLAIMS TO FAME

CLAIMS TO FAME

Celebrity in Contemporary America

JOSHUA GAMSON

UNIVERSITY OF CALIFORNIA PRESS
BERKELEY   LOS ANGELES   LONDON

University of California Press
Berkeley and Los Angeles, California

University of California Press, Ltd.
London, England

© 1994 by
The Regents of the University of California

Library of Congress Cataloging-in-Publication Data

Gamson, Joshua, 1962–
    Claims to fame : celebrity in contemporary America / Joshua
Gamson.
        p.   cm.
    Includes bibliographical references and index.
    ISBN 0-520-08352-0 (alk. paper). — ISBN 0-520-08353-9 (pbk. :
alk. paper)
    1. Celebrities—United States—History—20th century. 2. Popular
culture—United States—History—20th century. 3. United States—
Social life and customs—20th century. I. Title.
E169.G25   1994
973.92′092′2—dc20   93-28188
                                                                               CIP

Printed in the United States of America
9 8 7 6 5 4 3 2 1

For Zelda and Bill,
in continual and loving celebration

Contents

Illustrations

Acknowledgments

Although I am tempted to blame them on television, the shortcomings of this book are my own. Although I am tempted to take full credit for them, the insights of this book would not have been possible without the support and companionship and ideas of many others.

Financial support made it possible for me to focus my energies and eat at the same time. The Doreen B. Townsend Center for the Humanities at the University of California at Berkeley provided a fellowship for the first year of research and writing, and a Spencer Fellowship from the Woodrow Wilson National Fellowship Foundation saw me through the second year.

Kenneth Turan at the *Los Angeles Times* and Cathy Fischer at Home Box Office were key to helping me get started in Los Angeles. They generously spent time orienting me to the entertainment industry and connecting me to interview subjects. Friends Britt Tennell and Carolyn Helmke made entertaining and insightful celebrity-tourism companions. In the San Francisco Bay Area, two teachers, Barbara Blinick and Jeff Steinberg, kindly opened their classrooms to me.

My thinking and writing were pushed along by the sharp, thoughtful comments and criticisms of a number of colleagues and friends. They often pushed in different directions, and I benefited from struggling with the variety of opinions. In particular, I am grateful to Todd Gitlin, Ann Swidler, David Kirp, Michael Schudson, Michael Burawoy, Gaye Tuchman, Charles Ponce de Leon, Leo Braudy, and Zelda Gamson. Naomi Schneider at the University of California Press went to bat for me and the book and saw me through the review process with directness, humor, and support. I am especially grateful to my father, Bill Gamson, who at critical points listened and helped me talk my ideas through, wandered with me through my brain, and sorted out the directions it was taking me.

In addition to my family, numerous other friends, Mark Murphy in particular, kept things in perspective when the project took over too much of me. They carried me away when I claimed I needed to work, accompanied me to foreign films when I had overdosed on American popular culture, and laughed with me when Jodie Foster and Madonna began making regular appearances in my dreams. For that I cannot thank them enough.

Finally, the voices heard throughout this book are those of numerous industry workers and celebrity watchers who volunteered to spend time and share their thoughts with me. With respect and gratitude to them, I hope that their voices and others join mine to keep the discussion going.

Explaining Angelyne

The oddity of Angelyne is as obtrusive as the breasts in her eighty-five by forty-four foot portrait near Hollywood and Vine. In that 1987 mural, as in subsequent Los Angeles billboards, Angelyne is leaning back under her own giant pink name, looking out from behind sunglasses and from under a bleach-blonde hairdo, one shoulder bare, Dolly Parton chest pushed front and center. She acts like a celebrity, according to *Los Angeles* magazine, stopping "for any Kodak-ready spectator, effortlessly gliding through her repertoire of soft-core poses," signing "scores of autographs on a never-ending supply of full-color picture postcards, adding a kiss to each, leaving her perfect-pink-lips imprint."[1] Yet Angelyne has never done anything noteworthy beyond the attempt to have note taken of her. According to *People* magazine, she is "untalented by her own admission" and "has nothing to offer but her inflated, billboard-size image."[2]

Talent has nothing to do with it: she wants to be celebrated not for doing but for being. "A celebrity is famous for being a celebrity," her assistant, Scott Hennig, explains to me. "She wants to be famous for simply being Angelyne, for being the magical, Hollywood blonde bombshell of the twenty-first century."[3] (And she is not, according to her own and various other accounts, a put-on character that she takes off at home, but simply Angelyne.) Her dismissal of talent is not accidental, but part of Angelyne's philosophy of celebrity. "What do you think a celebrity is?" she asks. "It's someone sent to us as a gift, to bring us joy."[4] She was born a celebrity-in-waiting and needed only to be introduced to the world. As she puts it in an interview in the *Los Angeles Herald Examiner,* "I never felt 'normal' until I became a celebrity."[5] Angelyne, says the *Herald Examiner*'s theater critic, is trying to "demonstrate that 'everyone can make it!'—presumably, with qualifications no greater than Angelyne herself. Warhol's prophecy fulfilled with a vengeance! A teeming horde of roseate superstars so multitudinous they swallow up the entire populace and eradicate, once and for all, the distinction between artist and spectator."[6]

From the beginning, however, her celebrity was consciously engineered. Her high-capital promotion was first assumed by Jordan Michaels, a rock 'n' roll manager and promoter,[7] then taken up in 1982 by Hugo Maisnik, a display-printing veteran who financed her image on bus shelters and later on billboards. "This is a multi-million-dollar project," says her assistant, perhaps, but not necessarily, waxing hyperbolic. Maisnik has developed an Angelyne-doll prototype ("it's beautiful, with enormous breasts") and has even considered using a laser technique to project her image "a mile wide on the clouds" ("just imagine it, Angelyne's picture and name, in bright pink lights, flashed across the sky worldwide"). "I look forward to Angelyne without Angelyne," he says, "when just her name is an entity in itself."[8] To some degree the strategy has worked. She has appeared in scores of magazines and on television programs not only in Los Angeles but in Australia, England, France, Italy, Spain, Japan, Germany, and Sweden, claims over 2,000 members in her American fan club, and even converted her billboard-generated notoriety into a small movie role (in *Earth Girls Are Easy*), in which she played a character exactly like the billboard Angelyne. Angelyne herself noted the simplicity of her strategy back in 1987: "I can feel myself getting more and more famous every day."[9] (See figure 1.)

It is tempting to dismiss Angelyne as just another sexist stereotype, given the most visible pieces of her strategy: the objectified body and commodified sexuality, the auto-shop calendar image, the appeal to the "male gaze."[10] And of course she partakes of those things, although in such an exaggerated form that her image could easily be taken as ironic commentary on itself. It is also tempting to dismiss her as amusing and trivial and unlikely to join the ranks of the glamour queens she emulates and cites. And she does also partake of the trivial.

As a story of celebrity, however, Angelyne is not dismissible, not anomalous, not an accident of history. In fact, she pushes a host of questions into high relief. A first set concerns the relationship in practice between fame and substantive claims to it. Is it possible to bypass work, action, achievement, and talent and head straight for notoriety? Is celebrity a

Figure 1. Celebrity as product: "I can feel myself getting more and more famous every day." Angelyne, ca. 1991. Photo: Richard Sullivan.

commodity that can be manufactured through publicity, not by building an audience but by building the perception that one already exists?

Angelyne also raises questions about celebrities' meanings as images and texts. What are we to make, for example, of her insistent superficiality, the dependence on a single image (her "logo," as her assistant calls it), the odd vision of "Angelyne without Angelyne," in which disembodied names alone are famous? What of the claim that celebrities are born with magical selves and the simultaneous visibly active publicity strategies, suggesting that she is being made a star even as she claims celebrity as her inevitable, natural fate?

Angelyne seems open, moreover, to a range of interpretations for those encountering her: a glamorous personality deserving of attention; a talentless, pathetic climber; a demonstration that anyone can make it; a campy, ironic comment on blatant fame seeking; a person, a persona, or a character. How is she understood? When the public reads about or takes snapshots of celebrities, how are these celebrity watchers interpreting the celebrities and their claims to attention?

I became interested in exploring the peculiarities of celebrity culture in graduate school, through my evening encounters with "Entertainment Tonight," a television program that can generously be called lightweight. When Mary Hart, the "ET" anchor whose celebrity derives from a chipper reading of teleprompted words about entertainers, received a star on the Hollywood Walk of Fame, I called friends, my mind spinning. When the *New England Journal of Medicine* reported that Hart's voice was triggering an unidentified viewer's epileptic seizures ("she experienced an upset feeling in the pit of her stomach, a sense of pressure in her head and mental confusion,"[11] perhaps a more common reaction to Hart than the report suggested), friends called me.

My interest went beyond amusement. I was astonished, confused. What were these people doing in my life? How had they gotten there? And why was I lapping this up, so thrilled by the details? I did not fit the stereotype of the bored and gullible viewer; I was an established cynic, a Ph.D. candidate from an academic family. If even I was so enthralled by the trivia, how varied might the population of celebrity watchers be, how diverse their activities? I began to tap into the weird world of what for many people in this country, including myself, had become the stuff of everyday life. I wanted first of all to unlock that strangeness.

How? What exactly requires investigation? This book does not directly tackle celebrity in every arena of contemporary life, but focuses on enter-

tainment celebrity, for several reasons. Entertainment is clearly the dominant celebrity realm in this century; it is also the most fully rationalized
and industrialized. It is therefore typically used as a model for the development of celebrity in other realms (politics, for example) and the model
against which critics tend to argue. Understanding entertainment celebrity
promises to help us comprehend celebrity as a general cultural phenomenon: its peculiar dynamics, its place in everyday lives, its broader implications. (Comparisons with other realms, explicit only in my closing discussion of political celebrity, should be kept in mind as we confront
entertainment celebrity: for example, do the worlds of television, literature, and politics operate according to the same production logics? Are
entertainment, medical, academic, and sports celebrities all of a piece?
Although the conclusions I draw regarding entertainment celebrity cannot
be applied to other domains without careful analysis, they do provide
ways to think through celebrity culture across these realms, helping us
to sort out dangerous games from healthful ones and warning signs from
signs of promise.)

Even narrowed to entertainment, the topic is huge. The analysis presented here breaks it down into the key elements making up any cultural
phenomenon: texts, producers, and audiences. Thus, in addition to giving
a composite sketch of the history of celebrity, Part I looks at selected
twentieth-century magazine, newspaper, and broadcast celebrity texts to
ascertain what has been and is being *said*. Next, based on interviews with
Los Angeles celebrity-industry workers (publicists, agents, managers,
bookers, producers, performers, and journalists) and on participant-
observation in celebrity-based settings (television-show tapings, award-
show spectator crowds, the Los Angeles tourist circuit), Part II focuses
on the present production setup. There, I try to determine what is *done*
to acquire, maintain, and make use of celebrity. Finally, Part III examines
self-designated celebrity-watching audiences, making use of focus-group
conversations, along with the observational data, to analyze how people
actively encountering celebrities *interpret and use* celebrity images. (The
Appendix takes up both the sociological theories informing this approach
and the research methodology taken to implement it; there I argue that
celebrity provides sociologists of culture with an especially striking and
challenging case study in the production and reception of culture.)

Distinguishing these main elements of the massive celebrity phenomenon clears paths that can then be linked. How do production processes
and interest-driven activities affect what is said and received? How do

these processes and activities show up in the text, and what happens to
the discourse when they do? How do audiences understand production
activities, and how do producers perceive audiences and build them into
their own work? The discussion is guided by the connections between
discourse, production, and reception of entertainment celebrity—and by
the gaps between them.

That is the overall tack the book takes in unpacking the celebrity phenomenon. But I am begging the question that ought to nag those who do
not share my peculiar, confused relationship to celebrity culture and thus
my peculiar need to make sense of it all: why bother? What difference
does any of this make? Why take Angelyne or Mary Hart or Michael
Jackson or Madonna or Tom Cruise seriously at all?

To begin with, as the saying goes, because they are there. They occupy
a large space in many Americans' daily lives, and that space has been
for the most part unexplored. Effective studies have approached stars
as textual phenomena ("images" and "signs"[12]) and as a status group
("power elites"[13] and "powerless elites"[14]), and interesting writers have
occasionally reflected on "the culture of celebrity."[15] The territory as a
whole, however—audience interpretations, in particular, but also the relationships between discourse, production, and audiences—has been tremendously underexamined.

The space celebrities occupy, we will see, is not necessarily a deep one,
and the experience of it is not necessarily weighty. The time, resources,
and energy devoted to it are all the more puzzling. Indeed, in this book
the often blatant shallowness of the entertainment celebrity arena is taken
as a starting point, and the challenge will be to mine the superficialities
for their depths.

I am among many, of course, who have waded these shallows. Mass
commercial culture has triggered compelling and vehement criticism for
quite some time, and particularly in the past several decades. Moored
in traditions both left and right, as varied and venerable as Marxism,
Puritanism, classicism, and republicanism, these now-familiar critiques
suggest that we take consumer culture very seriously.[16] Contemporary
culture is seen as ugly or dangerous, a symptom of an American decline
into decadence, ignorance, and triviality, or a cause of such declines.
Surface has overwhelmed substance, image has overtaken reality, truth
is "submerged in a sea of irrelevance,"[17] imitation and copying have dis-
placed originality and imagination. Passivity has replaced involvement,
the values of "life-style" and consumption have pushed aside those of

work and production. Commercial culture is system-preserving distraction, an "opiate," an ideological tool, its satisfactions illusory.

Commercial culture, it is argued, guts public life through both "complacency and the inappropriate transfer of consumer values to other arenas of life."[18] We Americans, argues Neil Postman for example, are "amusing ourselves to death." Public discourse is rendered "simplistic, nonsubstantive, nonhistorical and noncontextual" by the packaging of information as entertainment.[19] Stuart Ewen similarly suggests that, under the culture of commerce, "information becomes style," history becomes "a market mechanism, a fashion show," and truth becomes "that which most people will buy."[20] Others, descendants of the Frankfurt Institute theorists of the 1930s and 1940s, forcefully suggest that the culture industry does crucial maintenance service for an exploitative social or economic system.[21] "Silly amusement, contrived distraction, and endless hype," Michael Parenti has recently asserted, for example, "become the foremost means of social control."[22]

A cornerstone of these arguments is that, as one recent pair of critics put it, "unreality has become in effect our primary mode of reference." New technologies can make "the unreal look so real that we cannot tell the difference between the two," and deliberate distortion can make "the unreal so entertaining that we no longer care about reality."[23] This is not only a pop-critical argument but one that draws on theoretical writings of poststructuralist literary criticism. Writing about "simulacra" and the "hyperreal," for example, Jean Baudrillard argues that we have entered "the age of simulation" in which "it is no longer a question of imitation, nor of reduplication, nor even of parody. It is rather a question of substituting signs of the real for the real itself."[24] We live in a world in which "the distinctions between object and representation, thing and idea, are no longer valid," a "strange new world constructed out of models or simulacra which have no referent or ground in any 'reality' except their own."[25]

These are all profound concerns, and concerns rightly focused on the tie between culture and the directions taken in social and political life. The implications for American *democracy* in particular abound. If information is provided according to entertainment criteria, how is meaningful public discourse possible? If having things is valued above doing things, how is meaningful democratic participation possible? If social control is achieved invisibly, through fun, how is social change possible? Does democracy remain democratic if authenticity and reality and truth are no longer discernible, if they themselves are mimicked, stylized, and marketed?

Few offer answers. Often a return is prescribed, a reversal, an overthrow of empty images. "The dominance of surface over substance must be overcome," says Ewen. "There must be reconciliation of image and meaning, a reinvigoration of a politics of substance."[26] Understandably, the question of how the prescription can be filled often goes unanswered, the difficulty of finding a way out noted in tones of frustration. When they do push further, those seeing dangers in commercial culture want to educate the public, building a sort of critical immunity. Postman, for whom the fundamental problem is the impact of television watching, claims that "the solution must be found in *how* we watch," in "media consciousness." Only "through a deep and unfailing awareness of the structure and effects of information, through a demystification of media, is there any hope of our gaining some measure of control."[27] Parenti argues similarly. "Resist we must," he writes. "The public is not able to exercise much democratic control over image manipulation unless it is *aware of the manipulation.* The first step, then, is to develop a critical perspective. When it comes to the media, *criticism is a form of defense.*"[28] Audiences, in order to face reality head-on, must be exposed to the people behind the curtain. Knowledge is power: by making the creation of commercial culture visible, it is often suggested, a more informed and oppositional stance can be built among those living within it.

This, then, is the most fundamental reason to get serious about billboard queens and television talk-show guests. Because its objects are so concrete and apprehensible—living, directly visible, human—celebrity is a choice arena in which to watch these alleged processes of commercial culture at work, to raise and examine questions about the directions American democratic life has been taking. Indeed, when their eyes turn directly to celebrity culture, social critics see concrete, embodied evidence of pathology. Celebrity might logically be seen (following William J. Goode) as a system of prestige, as (following C. Wright Mills) "the American forum for public honor." Mills interpreted the professional celebrity as "the crowning result of the star system in a society that makes a fetish of competition. . . . It does not seem to matter what the man is the very best at; so long as he has won out in competition over all others, he is celebrated."[29]

The more common claim, however, is that this portrayal is outmoded, almost nostalgic. Instead, it is argued that "celebrity has entirely superseded heroism,"[30] a perspective captured by Daniel J. Boorstin's well-known definition of the celebrity as a "human pseudo-event," a person who is "known for his well-knownness."[31] The phenomenon itself is a sign of cultural emptiness and groundlessness. Recently able to manufacture fame, we "have willingly been misled" into mistaking the signs of greatness for its presence, confusing "the Big Name with the Big Man." Americans may fetishize competition, but they have allowed the commercial cultural enterprise to render competition meaningless. The winner is not the "best at" anything, except of course at getting attention. In fact, even if we wanted to find heroes, "Big Men" (and Women), we now have little hope of distinguishing them from pseudo-heroes. "Our illusions are the very house in which we live," wrote Boorstin. "We risk being the first people in history to have been able to make their illusions so vivid, so persuasive, so 'realistic,' that they can live in them."[32]

Boorstin's persuasive take on fame has soundly dominated the bits of mainstream intellectual writing on celebrity that have since appeared, as illustrated by the following snippets from a 1978 *Harper's* essay by John Lahr:

> Visibility is now an end in itself. . . . Celebrity turns serious endeavor into performance. Everything that rises in America must converge on a talk show. . . . Whoever is the most visible holds the most sway. Modern politicians (Hitler, Eisenhower, Nixon) have understood this and taken lessons from actors. . . . Attention-getting becomes the national style in which gesture replaces commitment. . . . The famous, who make a myth of accomplishment, become pseudo-events, turning the public gaze from the real to the ideal. . . . Fame is America's Faustian bargain: a passport to the good life which trivializes human endeavor. . . . Fame dramatizes vindictiveness as drive, megalomania as commitment, hysteria as action, greed as just reward.[33]

Barbara Goldsmith, writing in the *New York Times Magazine* in 1983, argues similarly that "we" neither distinguish nor care to distinguish real from imitated quality.

> The line between fame and notoriety has been erased. Today we are faced with a vast confusing jumble of celebrities: the talented and the untalented, heroes and villains, people of accomplishment and those who have accomplished nothing at all. . . . We no longer demand reality, only that which is real seeming. Our age is not one in which the emperor's golden nightingale is exposed as valueless when the true pure voice of the real bird pours forth, but one in which the synthetic product has become so seductive and malleable that we no longer care to distinguish one from the other. . . . As our lives become more and more difficult to comprehend, we become so accustomed to retreating into our illusions that we

forget we have created them ourselves. We treat them as if they were real and in so doing we make them real. Image supersedes reality. Synthetic celebrities become the personification of our hollow dreams.[34]

James Monaco, introducing a collection of essays on celebrity, suggests that celebrity involves a recognition of social life's inherently fictional nature.

Before we had celebrities we had heroes. . . . Now, what these hero types all share, of course, are admirable qualities—qualities that somehow set them apart from the rest of us. They have *done* things, acted in the world: written, thought, understood, led. Celebrities, on the other hand, needn't have done—needn't do—anything special. Their function isn't to act—just to be. . . . The qualities of our admirations are distinctly different, and the actions of heroes are often lost in a haze of fictional celebrity unrelated to the nonfictional heroism. . . . Already it's clear that the once essential differentiation between fact and fiction no longer operates usefully. Truthfulness—verism—is an adolescent affectation. No one presents himself directly, even among friends. Everyone is more or less fictional, made up, constructed.[35]

The themes repeat themselves: the trivialization of endeavor, commitment, and action; visibility as its own reward; the elimination of distinctions between deserving and undeserving people; the seductive replacement of real life with artificial image; and the increased inability to make such distinctions—even more important, the lack of interest in making them.

These themes are crucial starting points for this book, but as arguments they leave many important questions unanswered and many important assumptions unjustified. A quieter, but nonetheless significant, set of voices has countered the hand-wringing critiques, arguing that commercial culture is not nearly as powerful, and those consuming it not nearly as powerless, as the critics propose. These voices demand closer attention to and greater respect for the consumers of commercial culture. "Is a consumerist orientation to goods necessarily passive?" asks Michael Schudson. "There are degrees of activity in consumption just as there are degrees of disengagement in labor."[36] Critics need to recognize, Andrew Sullivan has argued in a similar vein, that "even within the captivity of consumerism, the consumer still has some room to maneuver: that she can choose this fantasy over another, this product over another; that she can outwit by mockery, humor—or even simply boredom—the schemes of an industry at much at war with itself as it is intent on capturing her."[37]

More fundamentally, these voices challenge social criticism's privileging of work as the grounding for human identity. "Why treat consumption, a priori, as peripheral to key matters of human fulfillment?" Schudson asks. Why assume, moreover, that satisfactions from commodities are necessarily "illusory"? "Normally they are quite real," he asserts. "The critics may see them as distractions, but they can also be seen as authentic sources of meaning."[38] The shallowness of style, Sullivan contends, can contain a liberation—a "genuine release from mundanity," a "fleeting freedom, but a freedom nonetheless"—that ought not to be disregarded.[39] Criticizing commercial culture as mystifying pap involves dismissing those consuming it, those living sometimes happily within it, as mystified dupes.

It is the ambition of this book to dismiss neither the concerns of the critics nor the pleasures and freedoms and meanings that participants in entertainment-celebrity culture derive. I mean to confront them with each other and to complicate the critiques, often smart but nearly always speculative, with my own research. I mean to turn the critical claims into questions. When I turn to the celebrity discourse, I want to know: What has been and is being said about the connection between celebrities' notoriety and their internal qualities? What have celebrity texts had to say about the celebrity industry through which celebrities arise? What happens to the celebrity text when it begins to include the story of its own production, when image making becomes visible? When I turn to the practices of the celebrity industry, I want to know: To what degree do celebrity producers in fact attempt to manufacture celebrities-as-commodities rather than discover deserving candidates? How are the tensions between the "natural" and the "artificial" practically managed? Do celebrity-industry workers try to keep their own activities hidden from public view, to protect their manipulations by masking them? When I turn to the celebrity-watching audiences, I want to know: What are they doing with celebrity stories, and what are they taking out of them? What relationship between merit and celebrity do they find? To what degree are audiences aware of production activities and to what degree are they "mystified"? Do they read the celebrity text as realistic representation or as fiction?

In pursuing the answers to these questions, honoring both critics of celebrity culture and its everyday participants builds in analytical tension. In fact, the pictures drawn in the pages that follow suggest that celebrity culture is itself built on major American fault lines: simultaneous pulls on the parts of producers and audiences alike to celebrate individual distinction and the equality of all, to demonstrate that success is available to all and available only to the special, to instate and to undermine a meritocratic hierarchy, to embrace and attack authority.

These broad cultural struggles are anchored, moreover, in everyday conflicts rarely noticed before. Who controls the various profits from visibility, who gets to cash in the currency of celebrity, who controls valuable information? These are the working issues for celebrity-industry workers. And audiences are often involved with the celebrity text in their own submerged power games: Who defines "truth" and "reality," who can be trusted and who cannot, when is manipulation acceptable and when must it be resisted? In the end, it is these cultural tensions and these everyday conflicts—and whether and how they might be operating in arenas outside of entertainment—that need attention, that promise nourishment from amidst the shallow, the amusing, and the odd.

Part One

The Celebrity Text

Chapter One

The Great and the Gifted:
Celebrity in the Early
Twentieth Century

"It is, we are sure," wrote the editor of the movie fan magazine *Silver Screen* in the 1930s, "impossible to be great part of the time and revert to commonplaceness the rest of the time. Greatness is built in."[1] In the late 1960s, a *TV Guide* writer took issue with this claim, describing a "peculiar machine" in American culture. "It was conceived by public-relations men," she wrote, "and it is a cross between a vacuum cleaner and a sausage maker. It sucks people in—it processes them uniformly—it ships them briskly along a mechanical assembly line—and it pops them out at the other end, stuffed tight into a shiny casing stamped 'U.S. Celebrity.' "[2] Two decades later, Andy Warhol's claim that "in the future everyone will be world famous for fifteen minutes" had become the most famous statement on fame. "Well, Andy, the future is now," wrote the editors of a 1988 *People* magazine report. "Fame's spotlight darts here and there, plucking unknowns from the crowd, then plunging them back into obscurity."[3] How did this central American discourse migrate from fame as the natural result of irresponsible greatness to celebrity as the fleeting product of a vacuum cleaner/sausage maker?

This is the story of two stories. In one, the great and talented and virtuous and best-at rise like cream to the top of the attended-to, aided perhaps by rowdy promotion, which gets people to notice but can do nothing to actually make the unworthy famous. In this story, fame is deserved and earned, related to achievement or quality. In the second story, the publicity apparatus itself becomes a central plot element, even a central character; the publicity machine focuses attention on the worthy and unworthy alike, churning out many admired commodities called celebrities, famous because they have been made to be. Contrary to ahistorical popular mythology, the stories have actually *coexisted* for more than a century, usually in odd but harmonious combinations—with seeds planted much further back in time. Over the course of this century, however, the balance between them has shifted dramatically.

It is this shift that I intend to trace. The roots reach far back into the history of Western civilization. As Leo Braudy amply demonstrates in his history of fame discourse, the ambition to stand out from the crowd, to be known by those not known to one, to make an impact on time, is not at all new. Alexander the Great, Braudy argues, "deserves to be called the first famous person" in that he sought "to be remembered not for his place in an eternal descent but for himself."[4] By literally mythologizing himself—constantly relating his achievements to those of established heroes and gods—he *created* Alexander the Great from Alexander III of Macedonia. Even the explicit manipulation of public image, the acknowledged gap between public and private selves so characteristic of contemporary politics, has some precedent in Julius Caesar's "taste for theater and symbolic staging," for which he was "stage manager, producer, and director" as well as actor. In fact, although he had been stabbed twenty-three times, Caesar managed to meet his death with an image-savvy act that previews contemporary American politics: he arranged his toga.[5]

It is often assumed, and sometimes argued, that the characteristics of contemporary fame are new, products of modern "mass culture" alone. A focused glance at history forces an immediate recognition that the basic celebrity motifs of modern America were composed long before the development of mass-cultural technologies. Beginning in earnest in the seventeenth century, tensions arose between interior and exterior selves, between public and private lives, and between egalitarian and aristocratic interests.

We can also tease out of history the crucial relationship of attention-garnering strategies and technologies to the shape of the fame discourse. Changes in the organization, availability, and visibility of fame technologies have pushed certain themes to the forefront and tangled the two stories—fame as rise to greatness and fame as artificial production—in particular, curious unions.

Coins, Speeches, Portraits:
Premodern Western Fame

The key Western traditions establishing notions of fame contributed themes that are now familiar. Roman fame celebrated public action "for the good or ostensible good of the state." The early Christian tradition developed an alternative, a "fame of the spirit," a "fame of being" rather than of action. Literary fame, a "fame of the wise, the private contemplator of time rather than its public master," took shape alongside and within these traditions. The pursuit of fame was, however, limited to those with "the power to control their audiences and their images"—that is, political and religious elites. The early discourses firmly established fame as the province of the top layer of a natural hierarchy.[6]

Moreover, those who would build fame were limited in their strategies and audiences. Images could be publicized and revised on coins, for example, but little information could be conveyed this way. Oratory, along with the sponsorship and composition of literary and historical writings, was a key strategy, but not far-reaching. These were worlds of "slow communication and brief lives," where audiences were not immediate but were developed over many years, "as certain figures gather[ed] around themselves layer upon layer of interpretation."[7]

In the sixteenth century, the new technologies of printing and copper engraving began to challenge the aristocratic fame discourse. They allowed for the widespread dissemination of images, with a more broadly based use of the individual face. "Faces," Braudy writes, "were appearing everywhere."

Images of the wise, the artistic, the holy, and the powerful began to be published widely as examples of contemporary heroism, alongside freshly minted models for the ways one could act, dance, dress, or even preach with the proper gestures and body movement. . . . Everyone who made a career in public—and the number of public professions was speedily increasing—was being made to realize how both art and printing could make him more symbolic, more essential, and more powerful. Whatever holy aura had attached to the image, whatever link with eternity was asserted by the book, was becoming accessible to all who cared to make their claim. . . . It was a new world of fame, in which visible and theatrical fame would become the standard.

By the seventeenth century the pursuit of fame was clearly becoming democratized. More and more people occupied the public stage—"merchants, tradesmen, and lawyers put on festivities as elaborately theatrical as those of royalty"—in front of an ever-expanding audience.[8]

The very early experience of fame, though, lacked more than media by which to immediately reach an audience; missing as well was a developed notion of individuality. What Braudy calls the "dissemination of the unique," initially through printing and portraiture capturing the individual face in the midst of life, awaited "the coming of a new sense of character."[9] The major social changes preceding the Renaissance opened a path for new experiences of the self: the breakdown of fixed, inherited social roles, the subsequent increased social mobility, and the new social interactions of the city, all meant a heightened awareness of the impact of other peoples' expectations on one's fate. In the new "market culture" especially, in which one was selling oneself on the marketplace, economic exchange was becoming "increasingly mysterious and opaque." "Without rituals and conventions to ensure that both parties were on the level, opportunities arose for exploitation and misrepresentation. A new premium began to be placed on 'performance,' on presenting manipulable 'fronts.' Men hid their motives and intentions from those who might use this information to gain advantage."[10]

A new, theatrical, other-oriented sense of self was growing up. Along with it, new anxieties developed about what a self *is*. The question began to be raised: Is the self a manipulable performance for others or an enactment of fixed character? The public realm began to be experienced as untrustworthy, "an endless round of confidence games," to be distinguished from the private realm, where the " 'real' self could be displayed."[11] The new notion of self, an exterior and an interior in questionable relation, laid the ground for a heightened play of images and, in turn, for increased individuation through those images.

By the time of the early American republic, then, the fame discourse began to accommodate the emerging market-self. New writings appeared to "explain and illuminate the 'mechanics of representation and misrepresentation.' "[12] With the dramatic broadening of fame's producers and audiences, fame began to be conceived not as the "validation of a class distinction" but as the personal possession of any worthy individual. In its democratized version, particularly strong in early America, the discourse was characterized by a "paradoxical uniqueness," a compromise between an aristocracy of the personally distinguished and an egalitarian democracy in which all are deserving. "Praise me because I am unique," went the logic, "but praise me as well because my uniqueness is only a more intense version of your own." The emphasis, still, was on an out-standing individual nature or character. But although the fame of the "great man" was generally one of distinctive inner qualities, they were qualities that could potentially exist in any man. (Women, almost entirely excluded from public life, were also excluded from this early mythology of public greatness.) The famous great man combined democratic egalitarianism and personal distinction, being "unprecedented without being un-recognizable."[13] Aristocratic and egalitarian strains were linked with the fragile splice of paradox.

Moreover, everyday life contained more and more ways to make greatness visible. The popular "cult" of George Washington, for example, transformed a man of "ordinary and unremarkable characteristics into an image of heroic proportions," according to Barry Schwartz. Through written and oral accounts of his early life and actions, through paintings, engravings, statues, bank notes, sheet music, children's primers, through physical sites linked to his exploits and named after him, and through ceremonies and holidays dedicated in his honor, "most Americans came to know Washington indirectly, through his cult, and his veneration depended on the capacity of that cult to keep him continually in the forefront of the popular imagination."[14] The story being told, of course, was definitively about his greatness, the public virtues that "earned" him fame, not about the primitive publicity media at the core of the cult. Yet built into the telling of the story was a hint of anxiety about those mechanisms at work building public reputation. The "real" Washington was to be found by considering his private life: according to early editions of Parson Weems's biography of Washington, it was not enough to judge Washington great on the basis of public character, which is "no evidence of *true greatness,* for a public character is often an artificial one."[15] The story of greatness as the root of fame quietly contained the skepticism born in the early production of images, the notion of a gap between the public and private self that can be bridged only by digging into the self's "interior."

The Sucker as Expert:
Barnum and Nineteenth-Century Celebrity

In the middle of the nineteenth century, a series of dramatic changes in the media of publicity and communication established celebrity as a "mass" phenomenon. Newspapers began to spread with the invention of the steam-powered cylinder press in the early 1800s. By mid-century, there had developed new technologies—the telegraph in particular—that allowed information to move without being constrained by space. The idea and practices of "context-free information" began to solidify, such that the value of information was no longer necessarily "tied to any function it might serve in social and political decision-making and action, but [could] attach itself merely to its novelty, interest, and curiosity."[16] Information was now transportable through space and, thus freed, could be bought or sold. With the arrival of the rotary press in the mid-1840s, the subsequent growth of widely available and affordable "penny press" papers, the founding of the newswire services, and the professionalization of reporting, encounters with the names and activities of many people one didn't know became a daily experience—and a business.[17]

The penny press, expressing the "heightened suspicion of public fronts," innovated reporting styles that "put a premium on exposure."[18] As the newspaper industry took off, publishers fighting for a competitive edge in the increasingly information-dense environment, spurred by the circulation wars and the introduction of "yellow journalism" in the last quarter of the nineteenth century, made stories about *people* a central feature of journalism. "What was vital," writes Richard Schickel, "was the symbol." In particular, newspapermen like Joseph Pulitzer and William Randolph Hearst sought "human symbols whose terror, anguish, or sudden good fortune, whatever, seemed to dramatically summarize some local event or social problem or social tragedy."[19] Names, in short, began to make news.

In the meantime, photography was taking a strong hold in the latter half of the century, with the halftone print perfected by the 1880s. Photography, of course, meant encountering not only a name and a description of a stranger but also a realistic image. Imaging was no longer in the hands of those who could paint or engrave, nor was it available only to the rich; now it was at nearly everyone's disposal. By the time of Abraham Lincoln, for example, the *carte de visite,* a calling card with photograph and signature, was in wide circulation. (Lincoln, in fact, said he owed his election in part to the *carte de visite* made of him by photographer Mathew Brady.)[20]

With photography, wrote Oliver Wendell Holmes in 1859, "form is henceforth divorced from matter." This is a divorce driven, Holmes points out, by economics. Matter is fixed, form cheap and transportable; "we have got the fruit of creation now, and need not trouble ourselves with the core." As a result, Holmes argued, "every conceivable object of Nature and Art will soon scale off its surface for us. Men will hunt all curious, beautiful, grand objects, as they hunt the cattle in South America, for their *skins,* and leave the carcasses as of little worth."[21] Like the new journalism, photography pushed toward the publicizing of surfaces and, by making "the dissemination of the face even easier than that of the reputation or the ideas," toward the publicizing of people.[22]

If anyone brought the "hunt for skins" to the American cultural scene, it was P. T. Barnum. Publicity stunts were standard early-journalistic fare and were often revealed; as early as 1835 the *New York Sun* boosted its circulation with a series purporting to describe life on the moon (four-foot tall, winged creatures with apelike features romping across lush landscape), suffering no damage with the revelation of the hoax.[23] But with Barnum and his claim to cater to the "sucker born every minute," the showman-publicist and the publicity system became active parts of the discourse on fame.

Barnum was, first of all, an innovator in the activity of press agentry. His subjects were superlatives—the best, the strangest, the biggest, the only—made superlative through image management. In his early days, these subjects were generally "freaks": the Fejee Mermaid (actually the top part of a mummified monkey attached to the bottom part of a dried fish); singing, dancing, joke-telling midget General Tom Thumb (Charles S. Stratton); Anna Swan, the "tallest woman in the world"; Siamese twins Eng and Chang. Later, he specialized in the huge spectacular: the circus, the American Museum. Throughout, writes one biographer, "his main instrument was the press, which he played like a calliope. While still young he learned the lesson that any publicity was good publicity."[24] His first hit, Joice Heth, was an ex-slave alleged to have been George Washington's nurse, announced by Barnum to be 161 years old. When her audiences dwindled, Barnum sent an anonymous letter to the papers, a tactic which soon became habitual. "The fact is," he wrote, "Joice Heth is not a human being [but] an automaton, made up of whalebone, india-rubber, and numberless springs." Sales took off again. Jenny Lind, the "Swedish Nightingale," was little known in the United States before her promotion by Barnum. After a flood of Barnum-promoted stories about her, she was met on arrival by some 30,000 people, under Barnum-created banners, and went on to a very successful national tour.[25] As Barnum himself put it, "I thoroughly understood the art of advertising, not merely by means of printer's ink, which I have always used freely, and to which

I confess myself so much indebted for my success, but by turning every possible circumstance to my account."[26]

Barnum was not simply publicly promoting the performers, however; he was publicly performing the promotion. He became an international figure for the *way* he focused attention to create fame and illusion. "First he humbugs them," a ticket-seller once told, "and then they pay to hear him tell how he did it."[27] Barnum himself was a show. In his multivolume autobiography, one of the most widely read books of the later nineteenth century, he revealed the tricks of attention gathering and image creation, taking readers behind the scenes with the humbug.[28] The activity involved playing with reality more than definitively marking it off. His was a newly active audience, "willing to be manipulated but eager to convey how that ought to be done more expertly."[29] He played to what Neil Harris has called the "operational aesthetic," a "delight in observing process and examining for literal truth" as a "form of intellectual exercise, stimulating even when the literal truth could not be determined."[30] Shuttling his audiences between knowing the tricks and believing the illusions, Barnum brought publicity mechanisms and questions of artifice to the forefront.

Film and the Early Twentieth-Century Star System

Barnum, however, was extraordinary. Attention getting and image management were common but practiced relatively unsystematically until the early twentieth century, when professional public relations and film technology began to develop. As industrial power grew in the first quarter of the century, so did conscious policies of managing public attitudes to retain that power. Corporations "began to *recognize* a public for the first time: business moved from ignoring the public, or damning it, in the nineteenth century, to advising and accommodating it through public relations, in the twentieth century."[31] The first independent publicity firm was founded in Boston in 1900. Ivy Lee, who had transformed John D. Rockefeller's image from callous businessman to magnanimous benefactor, relentlessly promoted "the art of getting believed in."[32] By the 1920s, led by Edward Bernays, the profession of "counsel on public relations" was well established; Bernays taught his first course in the field in 1923 at New York University.

The new publicity professional represented a departure from showman press agentry. The "art" was not simply getting attention (any publicity is good) but "getting believed in" (only publicity that promotes the desired image is good). The public-relations counsel, Bernays argued, "is not merely the purveyor of news, he is more logically the *creator* of news."[33] The growth of public relations thus involved radical changes in the ideology and practice of news. "What had been the primary basis for competition among journalists—the exclusive, the inside story, the tip, the scoop," writes Michael Schudson, "was whisked away by press releases and press conferences." Image management, which had earlier been haphazard, was now a profession; and newspapers, which "had once fought 'the interests,' now depended on them for handouts."[34]

This period also marked the birth of modern American consumer culture.[35] Over the last quarter of the nineteenth century and the first quarter of the twentieth, amusement activities moved rapidly into the center of everyday American life. As the national product grew (tripling between 1870 and 1920), the work week declined, and household expenditures, especially in consumer goods such as "amusements, leisure pursuits, clothes, appearance, furniture, and automobiles," exploded (tripling between 1909 and 1929). As women entered the work force, they became a new consumer power; as urban areas grew (from 28 to 52 percent of the population between 1870 and 1920), they provided new, centralized markets.[36] The business of leisure was booming. As celebrity became systematized in the early twentieth century, the leisure-time business of "show" was, not surprisingly, its primary arena: famous people as entertainment and entertainers as famous people.

This new system grew up, of course, around the new technologies of film. In 1894, the world's first kinetoscope parlor opened in New York City. Within a few years, short moving films had been integrated into the preeminent popular entertainment of the time, vaudeville, which provided easy access to a receptive audience. The films were short, and vaudeville's presentational format accommodated them easily.[37] By 1905, a new distribution system ushered in a boom in film exhibition. The nickelodeon—nickel-a-show displays in rented storefronts, restaurants, or amusement parlors, based primarily in urban, immigrant neighborhoods—dominated until around 1912.[38] In 1908, 400 small theaters, up from 50 in 1900, showed movies to approximately 200,000 people daily in New York.[39] An estimated 8,000 to 10,000 nickelodeons were in operation around the country.[40] The possibilities for mass, industrial production of film entertainment were becoming clear.

The custom in stage theater, touring companies, burlesque, and vaude-

ville of using featured "players" (actors) to attract audiences had not
made the transition to early film. Filmmakers in the first decade of the
twentieth century sometimes referred to players simply by "singling out
a striking physical feature of the nameless owner"—such as "the girl with
the curls," "the sad-eyed man," "the fat guy."[41] In part, players were not
named and advertised because "names" cost money. In part, early film
directors "saw their art as separate from the entertainment popular with
the rich and the immigrants" and subordinated character to the "larger
message of the plot."[42] Finally, exhibition in nickelodeons—twenty- to
sixty-minute programs, morning to midnight, often changing daily—was
a handicap to the emergence of film stars since, with "no time for word-
of-mouth publicity to build up a following" for actors, "they might not
be available for very long when the fans wanted to see them."[43]

How, then, did the American star system begin to emerge? Most film
historians locate the innovation in the bitter struggles for domination of
the new film industry.[44] In 1908, Edison and Biograph joined forces to
form the Motion Picture Patents Company (MPPC), which essentially
controlled the industry. Independent producers actively opposed and
competed with the MPPC. Although there is some dispute among historians about whether independents or trust companies were the first to promote their players, it is clear that the breakdown of film anonymity arose
out of this climate of competition.[45] In March 1910, for example, Carl
Laemmle, in an attempt to give his independent production company an
edge, demonstrated the possibilities of star building. He hired Florence
Lawrence, whose face was already recognizable as "the Biograph Girl,"
and apparently planted a story of her tragic, untimely death. In Barnumesque style, he subsequently denounced the story as a lie and as proof
announced Lawrence's appearance in St. Louis, where she made a tremendous publicity splash.

Industry competition also pushed developments in film production.
Most important, single-reel programs were replaced by feature-length
films, which by 1915, clinched by the success of D. W. Griffith's *Birth
of a Nation*, became the norm.[46] The feature film, with higher production
costs, "required a special and individualized promotional effort" and a
new marketing and distribution system not met by nickelodeons.[47] Studios
began to draw on established actors from the stage to promote these new,
more expensive films. In 1909, the Edison Company began publicizing
its acquisition of theatrical players from Broadway producers; in 1910,
Leman and Vitagraph introduced lobby-card photo displays of their act-

ing companies.[48] Also in 1910, the first movie fan magazine, *Photoplay*, was founded, followed quickly by others.

Movie manufacturers, now firmly committed to mass production, adapted the star system to the industry's needs. In particular, producers needed product differentiation to stabilize demand and price, especially crucial given the intangibility of the film product. Early attempts at demarcating their products without using players had not been especially successful. At first, producers used their own trademarks, which apparently were not distinguishable enough to fans. Next, they tried narratives. In 1911, *Motion Picture Story*, an early fan magazine, asked its readers to choose their favorite film stories, and, "instead of the expected answers, the magazine was deluged with inquiries about favorite players. The fact that audiences distinguished films by stars became inescapable, and accordingly, the producers began to utilize talent as a successful strategy for differentiation."[49] Knowledge about players became key, providing a progressively "more elaborate grid through which the actor's identity could be specified and differentiated, and thus a more supple and powerful means of promotion."[50] The advantages of the star system had become abundantly clear to film manufacturers, and the studios moved quickly to institutionalize it.[51]

By the 1920s, film performers were essentially studio-owned-and-operated commodities. The system was extensive and tightly controlled—successfully so because of the high integration of the industry—encompassing production, distribution, and exhibition of films.[52] Studio control of actors' images was anchored in legal contracts. The usual contract for stars and feature players tied them to the studio for seven years; each year, the studio could either renew (with a set salary increase) or drop. While some employees were very well compensated, they often had little control over the direction of their careers and could even be "loaned out" for appearances in damaging movies as a disciplinary measure. Typically, an actor agreed to "act, pose, sing, speak, or otherwise perform solely and exclusively" for the contracting studio, to promote films through personal appearance tours, and to give the studio control of his or her name and likeness in advertising and publicity. Buster Keaton's contract went so far as to forbid him from laughing in public.[53] After the conversion to sound, contracts were amended to allow substitution of one actor's voice by another at the studio's discretion.[54]

Controlling an actor, of course, did no good unless he or she could become a semiguaranteed draw. Despite technological and organizational changes in the film industry, the strategies developed during this time for manufacturing and using celebrity remained essentially intact until the early 1950s—and many remain today. Some celebrity building was conducted through simple fabrication. "In those days," veteran public-relations man Henry Rogers says, "we had absolutely no scruples, no ethics, no morals, no nothing." Rogers recalls his strategy for giving Rita Hayworth a boost:

This was really a great hustle. One day I sent Rita Hayworth, who was a small-time player under contract, a telegram. I made up the name of an organization, and I made up the name of the president, and I told her this organization had selected her as the best-dressed offscreen actress in Hollywood. I made this up out of the proverbial whole cloth. She called me one day and said, "I have this telegram you should see." So I went over, and I said, "I'm going to do something with this." And I went to the West Coast editor of *Look* and said, "I have a helluva story for you. Here is a girl who nobody in Hollywood knows, and this distinguished organization selected her as the best-dressed. You should send a photographer out to her house and shoot the wardrobe and do a layout of this girl." Now that was the biggest lie, because she had no clothes. Two days later he called and said he was sending a photographer out. So we convinced the general manager of Saks to loan us probably fifty dresses, and we told them we would say in the magazine that she always buys her clothes at Saks. That layout resulted in a cover on *Look* magazine, and that really launched the career.[55]

Rita Hayworth was preceded by Theda Bara, an actress with no established onscreen reputation who was given a name and an exotic background to establish her reputation offscreen. She was publicized as the Egyptian offspring of "a sheik and a princess, given in mystic marriage to the Sphinx, fought over by nomadic tribesmen, clairvoyant and insatiably lustful." The public personality, built by exhibitor and producer William Fox, would match the future screen image; her 1914 publicity tour preceded her films. Fox popularized Bara "by using the attributes of stardom as a substitute for it."[56]

This merging of screen roles and offscreen personality was central to studio star making, though usually accomplished with less direct fabrication. Studios would essentially "test market" the image through fan mail, sneak previews, exhibitor preferences, and box office grosses;[57] then promote the personality through advertising, stunts, rumors, and feature stories and photos; then release and exhibit their films in premieres and opulent theaters that underlined the stars' larger-than-life images.[58] Finally, the studio publicity departments took over to match the star's personal life with the traits of the screen character. "The publicity would be in accordance with the roles that they were trying to sell," Henry Rogers says. "So when MGM knew that Joan Crawford was playing a hooker in *Sadie Thompson,* the publicity that was going out at the time would be very racy, and the still photos of her would be very sexy." Publicity, advertising, and "exploitation" crews—organized together like newspaper city rooms, and with 60 to 100 employees at their height—would actively create and manipulate the player's image.

To begin, the department manufactured an authorized biography of the star's personal life based in large part on the successful narrative roles of the star's pictures. The department would disseminate this information by writing features for fan magazines, press releases, and items for gossip columns. A publicist would then be assigned to handle interviews and to supervise the correct choice of makeup and clothing for public appearances. Finally, the department had glamour photographs taken that fixed the important physical and emotional traits of the star in the proper image.[59]

The "audience was assured that the star acted identically in both her 'real' and 'reel' lives."[60]

Like the new public-relations profession, the studios depended on manipulating not only attention but also belief. Critical to the early building of stars was the building of an image that did not *appear* to emanate from the studio. The studios, as gossip Hedda Hopper described them in her autobiography, lived in "stark terror of God's honest truth" about the machinery through which they produced "illusion"; they "couldn't afford to let the public glimpse the facts behind the fiction."[61] Studio press departments operated not only as promoters but also as protectors; press agents "were extremely successful in quieting the doubts that arose from the frequent lack of correlation between a star's skill and his or her success," and columnists "spent more time covering up dubious behavior than they did exposing it."[62] When scandals did explode—as they did often during the 1920s and 1930s—they were frequently used to produce more interest in a star, as long as they remained under studio control.[63]

These publicity activities took place within the power-from-the-top studio, with vertical integration allowing firm, though not seamless, jurisdiction. Moreover, the appetite for films, film stars, and their movie and private lives had by the 1920s become voracious. By the 1930s, Hollywood was the third-largest news source in the country, with some 300 correspondents, including one from the Vatican.[64] The most important outlets for celebrity stories were the film fan magazines (*Photoplay, Modern Screen,* and *Silver Screen* each had monthly circulations of nearly half

a million), the columns of gossip writers such as Hedda Hopper and
Louella Parsons (and, publicizing a broader range of people, Walter Win-
chell in New York), and profiles in general-interest periodicals.[65] With an
eager and sensationalizing press in place by the 1920s, and an integrated,
oligopolistic film industry—by 1930 dominated by the "Big Five" studios—image and information control were not especially difficult to
manage.

Routes to public visibility other than this production system still ex-
isted, of course, but the process had entered a period of industrialization.
The components of celebrity in the first half of the twentieth century were
visual media as "the prime arbiters of celebrity and the bestowers of
honor,"[66] a developed profession of public-image management, and an
elaborate and tightly controlled production system mass producing entertainment celebrities for a widely consuming audience.

Discovering the Gift:
Explanations of Fame in Early Texts

Greatness in its more traditional, aristocratic formulation—virtue, genius,
character, or skill that did not depend on audience recognition—remained
a strong model in many early magazine texts. "Greatness," asserted a
1930s author in *American Magazine,* "is always productive, never receptive. It is both imagination and will which give the genius his strength."[67]
The notion of a correspondence between greatness and fame, however,
was clearly threatened in the early consumer culture. The elite-serving
Vanity Fair, for example, was forever striving to distinguish the truly
"great" Hall of Famers from the merely popular.[68]

These postures were defensive, and understandably so. By the 1920s
the typical idols in popular magazines were those of consumption (entertainment, sport) rather than production (industry, business, natural sciences). By the 1940s, almost every hero biography featured a hero either
"related to the sphere of leisure time" or drawn as "a caricature of a
socially productive agent."[69] At the center of this new consumerist heroism were Hollywood and the movie stars. Hollywood represented a "leisure utopia," and "film idols presented national models as leisure experts."[70] Most writing about famous people reported on their private
lives and personal habits, their tastes, romances, likes, and dislikes. Fan
magazines took this sort of story to its extreme, reporting on the specifics

of "how stars spend their fortunes"; exhibiting his home, her pets, their swimming pools; providing their beauty secrets, dietary preferences, expenses, travel plans; offering advice from Douglas Fairbanks and Bette Davis.[71] While Ginger Rogers explained "why I like fried potatoes," Hedy Lamarr spelled out why "a husband should be made to shave."[72] Although entertainers were the clear model, all public figures met in this field of tastes: Greer Garson "likes potatoes and stew and never tires of a breakfast of porridge and haddock," while Mahatma Gandhi's "evening meal is simple—a few dates, a little rice, goat's milk."[73]

Not only did attention shift to entertainers and their personal lives, but these famous entertainers also underwent a gradual demotion of sorts over the first half of the century. Early on, the stars were depicted as democratic royalty (Mary Pickford and Douglas Fairbanks reigning), popularly "elected" gods and goddesses. Lifestyle reports focused on "the good life," the lavish Hollywood homes, the expensive clothing, the glamour those watching could not touch. But, pushed by the development of sound and film realism—and, I'll argue below, by deeper difficulties—the presentation by the 1930s had become more and more mortal, as "prettified versions of the folks who lived just down the block."[74] Rather than the ideal, celebrity was presented in the pages of magazines such as *Life* and *Look* as containing a blown-up version of the typical. "Stars now build homes, live quietly and raise children," a 1940 *Life* article explained. "Their homes, once gaudy and too ornate, are now as sensible and sound in taste as any in the country." And, as always, *Life* had the pics to prove it: "candid" shots of Merle Oberon playing blindman's bluff with her nephews on a suburban lawn, Brenda Marshall eating her "frugal breakfast" in a simple, bachelorette kitchen.[75] "Stardom?" said Clark Gable in *Screenland*. "I'm satisfied that it's a real job that will keep me out of mischief."[76] "The news from the rumpus rooms and the barbecue pits of the famous," as Richard Schickel describes it, "conveyed through the layouts in the Sunday supplements, the profiles in the thick, slick magazines, was that not only their pleasures, but their most basic values were virtually indistinguishable from our own—despite the fact that they were better supplied with terrific recreational equipment."[77] (See figure 2.)

Such ordinariness promoted a greater sense of connection and intimacy between the famous and their admirers. Crucial to this process was the ubiquitous narrative principle of the "inside" journey into the "real lives" of celebrities, lives much like the readers'. Other common themes in

Figure 2. Stars as typical: Judy Garland "plays" baseball, 1937.
Photo: Kobal Collection.

entertainment celebrity texts of the time—love lives, the "price they pay for fame," the desire to be just like the reader, the hard work of gaining and retaining success—further tightened the narrative links between the audience and the celebrated. Celebrities, in fact, began to address readers directly, often as confidantes: "I regret more than I can say that my marriage with Hal Rosson did not work out," wrote Jean Harlow to her "*Screen Book* Friends."[78] Joan Crawford confessed in a 1928 *Photoplay* that she hadn't told her life story because "I was afraid to tell it to you. You have one idea of Joan Crawford, now you are going to have another."[79] Bette Davis offered answers to "your problems" in 1942's *Photoplay,* but with a disclaimer: "I am merely giving my personal opinion," a letter from Davis states, and "my advice must not be considered authoritative in any instance."[80]

Yet if they were so much like the reader, why were celebrities so elevated and watched? Celebrity texts updated the early American paradox of egalitarian distinction. Rather than for public virtue or action, the celebrity rose because of his or her authentic, gifted self. A fame meritocracy was reinscribed in the new, consumerist language: the celebrity rises, selected for his personality (revealed through life-style choices), an irrational, but nonetheless organic, "folk" phenomenon.[81] The theme of the discovery of greatness, earlier termed a greatness of character, was translated into the discovery of a combination of "talent," "star quality," and "personality."

The luck of the lucky star, for example, is that she got the "break" that allowed her to rise. "Nobody knows," a 1940 *American Magazine* article told its readers, "when or where one of these will bob up."[82] Jean Harlow, driving some friends to a studio luncheon, came to fame "quite by accident," moving "from extra to star."[83] The stories in their purest form suggested that a star would not rise, or bob up, even with a lucky break—unless she had what it took. As Edgar Morin found in looking at how-to-be-a-star handbooks, "luck is a break, and a break is grace. Hence, no recipe. . . . What matters is the *gift*."[84] It could be cultivated, certainly, and for that reason hard work was important; without it, one might never find out if one had the gift that would be demonstrated by the break. Sometimes, as in the lucky break's corollary, the discovery story, one did not need to work, just *be:* Lana Turner sitting in the soda shop. Fame, apparently, would come to those destined to be famous and pass over the doors of the undeserving.

This tautology (how do we know the famous deserve fame? because they have it) is the core of the dominant early story of fame. Talent was often mentioned but rarely treated as sufficient. The only stars who survived, an early *Photoplay* suggested, were the ones "who had that rare gift designated as screen charm or personality, combined with adaptability and inherent talent."[85] Clark Gable "deserves his pre-eminent place" because "there's no one else exactly like him."[86] What it took to rise—"star quality," "charisma," "appeal," "personality," or simply "It"—was never defined beyond a label, even "ineffable."[87] Whatever it was, though, the texts made it clear that stars had always had it. Fame, based on an indefinable internal quality of the self, was natural, almost predestined.

The celebrity's background thus took its place as a demonstration that, put simply, a star is born. Ruby Keeler was "born with dancing feet."[88] Greta Garbo had "a certain force within her." Look back at Greta's childhood, the "first true story of Garbo's childhood" demonstrates, and you'll see that the "urge" was always "in her," that "she was a born actress."[89] This presentation of childhood did not build a personal history so much as locate in the famous a nebulous *essence* that explains their fame. Lowenthal's description of consumption-idol biographies aptly sums up fan and general magazine portrayals as well:

Childhood appears neither as prehistory and key to the character of an individual nor as a stage of transition to the growth and reformation of the abundant diversity of an adult. Childhood is nothing but a midget edition, a predated publication of a [person's] profession and career. *A [person] is an actor, a doctor, a dancer, an entrepreneur, and [she or] he always was.*[90]

Greatness is built in, it is who you are. If one works at it, or gets a lucky break, it may be discovered. If it is discovered, one becomes celebrated for it, which is evidence that one had it to begin with.

What do we make of the characteristics of these texts, the focus on leisure idols and leisure habits, the gradual move toward ordinariness, and the logic of the discovered gift? In many ways these early texts simply reassert in a new cultural vocabulary that those in the public eye are there because they deserve to be. But why *not* continue to focus on glamorous and extravagant consumption habits? Why increase the intimacy between star and reader through inside stories? The answer comes clear when we bring the production system back into the picture: the new publicity professions and the studio system, which, however tightly controlled, were neither seamless nor invisible.

Exposing the Gift:
Publicity in the Early Texts

The publicity system was clearly visible and commonly noted in these texts. "Everyone thinks he knows everything there is to know about moving pictures," a *Collier's* writer said in 1920. "Small wonder. The knowledge has been poured down our not unwilling throats by the photoplay magazines, the press agents, the newspapers, the censors, the critics."[91] Initially, this knowledge was not a problem. The studio star system was, for the most part, accommodated quite comfortably into most stories as the final step up the ladder. If the ineffable quality was discovered—and properly publicized, the story often added—one became celebrated. Like hard work, the studio could not create a star from the ungifted. *Life* reported, for example, that starlets spent their days in training "that would wilt all but the most determined" (hard work). They were "told what to do, what to say, how to dress, where to go, whom to go with" (studio control). Yet the studio couldn't make them into something they were not: "Only if they obey implicitly and only if, in addition, by some magic of beauty, personality or talent, they touch off an active response in millions of movie fans, will a few of them know the full flower of stardom" (indefinable essence).[92]

The management of publicity was itself generally presented in a way that posed hardly a threat to the notion of natural, deserved celebrity. Stories of "ballyhoo" press agents persisted, claiming that "the old hokum still gets newspaper space better than anything else";[93] behind each movie premiere, *Reader's Digest* told, was "a group of harried, sardonic studio press agents . . . [pulling] the strings."[94] This Barnumesque figure was portrayed as a harmless, amusing promoter—harmless because of the visibility of his tricks. The new public-relations counselor had, according to most stories, the same aim as the old showman press agent, to "boost the fame" of public figures. Only his style differed: he wore a suit instead of "a sun-struck plug hat and molting fur-lined overcoat" and depended "more upon his typewriter and truth and less upon the imagination."[95] Since he favored building on facts rather than fiction, he could only amplify a preexisting condition. While new inventions meant "an engine of publicity such as the world has never known before," Walter Lippmann wrote in *Vanity Fair* in 1927, that machine "will illuminate whatever we point it at. . . . The machine itself is without morals or taste of any kind, without prejudice or purpose, without conviction or ulterior motive."[96] By the 1930s, this new publicity machine had taken a permanent place in the discussion of celebrity.

Although Lippmann pointed out that "newspapermen" were the ones doing the pointing, the dominant notion of publicity as it appeared in early celebrity texts was of a neutral machine illuminating what "we," the public, wanted to see in the spotlight. The standing model of celebrities as rising organically from the populace would otherwise be jeopardized: if the studios or the newspapers controlled the "machine," people could enter the spotlight not because of popular election but because of manu-factured attention by interested elites. In these stories, the "public," mod-eled as a unified, powerful near-person forever casting its votes for its favorite personalities, became a crucial character in its own right. The notion of the public as an entity that "owned" both space and the public figures inhabiting it runs consistently through both general and fan maga-zines. In a 1932 *Vanity Fair,* Mussolini, the Prince of Wales, George Bernard Shaw, William Randolph Hearst, and others romp in bathing suits "On the Public's Beach."[97] The public, forever "fickle," was increas-ingly credited with *control* of celebrity.

As celebrities were being demoted to ordinariness in narratives, then, the audience was being promoted from a position of religious prostration. The public became the final discoverer, the publicity machine shifting the spotlights according to the public's whims. Myrna Loy tells "all you little Marys and Sues and Sarahs who wish you could be movie stars" that she is, in fact, at their service.

I'd like to tell her in good plain English that I am not my own boss. I'd like to tell her that I serve not one boss but several million. For my boss is—the Public. My boss is that very girl who writes me herself and thousands like her. It is the Public that first hired me, and it is the Public that can fire me. The Public criticizes me, reprimands me.[98]

The celebrity as public servant displaces difficult questions in the relation-ship between "authentic" greatness and publicity activities. It affirms the notion that celebrities are cream risen to the top while allowing the vague criterion of "personality" to coexist with the newly visible power of the publicity "machine." *You* control the machine, it says. If *you* don't like me, *you* can grab the spotlight and throw it onto someone else more worthy. Elitism and egalitarianism, long engaged in a submerged battle, take on a new mutation here. The antiegalitarian implications of both a celebrity elite and elite-controlled publicity are tempered by the emphasis on audience control. Desert and publicity live together.

In a remarkably obsequious, and revealing, rumination on the question of "Why did I slip?" Robert Taylor turned to the fans in control, whom he hoped had come to "accept me as a friend." "Maybe temperament is the trick that captures the public imagination. Should an actor be erratic and difficult, or should he be business-like, stable, and quiet? That's a tangled question, too. Because it seems if you're too 'colorful,' people resent you; if you're too tame, they're bored.... Maybe I should put on an act."[99] Taylor's article, while it contained the characteristic direct apostrophe and bow to the power of the public, also revealed a theme that grew in early texts along with that of public control. What image should I put on? he asks. The assumption that people are famous because of who they are, an authentic self, gets left behind as Taylor suggests that he will be who you want him to be. In one, audiences discover; in the other, audiences dictate.

Indeed, as the power of the audience to create stars to their liking became a stronger narrative ingredient, an alternative story line also developed. The more active the audience, the more celebrity is suspect as an artificial image created and managed to pander to that audience. Terms of commerce began to enter the discourse, still subordinated to terms of greatness and quality, but there nonetheless. Commercial creation and the marketing of false public images (as opposed to publicizing of true selves) began to surface as an explanation of fame. Myrna Loy, significantly slipping between public as boss and studio as boss, complained that

I daren't take any chances with Myrna Loy, for she isn't my property.... I couldn't even go [to the corner drugstore] without looking "right," you see. Not because of personal vanity, but because the studio has spent millions of dollars on the personality known as Myrna Loy. *And I can't let the studio down by slipping off my expensive mask of glamor. I've got to be, on all public occasions, the personality they sell at the box office.*[100]

Marlene Dietrich, a 1930s *Motion Picture* writer argued, was nothing but manufactured glamour. Through the use of publicity stunts, lighting effects, photography, and Dietrich's single talent—"simulating glamour"—she became famous. "The difference between Miss Dietrich in real

Figure 3. The mask of glamour: Carole Lombard, 1933.
Photo: Kobal Collection.

Figure 4. The mask removed: Bette Davis tests the water, 1952.
Photo: Kobal Collection.

life and Miss Dietrich in the photograph," he wrote, "was the difference between a handsome woman and one built up by studio artifice into a glamorous idol."[101] Here was taking shape a story that gained steam as the century progressed: studio artifice, in search of box office sales, created images that had little or nothing to do with the actual persons behind them. As early as 1931, the *Nation* wrote that fame "is largely manufactured and that those best known are those who have seen to it that they should be."[102] By 1944, an *American Mercury* writer was arguing that celebrity had become a "lush, weedy thing" choking "many a rare plant of genuine accomplishment"—a perspective that would become more popular in the following decades.[103]

This skepticism about the connection between celebrity and authenticity updated earlier anxieties about the trustworthiness of public selves. It was, however, largely muted in most celebrity stories. To a degree, this was simply accomplished through studio control. When Clark Gable suggested in a 1933 *Photoplay* interview, for example, that "I just work here. . . . The company has an investment in me. It's my business to work, not to think," his statement was considered "frank enough to be dangerous and the studio thereafter began to 'protect' Gable from unguarded utterances."[104]

But the skepticism heightened by increasingly visible publicity activities was contained more commonly by being acknowledged: by pulling down "the expensive mask of glamour." Here we arrive at the key to the drive toward "ordinariness" in early texts. By embracing the notion that celebrity images were artificial products and inviting readers to visit the real self behind those images, popular magazines partially defused the notion that celebrity was really derived from nothing but images. Celebrity profiling parked in exposé gear, offering instructions in the art of distinguishing truth from artifice, the real Dietrich from the fake one. Once you get to know the real one, the texts implied, you will see why you were right to have made her famous—or why, for that matter, she ought to be dropped from the firmament. Similarly, magazine photography began to move from "posed" glamour shots (the subject fixed, inactive, reminding the viewer that this is a photo) to the "candid," naturalistic shots of *Life* and *Look*, "how they look morning, noon and night"[105] (the subject as herself, caught in action). (See figures 3 and 4.) The at-home-with-the-famous "inside story" was central to this process. The glamorous celebrity was thus sacrificed for the more "realistic," down-to-earth celebrity. Intimacy, bolstering belief, was offered up. Manufactured images, then, would be harmless to allegiances. The public could discover and make famous certain people because it (with the help of the magazines) could see through the publicity-generated, artificial self to the real, deserving, special self. The distrust of public fronts was undercut by the promise of the private life exposed. The story of celebrity as a natural phenomenon rewarding the deserving was joined—quite shakily—with the story of celebrity as an artificial product.

Chapter Two

The Name and the Product:
Late Twentieth-Century Celebrity

In the old days, fame was the result of achievement. After a body of work, performing artists acquired a certain status, which was the natural consequence of accu-
mulated excellence. This inspired others to follow in their footsteps, to work just
as hard to emulate those successes. Today, in this streamlined age of labor-saving
devices, we know there are quicker methods with which to achieve notoriety.
With the refinements of hype, the ultimate 20th-century invention, it is now
possible to purchase fame through media manipulation, to acquire it by dogged
self-promotion or simply by association.

(Charles Marowitz,
"The Angel of Publicity," p. E1)

As historical analysis, Marowitz's grounding of the separation of fame
and achievement in recent "refinements of hype" is not exactly on target.
The link between "status" and "excellence" has never been absolute, and
the gap between them began to be actively widened before the twentieth
century—although, as we will see later in detail, celebrity has certainly
become increasingly industrialized. As historical artifact, however, the
argument hits the mark. Hype, purchase, manipulation, self-promotion,
association have become central elements in celebrity discourse. How so?

Most critical to these developments was a shift in the organization of
the film entertainment industry from which celebrities were emanating.
In the late 1940s and early 1950s, the film industry was jolted from several
sides. In 1948, the Supreme Court, in the antitrust case *United States v.
Paramount Pictures, Inc. et al.,* unanimously sided with the Department
of Justice in its charges against the motion picture industry. The "Big
Five" studios were ordered to divorce their theater exhibition holdings

from the production and distribution ends of their business and cease the block booking of films that had essentially guaranteed sales.[1] The industry also faced a box office crisis, greatly aggravated by television, which was fast displacing film as the dominant leisure-time activity. American television took off quickly: the number of sets in use in 1947 was around 14,000 and by the next year had shot to 172,000; by 1950, there were four million sets, by 1954 eight times more, and by the late 1950s television was in 90 percent of American homes.[2] Suddenly, the studios were struggling for an audience.

The shake-up of the movie studio system brought both changes for existing companies and new entrants into the field. Independent production companies began to grow. Studios shifted to contracting on a picture-by-picture basis rather than "owning" workers for longer periods. With studios pulling back from long-term control, talent agents, whose role earlier had been marginal, moved in, taking on tasks left undone by the studios: cultivating "talent," selecting "properties" to develop, taking "the long view." Agents began to be important power brokers, and the "packages" they offered—a writer, a script, a star or two, sometimes a director—became (and remain) the currency of the industry.[3] Eventually, despite changes in ownership patterns, the system stabilized in its new form: the major studios still dominated, though now they collaborated with the television industry and with talent agents and agencies, absorbing independent production.[4] While the economic drive toward a star system remained in this changed environment, new players entered the game from the now-dispersed subindustries of star making and from the new television industry, and strategies began to shift to meet the new environmental requirements. (In this chapter, the contemporary system and its workers—the authors of the celebrity discourse—are quickly sketched. They are given life in the chapters that follow.)

As studio control was necessarily relaxed and the studio image-maintenance activities became dispersed into an independent publicity profession, film stars in the 1950s became "proprietors of their own image," which they could sell to filmmakers. Whereas under the old system studios intervened to "enforce an overlap between the star image and character," under the new one this strategy of control was relaxed, and stars began "to show a distance from their own image."[5] Independent publicists, assistants in the management of public images (and often the controllers, in place of the celebrities themselves), became powerful players.

In the meantime, the new publicity profession was struggling to establish itself—through public relations for Public Relations—and taking more sophisticated shapes. Following World War II public relations (PR) grew "from a one-dimensional 'press agentry' function into a sophisticated communications network connecting the most powerful elements of our society." By the early 1950s PR was firmly institutionalized, and by the mid-1980s a conservative estimate put the number of public-relations professionals in the United States at around 100,000.[6]

This growth contained several components that affect celebrity. First, the overall trend toward delineating and targeting specialized market niches in product development, advertising, and sales has meant that the task of garnering and shaping attention has become progressively more "scientific." Strategies center on zeroing in on the perceived needs, desires, and knowledge of particular publics, seeking to attract and then sell the attention of segments of the mass market, matching certain populations to specific messages and vehicles. Beginning in the early 1960s, with the "values and life-styles" research of the Stanford Research Institute, the advertising industry had slowly abandoned class-based marketing for marketing that "hones in on a consumer's 'lifestyle' (marital status, education, region, sex) and 'attitudes' (religion, ambition, optimism, etc.)."[7] The mass media have headed in a similar direction. By the 1960s, for example, specialized publications had taken over the circulation lead from general-interest magazines. By the mid-1970s, television was shifting from mass to segmented marketing as well.[8]

Second, as the daily practices and interests of PR operatives and journalists, aligned since the 1920s, moved closer over these decades, arenas traditionally perceived as nonentertainment (news in particular) have come to depend on the practices of the entertainment industry, and celebrity in particular. Not surprisingly, as PR has developed new tools and become better at providing for journalists, news has become increasingly dependent on public-relations practitioners as sources: a 1980 *Columbia Journalism Review* survey of a typical issue of the *Wall Street Journal,* for example, found that 45 percent of the day's 188 news items were based on press releases.[9]

Third, the technologies for providing a visual image that *imitates the representation* of an activity, event, or person, rather than representing it directly, have become highly developed. Publicity practitioners, especially by making use of new video technology, have become masters at delivering entertaining news to news organizations. The electronic press release, "imitation news," is now commonplace. Originating in the film industry, these releases have "the feel of a genuine news story, right down to the imperfect oratory as the interview subjects gather their thoughts on camera." In entertainment PR, these releases are often highly advanced and widely used: some include multiple stories (personality profiles, "news features," etc.) on a dual sound track that allows a reporter to dub in his or her own voice; and some include art work, scripts, and "teaser" commercials for the news program to use. Studios send video interviews into which local reporters can insert tapes of themselves asking questions, thus appearing to "be rubbing elbows with the Hollywood elite."[10]

Finally, beginning in the early 1970s, the outlets for publicity have exploded with the success of magazine and newspaper writing about "people" and "personality" and, more recently, broadcast "infotainment." At the head of the pack has been *People* magazine, founded in 1974 to "focus entirely on the active personalities of our time," on "people—especially the above average, the important, the charismatic, the singular."[11] With *People*'s success, imitators quickly followed, so many that, three years later, *Newsweek*—itself caught up by the celebrity sell—reported that "the doleful fact is that the celebrity industry has reached the point at which the demand is outstripping the supply."[12] This has meant a need for more subject matter, and more opportunities for recognition: literally more editorial space for those aspiring to fame or to regain faded recognition, for star-for-a-day ordinary people, and for celebrities from untapped fields. "We're scouring every facet of American life for stars," said *People* magazine editor Richard Stolley in 1977. "We haven't changed the concept of the magazine. We're just expanding the concept of 'star.' "[13]

Television, with its constant flow, enormous reach, and vast space-filling needs, has from its initial boom provided the most significant new outlet for image creation. By the mid-1960s, adults and children were on average watching nearly four hours of television a day.[14] Like personality magazines from the 1970s on, television from the 1950s on provided more space for more faces. Moreover, television's new characteristics—its small proportions and at-home location—literally down-sized the celebrity. "Famous folks," as Richard Schickel points out, are brought "into our living room in psychically manageable size."[15] Sitting in the dark under a movie screen, watching Charlton Heston as Ben Hur, a viewer might feel as if Heston could reach right down and pull her in; sitting in front of a television screen, watching Heston in a sweat shirt chatting with Joan Rivers, the viewer could almost reach down and pluck *him* out. Other characteristics have also arguably effected changes in celebrity development: tremendous repetition, allowing greater familiarity;[16] an increased "illusion of intimacy" between celebrities and audience built through "reality" programming, talk shows most significantly;[17] and a near-total dependence on a sophisticated ratings system, leading to rapid turnover as executives try to hold onto the few perceived "hit" elements and replace the elements that may not be selling. Focus, though repeated, is diffuse; turnover is rapid. Attention, on television, is easier to get and more difficult to hold onto.

Celebrity Making Revealed: Late Twentieth-Century Texts

The narratives about and explanations of fame that were developed in the earlier part of the century have remained commonplace, even dominant. "Call it star quality, star power, maybe even star magic," a 1991 *USA Today* article suggested, sounding exactly like articles from six decades earlier. "Those who possess star quality have it onstage and off. . . . Star quality can be spotted and nurtured. But it cannot be created. Not ever. . . . Star quality is real and shining—and here to stay."[18] Where some texts continue to use magical terms to account for the natural rise of celebrities, others continue to attribute it to "hard and often anxious work, insisting that whatever the stars had, they earned."[19] Their success, in either case, is a merited one: either because their natural charisma is recognized or because they fulfill the American dream, becoming stars through their own blood, sweat, and tears.

The changes in the apparatus and practice of publicity in the post-glamour, television-dominated era have, however, seeped into the texts. The challenge from the manufacture-of-fame narrative has greatly amplified. No longer under institutional guard, it has become a serious contender in explaining celebrity. With *TV Guide,* which began in 1948, then quickly grew in circulation and has, since the early 1970s, been one of the two top-selling magazines in the United States, celebrity making as a business moved from a peripheral to a central theme. "Why," a 1953 article asked, "is there a lack of star-studded names in TV dramas?" The answer is simply that "building a 'star' " costs too much, and "few, if any, performers make the top without the Big Buildup. It's a selling job that requires an organized bunch of legmen, plenty of time and lots of cash."[20] The presence or lack of stars was not, in this story, seen as a question of talent or personality resources but of sales resources. A few years later, one performer's summary of the "feeling among performers" about answering fan mail stands in stark contrast to earlier treatments of mail answering and autographing as a sort of public service. "Stardom is a business," she says matter-of-factly. "It would be bad business to ignore a fan."[21] A "shrewd agent," a shrewd agent tells readers in a later article, "knows how to make Hollywood pay, *what image is wanted on the market, where shortages exist, how to fill niches.*"[22]

Visible links between celebrity and selling were not new. Fame as a sales device had been evident within advertising early on, primarily through endorsements. Beginning in the 1950s, however, celebrity began to be commonly represented not only as useful to selling and business but as a business itself, created by selling. Along with the old-style "what success does to the stars" and "life at home with the stars" stories, for example, *TV Guide* showed stars bickering over billing, arguing that "I'm a piece of merchandise. The bigger they make my name, the more important I am. And, the more important I am, the more money I'm worth."[23] This stance, which in the days of tight studio control was rare and sometimes punished, rapidly became commonplace. Terms began to change: the celebrity was becoming "merchandise," "inventory," "property," a "product," a "commodity," while the fans were becoming "markets." Star production, said a 1962 *New York Times Magazine* author, "is as ritualistic in its way as a fire dance." The celebrity is an "investment"—"like all raw materials, they often require a good deal of processing before they are marketable"—and that investment "must be protected."[24]

As the treatment of fame as produced and the famous as commercial products took hold, the entertainment media pursued the question of exactly how that production worked. Entertainment production began to be revealed. A 1967 article in *TV Guide* offered instructions in "how to manufacture a celebrity." Detailing the case of Barbara Walters, the author demonstrated how the "mechanical assembly line" created celebrities from raw human material: Walters was picked up in small feature stories, then profiled in *Life* and *TV Guide*. After being provided with professional recognition, she was "piped into the lecture circuit" and later into commercials, which turned her into a "personality." Then "certain characteristic things began to happen to her—none of which had anything

to do with her professional skills." She became "courted as a 'name.'"
Her wardrobe, home, and cosmetic habits were women's magazine topics;
she appeared on talk shows and at "fancy" parties. Even Walters recog-
nizes her own manufacture, chatting "candidly about the meaningless
mechanics of fabricated fame."[25]

Several years later, a press agent was quoted saying that his client,
Ann-Margret, could initially have been "sold . . . as anything": "She was
a new product. We felt there was a need in The Industry for a female
Elvis Presley. We mounted her on a billboard on Sunset Strip with her
legs around a motorcycle. *I saw emerge a star without the benefit of major
industry achievement.*"[26] A *TV Guide* article quoted the coordinator of
a star-grooming program. The "whole thing nowadays" is "just a big
machine. When they push the button, they grind out the name."[27]

"Make no mistake," the article continued, "the people who push the
button nowadays . . . are primarily publicity people." Although the focus
on the celebrity-making machine brought individual publicity people into
the spotlight, in many respects the representation of the publicity system
remains as it was in the 1930s and 1940s: subordinated to innate characteristics—sometimes talent, usually the same vague notions of "star quality" and "personality." Arthur Godfrey, for example, told *TV Guide* in
the 1950s that performers must have "intelligence in their faces . . . plus
industry"; another talent spotter said she looked for "talent, sincerity,
ability to be original and butterflies" in the stomach, also noting, as an
aside, "the advantages of a good manager."[28] These definitions of the
"stuff" that "stars are made of" have persisted. In 1988, Geraldo Rivera
asked a personal manager and two television producers to tell his TV-
show audience what "star quality" is. Their answers echo the early texts:
"I would say it's potential," says one; "it's the ability to feel," says another; it's "the ability to light a television up or a movie screen."[29] In
these cases, image managers have continued to be portrayed (often by
themselves) as giving the public what they want, not by creating it but
by discovering and publicizing it.

In other discussions of celebrity-production and -control activities,
though, the concept of "quality" has been dismissed as irrelevant and
old-fashioned and replaced by the idea of "image." Where once an agent's
job was to discover star quality, now the shrewd agent discovers a market
and manufactures a celebrity product to suit it. A 1963 series on "gentlemen of the pressure" opened with an illustration of a giant hand holding

a television screen, on which the word "images" is written; behind the hand, operating it through a panel marked "networks," is a messy, motley group of people; in front of it, a happy, smiling audience looks at the screen. "A mixed breed of nonobjective salesmen have found a home in the house of TV," the author warned, selling "affection for personalities, products, corporate entities and ideas." Their effects are "a little frightening," and "although they prefer to work in the shadows, they leave their traces on every TV screen in America."[30] Press agent Helen Ferguson, one profile notes, "provides the effective kind of image demanded by her clients." She does so successfully, objects a magazine writer quoted in the profile, because "when you finally get to one of her stars and ask a question, Helen answers. . . . What you always get is a Helen Ferguson portrait." Nonetheless—and again, the commercial system is noted and accepted in the text—"she has the people we have to have and we just take it her way."[31]

The interview process, which had earlier been seen as simply a means of revelation, began to be dissected as a means of image control. "The impresario of the Hollywood interview is the press agent," wrote one journalist, "who is trained to assess the writer and publication and then cut off at the pass embarrassing situations."[32] Another described how "stars and their press agents will arrange a location that will fortify the basic image they wish to present to the public," will "channel the discussion into those very few areas where the star can excel conversationally," and "look upon The Interview as an opportunity to convince the world at large that they are something quite different than they seem to be."[33]

Publicity agents and managers have been drawn into the narrative, coaching the public figure in "how to look cool in talk-show hot seats," sitting next to (or even replacing) the celebrity during an interview, overseeing the touching up of photos.[34] "Publicists rule the day," a 1986 *Rolling Stone* article explained. "The bigger the star, the more power the publicist wields. And this power enables publicists to choose the photographer for a fashion shoot, pick a sympathetic writer for an interview or demand the cover of a magazine."[35] Several years later, *Time* outlined how celebrity is "available to any Manhattan couple with about $100,000 to squander" by adopting the right charities, being photographed at the right spots, and hiring public-relations counselors, who "now serve everybody from models and movie stars to lawyers and landlords."[36] These are not the harmless "ballyhoodlums" revealed in some early twentieth-century texts but sophisticated business operators. Throughout these texts runs a tremendously heightened self-consciousness about the systematic production of celebrity and celebrity images for commercial purposes.

Enjoy the Hype: Instruction and Irony

With increased visibility, the problems that had surfaced occasionally in the first half of the century have deepened during the second. If celebrities are artificial creations, why should an audience remain attached and lavish attention on their fabricated lives? How can stars be both true and false? Artifice has moved to the foreground, and with it the old distrust of the market-self, the self that performs, cons, sells. These are the questions with which contemporary texts must cope.

Many texts have brought to fruition the behind-the-scenes, inside-dope style begun earlier, instructing the reader further in reading performances, finding the "real" behind the "image." This writing acknowledges the gap between image and reality but denies that bridging it is a problem, especially with television, an unfoolable medium that cannot help but transmit an "accurate, searching image."[37] "The TV camera has an X-ray attachment," Arlene Francis told *TV Guide* readers in 1960. "It pierces, it penetrates, it peels away the veneer. It communicates the heart and mind of man."[38] In nonvisual encounters, writers themselves provide the tools for seeing the truth. For example, by interpreting the facial traits of celebrities—ear position, nose shape, eyelids, chin—a 1980s author promises to uncover their "secrets," the "private side of these public figures."[39] Anchoring this argument, not surprisingly, is the old-fashioned search for a person's "genuine," internal characteristics. If viewers have difficulty peeling away the veneer, they simply need better viewing tools, and readers can depend on the writer to help uncover the person underneath. This is still the most common stance in what remains the standard celebrity text, the profile. With the proper guides, one can distinguish true personality from false.[40]

Many texts, though, have become more unabashed and unapologetic about artificial authenticity, instructing readers in how to be more sophisticated in recognizing and using it themselves. Groucho Marx's "You Bet Your Life," *TV Guide* disclosed, "represents the finest manufactured spontaneity television has yet known." That, the article claims, is simply professionalism, the business of "concocting entertainment."[41] A 1950s article prompted readers to pay attention to television stars' familiar, unconscious gestures, which, converted into conscious performances like Eddie Cantor's eye-popping, could "serve as trademarks."[42] By the 1980s, *Rolling Stone* was sardonically claiming that the key to everyone's inevitable encounter with fame is preparation: "No self-respecting modern person should be without fifteen minutes' worth of the props, costumes and condiments that are vital to the maintenance of fame."[43]

A final set of "instructions" has taken the inside-story theme a small, subtle step further. By the 1950s, how the publicity system works both to manufacture celebrity and to fabricate sincerity were already central topics: stories covered press agents, deals, and the arts of appearances. As such stories have become more common (especially with the growth of "infotainment" in the 1970s and 1980s), the audience has been instructed not simply in viewing the self behind the image (what the star really thinks, wears, does) but in viewing the fabrication process (how the celebrity is being constructed to amuse). Armed with knowledge about the process, the audience doesn't need to believe or disbelieve the hype, just to enjoy it. (See figures 5 and 6.)

An ironic, winking tone in these revelatory texts is one of the clearest developments in the latter part of the twentieth century. Irony is strongest in magazines aimed at young, educated people. At least one magazine, *Spy,* has made its name and money from the combination of inside dope and mockery. A regular feature lists the number of mentions given particular people in Liz Smith's gossip column. An April 1989 cover story on "celebrity garbage" offers "coffee grounds of the rich and famous—a scientific, sanitary and not at all unseemly SPY investigation"; a June story traces "the current bull market for selling one's soul" for attention. A 1990 cover story on "building a better celebrity" reports on "what America thinks about celebrities, what celebrities will do to keep themselves celebrated, what nobodies will do to become famous," and features a mock-scientific survey and analysis of public opinion, giving percentages of people believing that Drew Barrymore is dead, agreeing that "nearly every celebrity has been to the Playboy mansion," or willing to sacrifice a limb to win an Oscar. The accompanying list, a "surgical history of celebrity," includes the celebrity's name, rumored cosmetic surgery—and their "publicist's denial."[44]

This approach is found not only in "hipster" magazines, however, but also in more mainstream ones. The audience has been invited to take its power further with a new, cynical distance from the production of celebrity and celebrity images. A 1962 *New York Times* piece was

Figure 5. Enjoying the humor in the hype: "Two actors," as they appeared in *Spy* magazine, 1992. Photo: Kevin Winter/DMI.

Figure 6. Celebrity-making revealed: "Cher enjoys a quiet time in a serene setting." *Spy* magazine, 1992. Photo: Philippe Ledru/Sygma.

accompanied by an eight-box cartoon of "the publicity trail to stardom," including an "appropriate airport arrival," a supper with a columnist to "let fall romantic secrets," a press-agent–arranged crowning as "queen of something or other," the provision of "photographic material for the press" by "hamming it up with the livestock," and a TV panel-show guest star appearance.[45] In a 1977 report on overcrowding in the "celebrity industry," *Newsweek* waxed sarcastic, suggesting the foundation of a "National Celebrity Commission to select, at the earliest possible age, a rotating galaxy of Designated People" who would be "scientifically schooled in the art of outrageous behavior."[46] A decade later, an *Esquire* writer claimed that the strategy of cloaking oneself in goodness by "[buying] a lesser disease, preferably one that primarily affected children," no longer worked since "all the lesser diseases were taken."[47] *Life* magazine consulted "industry bigfoots" on how Clark Gable would fare if he started out today. The experts recommended plastic surgery ("deflating those wind socks"), publicity control ("a spin doctor"), image building ("have him sitting at ringside for fights and Laker games"), and television series and talk shows. "Were Gable a young actor today," the article concluded, "he would require careful packaging to make him the King of this era."[48] (See figure 7.) A 1982 *TV Guide* article traced the "three stages" of stardom, each turning on the manipulation of image and publicity apparatus: in stage one, the performer is eager, and "you see, hear and read about him or her everywhere"; in stage two, the successful celebrity is temperamental, and appearances now "depend on the publication, the subjects *not* to be discussed, who else will be in the story, whether or not the cover will be included"; in stage three, "the great holdout," the star exits, because "nothing is right."[49] Each stage is a pose. The reader, armed with a cynical knowledge about image-manipulation strategies, is being told how to read the pose as a pose. Instructively, what lies behind the pose is not taken up.

Irony has also become a common piece of celebrity public personas. "A self-mocking sense of humor," according to casting directors in a *TV Guide* story, "is a key ingredient in star quality."[50] Celebrities are often caught "simultaneously mocking and indulging their icon status," Todd Gitlin argues, describing a collection of *Rolling Stone* photographs. "New-style stars flaunt and celebrate stardom by mocking it, camping it up, or underplaying it (in public!). . . . The star now stands apart from glamour, and comments (often ironically) on it."[51] In the June 1989 *Esquire,* then Republican Party leader Lee Atwater, joining the posing of entertainment celebrities, saluted the audience with his pants around his ankles.[52]

Why this combination of exposure of the celebrity- and image-manufacturing processes and making fun of them? On one level, the ridiculing of glamour by celebrities is another star turn, much like tabloid revelations of the "true self," updated to accommodate the visibility of glamour production. Celebrities, Gitlin suggests, invite their admirers to revere them for being "too hip to be reverent or revered."[53] The constant visibility of publicity mechanisms works similarly on another level, defusing a threat to admiration by offering the audience the position of control. Celebrity audiences are treated to the knowledge of how they, and others, become the "sucker born every minute"—and thus avoid becoming the sucker. This is what one friend of Warhol describes as "the Warhol attitude": "You can have your cake and eat it, too. You can wallow in all the marvelous successes of modern-day American life and at the same time be superior to it because you're mocking it at the same time that you indulge in it."[54]

Invitations into the production process, and an ironic stance about it, operate much like the invitations into the "real lives" of the famous

Figure 7. The knowing, ironic stance: "As one of the gang in *Magnum, P.I.,* our hero would acquire the necessary macho image." Clark Gable as he appeared in *Life* magazine, Spring 1989. Photo: Lou Valentino Collection.

(which continue from the 1920s). They partially defuse the threats it makes to the notion that fame is rooted in character traits, that admiration of celebrities is grounded in merit. Who is real? Who has "star quality" or "talent" or "greatness"? Who actually deserves attention? These questions, still circulating from the earlier fame story, are unanswered—this time because they are largely rendered moot. Mark Crispin Miller's comments about televisual irony have more general application here:

> TV seems to flatter the inert skepticism of its own audience, assuring them that they can do no better than to stay right where they are, rolling their eyes in feeble disbelief. . . . [Each] subtle televisual gaze . . . offers not a welcome but an ultimatum—that we had better see the joke or else turn into it. . . . [The] TV viewer does not gaze up at the screen with angry scorn or piety, but—perfectly enlightened—looks down on its images with a nervous sneer which cannot threaten them and which only keeps the viewer himself from standing up.[55]

Through irony, these celebrity texts reposition their readers, enlightened about the falseness of celebrity, to "see the joke" of the performed self or become it. Cynicism, irony, and invitations behind the scenes engage where tuning out would be quite logical.

The contemporary texts promoting the story of artificial production do not simply tell that story, though; they luxuriate in it. The irony is more than defensive; it is proud. These texts offer telling new resolutions to the underlying cultural tensions. The anxiety about public selves, for example, is no longer met only with the continual promise of personal revelation. The private self is no longer the ultimate truth. Instead, what is most true, most real, most trustworthy, is precisely the relentlessly performing public self. New sorts of revelations are offered: the details of how and when and by whom the public self is constructed. Ubiquitous Barnums reappear, and with them the fascination with the mechanics of manipulation.

The artificial-manufacture story also offers a strange new interplay between hierarchy and egalitarian democracy. On the one hand, it brings its own radical egalitarianism: a world where attention will be distributed more evenly, if in shorter increments; a world where stardom is more accessible since the inborn requirements are fewer; a world in which anyone who can lip-synch can feel the glow of celebrity. On the other hand, it celebrates (even as it attacks) a new, powerful elite: the media, the industry, the star makers, able to make and control images, able to direct mass attention through marketing machinery. This new vision of authority, of systematic control and manipulation by the star system and its workers, deserves careful attention.

Part Two

The Production of Celebrity

Chapter Three

Industrial-Strength Celebrity

Within the last century, and especially since about 1900, we seem to have discovered the processes by which fame is manufactured. Discovering that we . . . can so quickly and so effectively give a man "fame" we have willingly been misled into believing that fame—well-knownness—is still a hallmark of greatness. . . . The celebrity is a person who is known for his well-knownness. . . . He is neither good nor bad, great nor petty. He is the human pseudo-event. . . . The hero was distinguished by his achievement; the celebrity by his image or trademark. The hero created himself; the celebrity is created by the media. The hero was a big man; the celebrity is a big name.

(Daniel Boorstin, *The Image,*
pp. 47, 57, 61)

Visibility is what every aspiring hostess wants, what every professional seeks. It is the crucial ingredient that can make lawyer X the most sought after in town, talk show host Y the most popular in her market, and surgeon Z the most highly paid in his city. This is the potential of industrialized celebrity manufacturing, the potential for elevating virtually anyone to a level of visibility unimaginable in any other age—and compensating that individual with unimaginable rewards. . . . Today, there is a whole industry that manages the business of transforming unknowns into celebrities, changing virtually every element of personality, appearance, and character that it is possible to change. The industry operates not by whim but by design, not by pride but for profit. . . . Wholly divorced from great deeds and accomplishments, *well-knownness itself* has obtained tremendous commercial value.

(Irving Rein, Philip Kotler, and Martin Stoller,
High Visibility, pp. 3, 4–5, 11)

Communication studies professor Irving Rein and his colleagues, writing over a quarter of a century after Daniel Boorstin's classic critique of commercial culture, happily embrace what Boorstin decried. They borrow from and agree with his analysis: fame is artificially producible and produced, well-knownness a salable and sold commodity, achievement divorceable and divorced from renown. The separation of notoriety from greatness, however, is taken as an indicator not of decline-of-civilization dangers but of unmined commercial opportunities. For them, the key question is not how to upend the manufacture of celebrities but how to make it more systematic. Their treatise, simultaneously a battle cry for the rationalization of the celebrity industry and a how-to book for aspiring attention getters, is in many ways the most clear statement available on the logic of the celebrity industry. Delving into the world of entertainment-industry celebrity workers, we witness pieces of that logic playing out. This chapter builds a portrait of celebrity production as a commercial industry much like other commodity-production systems: those working within it speak primarily in the language of commerce and machinery; they are organized industrially, with production tasks divided between tightly linked subindustries; marketing plays a key role in matching products to distributors and consumers, depending especially on strategies of product transformation and the building of consumer loyalty.

It is important to begin with the analytical distinction between two sorts of "products" that are typically conflated by those working with and observing celebrities. Since both usually reside within the body of the performer and in practice bleed into each other, actor and star are understandably fused in discussion. Nonetheless, the distinction between them is key. The strategies for developing and marketing each differ. The aspirant or performer is on the one hand a *worker,* and what is developed and sold is the capacity to play a role and the actual work of playing the role. This is the entertainer's more "traditional" aspect: the aspirant's qualities and abilities (not necessarily talent, also often looks alone) are the basis for decision making. On the other hand, he or she is a *celebrity,* and what is developed and sold is the capacity to command attention. It is here that knownness, separated from quality, is the basis for decision making. My attention is directed primarily to the latter aspect of entertainment celebrity. In fact, I will argue, in agreement with both Boorstin-style critics and Rein-style apologists, there is a good deal of commercial pressure to simply allow the actor as worker to be subsumed by the celebrity as celebrity. How does this production system actually work, and what illuminations do its workings provide? What is the evidence, to begin with, that it is in fact a production system, that celebrities are "products" manufactured in an "industry?"

The Organization of Industrialized Celebrity Production

From a distance, there is the suggestion of glamour: the movie theater is lit by search lights and a red carpet, held down by red tape, stretches across the sidewalk in front and up to the theater entrance. Distance is all a spectator is allowed on this occasion, a premiere screening of *Sleeping with the Enemy*. Fans or curious passersby are kept behind barricades across the street from the theater. "It's not just that we don't need the fans around," a publicist says. "In fact, we don't *want* them around." Behind several red soft-rope barriers along the edges of the carpet are groups of media workers, roughly divided into broadcast press, print journalists, and paparazzi. "Inside" the roped-off area seven or eight publicity workers from the film's studio, Fox, mill around in the brightly lit aisle. They talk with each other, sometimes with familiar journalists. They are dressed semicasually, semihip, as are most of the people attending the event.

For the publicists, this is work, just another premiere. Their tasks are divided. One is doing what she calls "red carpeting" or "celebrity spotting" so that the press can be fed information about who is pulling up. Another is responsible for hosting broadcast press, which involves, she says, getting them positioned physically and finding out whom they want to interview and trying to make sure that it happens. Another does the same for print. Another is keeping a list of celebrity attendees to coordinate later with a Fox staff photographer.

The broadcast publicist positions a crew from "Entertainment Tonight." The cameraman asks the interviewer about their plan that evening. Are they going to "stay for reacts"? They'll leave and come back, is the reply, even though "there's not even a party." Their coverage of these events is routine; they cover every premiere, which right now, during the "slow season," is one or two a week but during seasonal heights (Christmas, summer) is more often. They chat about "getting Julia and Kevin," the stars of the film, and then the conversation drifts into the subjects occupying most of the other journalists and camera crews: the weather, a recent LA plane crash. The "ET" crew is dissatisfied with its spot and tries to move across the aisle. Jasmine, a Fox publicist, stops them, sternly telling them that she can't allow it because others will then want special privileges as well. This elicits a series of mumbled complaints from the crew: publicists are always in the way, both physically blocking "clean" shots (not surprisingly, given how many of them are swarming in the small aisle) and by blocking opportunities to interview celebrities. "They're supposed to be here to help us," the cameraman complains. He turns to a publicist, who responds like a person who is always having to defend herself, and sarcastically suggests that if she'd only move a little bit to the right she could more completely block his shot.

Another challenge presents itself as the crowd begins to file into the theater, in that "civilians" are mixed in with celebrities. The "ET" journalist spots the celebrities and informs the cameraman, sometimes using their names, sometimes any identifying feature ("girl from sitcom, red dress"). "I use the paparazzi," the "ET" interviewer says, distractedly eyeing the crowd. There is a cuing at these events: as celebrities arrive, camera-flashing paparazzi call their names over and over in an attempt to get them to look directly at the camera ("Shirley! Shirley! James! James!"), and the names quickly make their way through the crowd, like information passed by chirping birds. The desirability of an arriving guest can easily be gleaned from the degree of frenzy in the bulb-flashing. As celebrities start appearing—Sidney Poitier, some television sitcom folks, semiknown actor Michael Ontkean—most pause for photographs. There is almost no verbal interaction between them and the photographers, and their responses to the experience range between veiled irritation and hamming, most falling in the center range of poised, polite, false smiles. A few do interviews, facilitated by a Fox publicist who has found out who "wants" them. Some, like Drew Barrymore ("our favorite," say the "ET" workers sarcastically), make a full circuit on their own accord, speaking with whomever. Some arrive with their own personal publicists, who either protect them from interviews or deliver them to specific contacts; Kevin Anderson is reluctantly shuttled to the "ET" crew, to whom he has been "promised" by his personal publicist. (The orchestration here is relatively low-key. At the Golden Globe Awards, celebrities are met by program organizers, who see to it that they pause at a series of posing stops and that they move on to avoid a celebrity-posing traffic jam.) Anderson is asked standard questions ("What will audiences get from this movie?" and "What was it like to work with Julia Roberts?") and gives standard answers ("It's like a roller-coaster ride, but intelligent and has a sense of humor" and "She's great, everything you'd expect her to be"). As he moves with his publicist to enter the theater, a Fox publicist begs him to do a few more interviews. "They'll hold the film," she says. That evening, or the next day, or the next week, the photos and interviews appear: television sitcom star in red dress at the opening of *Sleeping with the Enemy,* Kevin Anderson discussing how Julia Roberts is everything you'd expect her to be.

Film premieres and award shows are perhaps the clearest examples of the industrial nature of celebrity work. They are precisely Boorstin's "pseudo-events." For most participants, they are not events to be experienced but parts of their job. Staged and stage managed by entertainment organizations, they are routinely, habitually covered by news organizations. They are consciously and carefully organized to facilitate the capture and dissemination of standardized celebrity images in magazines and on television. These are true assembly lines, small parts in the more elaborate manufacture of fame: publicist brings person to media, person pauses, photographer shoots, person becomes image, image is disseminated. Labor is divided. Media workers, eager for celebrity images for sales purposes, shoot the same standard-pose photos and ask simple questions that receive standardized answers. Entertainment-industry publicists and celebrities, eager for coverage for promotional purposes, provide easy but controlled access to celebrity images. The operation is mechanical, designed, routine.

The premiere displays two key industrial elements of the celebrity system. Paid specialists surround the celebrities to increase and protect their market value, and linked subindustries make use of celebrities for their own commercial purposes, simultaneously building and using performers' attention-getting power. The authors of *High Visibility* argue this directly: celebrities develop primarily (though not exclusively, and differently in different fields) through a system organized to turn them into brand-name products, "manufactured, just as are cars, clothes and computers."[1] Talent, says personal manager Jay Bernstein, who recently ran an I'll-make-you-a-star campaign, is only "35 percent of making it in Hollywood."

The other 65 percent is having the team behind you. If Laurence Olivier came out and you didn't know who he was, I don't think he would make it on talent alone. I've met a lot of talented waiters that are still waiters. The bigger the team the better off you are. As long as it's a good team. If not, it's like Switzerland invading Russia. You need an Air Force, Marine Corps, a Navy. You need all the help you can get.[2]

Indeed, celebrities often give these specialists up to 50 percent of their income. In many cases organized into professional associations, the specialists form support industries around the development of celebrity products: personal publicists and public-relations firms handle the garnering of media coverage and help manage the packaging of the celebrity; agents, managers, and promoters handle representation, affecting the pricing and distribution of the celebrity; coaches and groomers of various sorts help with the presentation. Linked industries, in particular the communication-media and entertainment industries, distribute the celebrity image to consumers. Celebrities are sold to consumers in specified or mass markets through these intermediate distributors, who buy and resell the celebrity product—either in the form of celebrity information (programs, magazines, newspapers) or celebrity performance vehicles.

Agents (who handle many clients, linking them to employers) and managers (who handle a small stable of clients, responsible for long-term as well as short-term planning) literally sell entertainers as workers. But they also necessarily sell them as celebrities. Since an already popular figure is clearly a less uncertain sales draw, a recognizable celebrity is easier to move through the pitching ladder. "You have to convince people that they either are a name or could be a name," says David Spiro. "No one's going to want to distribute a film with a bunch of nobodies, unless for some reason it's *War and Peace*." Behind this, of course, is the long-standing logic of the "star system": audience loyalty to a celebrity is used to "guarantee" audience purchase of tickets to the celebrity's vehicle.

Celebrity itself is thus commodified; notoriety becomes a type of capital. Famous people are widely referred to within the entertainment industry simply as "names" (and the parallel term "somebody" is in wider use outside of the industry). By some criteria, such terms are odd, nonsensical, nondescriptive: everyone has a name, everybody is somebody. They hardly seem to communicate distinctive characteristics. In the context of the celebrity industry, the word "name" aptly summarizes the relevant commercial characteristic: recognition by consumers as a brand, familiarity in itself. The perceived ability to attract attention, regardless of what the attention is for, can be literally cashed in.

Day-to-day industry activities are logically geared toward building and profiting from the attention-getting capacities of performers. Publicists of a variety of kinds thus abound. Studio and network publicists are responsible for getting attention to a film or television program; unit publicists are hired by studios and networks to handle on-the-set publicity; and independent personal publicists, of varying power levels, are hired by individual clients to get them attention. Their role is absolutely central.

"There are too many people out there pushing for the space," says publicist Amanda Weber. "Eventually you have to get a publicist. Without one, if you're popular you have no control over publicity, and if you're not popular you're not going to get that popular because you won't have somebody pushing for the space for you."

Different players profit differently from celebrity. Personal publicists and their firms head up what can be seen as a team of *independent celebrity producers,* whose main concern is with individual personalities; *entertainment institutions* and the *entertainment-news media* each operate with a different set of concerns. Most commonly, independent celebrity producers make a profit by feeding performers into the entertainment industry: a publicist increases the perceived value of a particular client by building name recognition; that notoriety is promoted and cashed in through agents and managers for jobs, profiting the client and his or her team (the agent, the publicist, manager, business manager, lawyer). Within entertainment institutions, one set of activities is undertaken in order to increase an entertainer's notoriety (to increase the likelihood of consumption of the studio's film in which the person performs). Sarah Tamikian, a cable network publicist charged with promoting a new show with an unknown lead actor, takes it as her task to "make him more of a celebrity," simply because "if he becomes a celebrity more people are going to watch the show." A second set of activities use the entertainer as a spokesperson for the project, thereby increasing her recognition through increased exposure. "The celebrity is the selling tool," says film publicist Janine Rosenblat. "You need the individual to get the press. That's going to sell some tickets." For the entertainment-news media, celebrities not only provide the obvious subject matter but are exploited to sell magazines or build ratings and thus advertising revenues. Celebrities are used explicitly by her program, says Ann Sandberg, entertainment producer at a network morning show, to "generate audience turn-on." "That's very often how we promote the show. If you turn on [the network], you'll hear that on tomorrow's show you'll see Jodie Foster. That's a much sexier thing to promote than, 'Tomorrow we're going to show you inside an asbestos laboratory.'" At his entertainment magazine, says Stan Meyer, "there is a concentration of what we call hunks in trunks on the cover. There's no shortage of Tom Cruise and Mel Gibson and Kevin Costner on our cover, whoever the flavor of the season is, because those covers time and again sell extremely well."

Celebrities are useful money-makers not only for the entertainment and entertainment-journalism industries but for smaller industries such as novelty and tourism companies. For twenty to twenty-five dollars, one can choose from several Los Angeles companies' "tours of the Hollywood stars' homes," which take passengers past the current or former dwellings of Dinah Shore, Elvis Presley, Max Factor, Sonny and Cher, Ronald and Nancy Reagan, and so on. Restaurants and salons routinely place photos of famous clients on their walls to attract and impress customers. When a tabloid-television anchorwoman had her hair redesigned (shorter, bobbier) at his salon, proprietor Emile Riley received over fifty-five phone calls from prospective new clients. (The incident was reported in the *Los Angeles Times,* and that clip, blown up to poster size, is on the salon's wall.)

Celebrity making is clearly, then, an established commercial enterprise, made up of highly developed and institutionally linked professions and subindustries such as public relations, entertainment law, celebrity journalism and photography, grooming and training, managing and agenting, novelty sales. As carriers of the central commodity (attention-getting capacity), celebrity performers are themselves products. Indeed, the commercial-industrial environment in which they are developed is underlined by the language and self-perceptions of those working within it.

Theirs is predominantly the language of sales and marketing. "Everybody has to be sold," says personal manager Arlene Dayton. Margaret Thompson's job at a major talent agency is to find "up-and-coming people and expose them to buyers"—film and television studios and production companies. Marc Beyer is a television network publicist. "Celebrities are commodities," he says flatly. "These are products. I'm a salesman. I say this respectfully and immodestly. I'm a great salesman, and I'm proud of that. It's my salesmanship that has served me well in publicity, because publicists if they're good make it as salesmen." Home Box Office publicist Richard Rothenstein had the task of promoting a relatively unknown actress, Lynn Whitfield, in a major HBO film based on the life of Josephine Baker. "It would have been easier to promote a well-known actress because you could have said, 'Windex.' You could have said the brand name. Instead, you're selling a brand new product." Products, brands, flavors, selling tools, commodities, names—these are common terms used by celebrity workers for their clients.

One also typically hears the language of industry. The metaphor of machinery, for example, is a common one. Marsha Robertson is a former unit publicist and a "market coordinator" for Twentieth Century Fox.

"It's like an automobile," she says. "If there's a big enough engine this thing is going to move."

You can take someone and give them the machinery. With these really beautiful men and women, they don't have to do a whole lot themselves. You just get them in the car, turn on the engine, point it in that direction. Everything else is set up for them. The media is there waiting, with the covers and the profiles. Just slot the right driver in and we'll take care of the rest. And the machinery can also be customized, like any car.

Promoting his two unknowns, Josephine Baker and Lynn Whitfield, became an "industry," says Richard Rothenstein. "I call it the Josephine Machine."

The subindustries involved in celebrity production are not simply distant links in a production chain. The relationships between them are much tighter than, say, the relationship between a glass manufacturer providing supplies to an auto manufacturer. The ties are reinforced in constant day-to-day contact, at frequent "events" such as premieres and parties, and by focused mutual interest. The obvious shared interest in attracting consumers via celebrities is the most general basis for connections between the various subindustries. In particular, the representation and publicity industries are tightly linked both to each other (to produce and sell celebrities) and to the entertainment and entertainment-news industries (who buy and distribute their products). In daily work life, the institutional bonds translate into a continuous and voluminous flow of letters, faxes, and phone calls between publicists, agents, managers, producers, lawyers, journalists, and editors.

Those representing aspirants and those publicizing them depend on one another for their livelihoods: an unknown is difficult for an agent or manager to sell, and an unsold client is difficult for a publicist to get covered. As one publicist describes it:

They have to have some work. Hopefully they have past credits or they're coming up in good projects. You can't just tell everybody, "Gee, they're great, they're going to be working some day." Sometimes we've actually gotten our clients work so that they have something to talk about. When we take on a client, if they don't have a good team it really hurts. Because nobody else is taking what you're doing and using it towards the betterment of that person's career. We do stuff that then should help the manager and agent, who should take it and use it. Then we have more stuff to work with, and it keeps going like that. They have to *use* what we do.

The capital of notoriety is cashed in by the aspirant and her team, who then convert it into more notoriety, then into better jobs and higher fees and increased profits for the whole team.

Similarly, entertainment and media institutions are linked to each other: plainly put, producers need coverage and editors need subjects. "We are a magazine that has a vested interest in to some extent creating celebrities, because these are the people you're going to continue to get stories out of," says one *People* magazine editor. "It's about money. You need someone who can sell the magazine." A national morning-show producer sums up her job requirement as ensuring that there are "two very promotable names of the highest quality and promotability on every day." It is exactly these "someones" and "names" that publicists (along with the performers and the rest of their teams) are in the business of building and providing. "Since America is a brand-name buying public," says Gene Schwam, president of Hanson and Schwam Public Relations, "a public relations firm has to establish the client as a brand name in the marketplace."[3] Both the publicist and the journalistic organization share this fundamental commercial interest in the creation and use of brand-name celebrities for consumption.

The Celebrity Marketing Process

HBO publicist Richard Rothenstein, publicizing *The Josephine Baker Story,* was charged with making unknown actress Lynn Whitfield a known quantity, both to attract viewers and to make her more useful as a promoter for the film. Initially, Whitfield was conflated with the Baker character she was playing, who was also largely unknown; Whitfield, in Baker poses, was sold to fashion magazines simply as a "beautiful black woman." But Rothenstein also relied on a popular story line, "the new discovery."

She was a black actress getting the black role of a lifetime. That was the pitch. It was this heavily sought-after part that every black actress, singer, and dancer and probably even some white people wanted, and it was given to Lynn Whitfield after one of these Scarlett O'Hara talent hunts, months and months. I'd say to people, "This is the kind of role that could be Fanny Brice in *Funny Girl,* it could be Streisand. It's the kind of role that makes or breaks an actor." It was, "Here's a respected black actress who's done amazing work and who now has a role that everybody wanted." Lynn is a very good actress, on and off. She molds herself. She gives good interview. So we tried to find a way to have her life story peg into why she was meant to do this movie. She could relate to the role, even in her struggle as a black woman and not being cast in certain roles in high school plays. We strategized how we were going to explain to people why she won, why she became Josephine.

The "Josephine Machine" succinctly illustrates the elements of industrialized celebrity marketing. Lynn Whitfield must become of interest in order to attract attention to the film product, and a large organization goes to work to make it happen; she is trained and tinkered with, her raw materials "improved" upon; impressions of her are managed by the organization; a familiar narrative—the big break that was meant to be—is consciously developed for media sales and audience identification.

The step-by-step marketing process involved in launching and maintaining a celebrity is analogous to that undertaken for any new product, according to the authors of *High Visibility*. They set out the process in pure form, more a prescription for rationalizing it than a description of its current state, and therefore provide a usefully clean, unambiguous, exaggerated sketch of celebrity marketing. Although I will later reinsert the mess and ambiguity, it will help to first see the elements clearly.

For the most part, the marketing model of celebrity has moved from random "discovery" and refinement to deliberate "breeding." What in cultural myths appear to be uncontrollable are, according to the authors, in fact quite achievable: talent, for example, is not God-given and fixed but "the product of such controllable forces as role modeling, expectation management, mentoring, timing, luck-seeking, strategic positioning, and geography." In many arenas, most aspirants share basic requirements, and marketing serves to "identify the best sector in which to compete, determine the best role for one to play, and help isolate the most productive audiences to approach." Most generally, the principle is to "analyze the image and characteristics that the aspirant possesses, as well as those that the sector expects, and transform the person to bring the two closer together."[4]

After analyzing the market environment and carefully defining a target market, the marketer either sells a ready-for-consumption client as best she can, treating the product as fixed ("pure selling"), finds a market niche and then searches for the most promotable aspirant to fill it ("market fulfillment"), or looks for ways to modify the client to "add value to the performer's ability to attract the market's interest" ("product improvement"). If this latter marketing style is undertaken, certain "techniques of transformation" are available. A "character"—that is, a "unique, or at least distinct, combination of factors that will distinguish one aspirant from the rest"—must be generated and developed; it must then be tested and refined through the manipulation of signs and symbols, appearance, voice, movement, behavior, and performed material; finally, it must be realized, the change internalized by the aspirant, who must feel from within that "one *is* the new self."[5]

To successfully launch a celebrity, the authors argue, one must understand well the workings and desires of audiences. "The ultimate selling strategy is to foster audience identification," they write. "Product marketers understand the process well: Measure consumers' self-images, demographics, and psychological needs, then provide them with products that embody characteristics which match and meet them." The primary strategy for forging the bond begins from the core understanding that audiences depend on stories for the transmission of information. "Dramatic Reality," somewhere between fact and fiction, is a controllable transmission of celebrity publicity.

If there is one thing that serves more than any other to involve audiences with celebrities, it is the storyline. The conscious design, manipulation, and promotion of storylines in celebrities' lives—up to the point of creating realities more dramatic than real life—constitutes the celebrity industry's major breakthrough in the 1970s and 1980s. Not content merely to wait for real life to supply drama, celebrity marketers, realizing the power of drama to propel aspirants to high visibility, have begun to manufacture it. Dramatic Reality consists of either (a) highlighting of the dramatic elements in celebrities' real lives, or (b) the deliberate and strategic mixing of celebrities' real lives with fictional story elements. . . . The ultimate goal is to make more commercially exploitable the audience's involvement with celebrities.[6]

Most celebrity stories, the authors argue, contain a mix of six major elements (including adversity, crisis, and unrelenting talent) and run along twenty-two popular story lines (such as little guy makes good, outrageous behavior, a great rivalry, the big break). Marketers ought to find the "best match" between these and their client-aspirant.

The most powerful forces bonding audiences to aspirants are those that deliver celebrity images: institutional sponsors and the communication media. It is thus crucial that the celebrity's performance vehicles be carefully selected to fit the marketing plan; this is the job of those managing celebrity careers. It is just as crucial that media coverage be carefully "managed"; this is the job of the public-relations practitioners handling celebrities. PR's business is to know "how to get into the media's coverage patterns," providing services and giving each story a legitimate hook to attract news coverage. By controlling that coverage, acting as the "voice" of the celebrity, the authors argue, PR "defines the celebrity's relationship with the audience. . . . Whether the fundamental stories are true or not, PR *always* amplifies and distills them for public consumption."[7] By linking the celebrity to the media delivery system, PR is critical for seeing that the Dramatic Reality of the celebrity life is delivered both in celebrities' "real lives" and in their " 'performance' lives." The delivery system must be carefully managed for full effect.

How close is the actual Los Angeles celebrity industry to the pure marketing system advocated in *High Visibility*? In a few cases, it seems to be mimicked in unadulterated form. One industry worker describes a contest in which a self-proclaimed star maker offers one male winner and one female winner the chance to become stars: candidates are attracted through an advertising campaign and screened on the basis of "talent, looks, and charisma"; the first cut is through photos, on the basis of looks, and the second and subsequent cuts are judged by "experts," on the basis of auditions, interviews, and dinner-conversation evaluations of charisma. Once the selections are made, a manufacturing process is begun. The "svengali" decides on the proper images, building them from the carefully selected raw material; a support team is provided; and once the candidates are properly transformed, connections are made with industry and media buyers. Here the path to celebrity is deliberate and manufacturer-initiated.

Many in the industry point out, however, that this kind of behavior is atypical, that most activity around celebrities is not premeditated. "It's not as calculated as all that," says Bob Merlis, vice-president for publicity at Warner Brothers Records. "We don't really send them to Motown charm school and turn them into little ladies and gentlemen." Marketing *logic,* however, is ever present, coexisting with but overshadowing the "it just happens" cultural mythology. Merlis, for example, continues by arguing that charm school is especially unnecessary because "the whole rebel offensive persona is not necessarily negative on the marketplace." Film production company publicist Jack Emilio attributes much of what works to luck, getting "the bounce." He suggests that often what happens by accident "is declared premeditated in hindsight." "There are people who will walk you through a campaign and say, 'We did this, this, and this. We had them wear red because it's a color that people identify with, and we had them turn to the left because that's the side that makes people

such and such,' and so on. But a lot of it just happens." Many celebrity
workers aim toward and take pride in treating their work as a deliberate,
if not fully realized, manufacturing process—so much so that they claim
to have calculated serendipitous events. If someone knew the formula for
creating a celebrity, industry workers insist, they would bottle it and make
a million bucks.

Usually, that line is part of an argument that there is no formula.
The mystical, vague, decidedly nonrational notions, rooted in 1930s' and
1940s' celebrity texts, enter the discussion: "star quality," "charisma,"
"a certain something." Managers and agents look for aspirants with "It"
or "star quality" and say over and over that finding them is "a big guessing
game" based on "visceral responses." (We will return to this theme of
"unknowability," common in cultural industries, in the discussion of the
producer–audience relationship.) Nonetheless, most activities are geared
toward finding the unfindable formula, and the "mystical" beliefs, when
scratched, reveal marketing behaviors beneath them.

The prevalent notion of the "lucky break," for example, often comes
up in industry workers' explanations of why "star making" is impossible
(in that opportunities for stardom are based on luck, which is not controllable); however, publicists' and managers' behaviors do not fully support
a belief that celebrity is uncontrollable. "I don't consider myself a star
maker at all," says Henry Rogers, cofounder of the powerful public relations firm Rogers and Cowan. "I kick open the door of opportunity for
stardom." While they cannot control demand on the mass market, publicists design much of their activity precisely to influence the industry opportunity structure, the "break" market. "I'm hoping that my efforts in
getting the awareness through the media," says Rogers, "will help them
to get a part in a picture that will achieve fame for them." The "lucky
break" is dismissed; opportunities are to be created, not awaited.

Similarly, many industry activities resemble the project of "discovery":
keeping an eye out for "It." Operationally, however, this sort of discovery
is closer to a market-fulfillment strategy. "Maybe there still are Lana
Turners," says manager Arlene Dayton, "but you don't plan a career like
that." Celebrity producers are salespeople and look first to the marketplace. "Star quality" can be read as another name for mass-market appeal,
that which makes one popular. Not surprisingly, the characteristics that
attract a broad array of people are difficult to pin down, guessed at with
"the gut." It is not surprising that what agent Rob Hass calls "taking the

pulse of the audience" evokes a certain mysticism since it involves taking multiple, often conflicting pulses.

When the mass audience is broken into particular subaudiences, however, the "formula" is easier to nail down—and discussions of mystical qualities tend to give way to rational, marketing terms. To do her job "realistically," Dayton must "steer [her] clients into an area where they can flourish"—that is, discern entertainment-industry market gaps. "What goes into it is my experience of seeing what works, what sells, what there's a glut of now, what there's a need for," says manager David Spiro. "Once I find out what you want to do, I have to see if it's feasible, and if it is, I market you in that way." Feasibility, and the possibilities for market fulfillment, are relatively discernible when the scope is narrowed from "the public" to "the industry." An aspirant can be selected, or steered, accordingly.

Selecting a marketable aspirant also makes daily work life much easier. Confidence in the consumption-readiness of a product allows salespeople to argue enthusiastically and honestly and saves them and their companies from costly and time-consuming product-improvement activities. Susan Rice, a local television programmer, argues that "you could probably create things that aren't there," but it's not worth the bother. "It's that old thing about tell the truth, you don't have to take as many notes. If you said, 'Take your secretary and make her a talk-show host,' I could do it over a period of time, but what a bunch of work, rather than taking someone with on-air talent and potential." Many managers and publicists point out that the more "special" a client is, the easier the sales job to producers, casting directors, or editors. "I've got to really believe in it," says Dayton.

I can't sell somebody that I don't believe is really talented. Some of the great stuff I've done for people through the years is because of my passion. I've had conversations with producers or casting directors where I've said, "You're not going to leave your office. I'm going to lay in front of your door and you're not leaving your office until you see my client." And that comes from passion. I don't think you can fake that.

Personal publicist Amanda Weber won't take on clients unless she's convinced they're "special" and have "something internal." Again, the reasoning is pragmatic. "They need to stand out from the crowd for me because what I have to do eventually," she says, "is make them stand out from the crowd. If it's somebody I don't believe in it's harder." Pure selling is easier with a distinctive product; there is indeed an incentive to find aspirants who are starting off with extraordinary qualities.

Extraordinary qualities are not, however, necessarily dependable and certain ones on the marketplace. "I used to think that if the person was sufficiently talented that it really caught my breath, I could sell that person," says Dayton. "I don't do that anymore. I look today not only for talent but for a certain amount of commerciality. Marketability." Discovery, in fact, is "bad business," points out agent Rob Hass. "Standard Oil doesn't do a lot of wildcatting. They usually let smaller drillers wildcat, and then they go in and pay a premium." Large talent and publicity agencies tend to allow smaller firms to do discovery and transformation; they then "buy" stars with established markets and sell them. "The people we deal with already have an established name," says Jerome North, an account executive at a major publicity firm, "so it's just a matter of contacting the press." Marc Beyer's description of his colleagues at powerful personal publicity firms captures the work-life and business advantages of picking up established stars rather than finding and building them:

The guys that handle Warren Beatty, Madonna, Cher, Liz Taylor, whoever, they could have been carpet-sample salesmen for twenty years and then they sign Kevin Costner, and all they'd have to do is sit here and their phone would literally ring off the hook. "No." "Yes." "No." "I'll get back to you." Not make one proactive call. My father sold telephones, and he had to come up with ways to get them to buy this crap. But with them, it's like selling Mercedes, it's like, "Would you like the leather interior? Was that the brown paint?"

Although those who can afford to will avoid the risks of discovery and product testing, most celebrity-industry workers are not in a position to sign Madonna and Kevin Costner. Instead, they must launch unknowns. These aspirants and their teams most clearly reveal the manufacturing and marketing logic of the celebrity system. David Spiro, who himself has a degree in marketing, tells clients to

take courses in marketing, because you should know more than anything else how to market yourself. You can market yourself well if you're smart. If you're not smart, you get with someone who's smart and can market you. It is all marketing. You can mold any way you want. Meryl Streep could have been Bette Midler. Bette Midler could have been Meryl Streep. Agents and managers will always try to change what's raw.

Once the "raw materials" have been selected, most teams (and again, the team includes the aspirant herself) begin to assess the expectations of buyers and tr to bring the characteristics of aspirants closer to them. Often, this pu h to fulfill perceived market demands leads celebrity handlers to advise clients to adapt themselves to those demands through "product-improvement" strategies. Dayton advises on "everything pertaining to the image of that person"—teeth, nose jobs, hair pieces—based on "where the industry is at and where you fit within that industry." Marla Keane tells of her boss's determination that the key to the selling of a female client—who in fact became a major television star—was nipples. "So she had nipples in every poster," says Keane. "In every photo session, she wore little rubber bands around her nipples so that they were always sticking out."

Publicists sell to a set of buyers who pay not in cash but in exposure and must convince the media outlet that this celebrity can meet their business needs. "It's more than just 'Will this be an interesting person?' " says Diana Widdom, a publicity director for Paramount Studios, of the criteria of those to whom she pitches. "It's 'Will this person sell magazines? How will these magazines look on the news racks?' " For stars with proven drawing power, these questions are easily answered. For lesser-knowns, however, the publicist faces a difficulty: since he must convince media buyers that his client can attract an audience, the aspirant must ideally already have notoriety in order to get some more. Publicists seek coverage routes that bypass this catch-22, and their job is one of constant persuasion. The least sure strategy is pitching the project alone (although journalists often note with dismay that this is the most common pitch) or the aspirant's talents alone. Publicists look primarily toward strategies that can garner coverage regardless of name recognition or ability. One avenue is looks. "Let's face it," says personal publicist Amanda Weber, "looks is a great commodity in this business, and it tends to carry over to publications and television and everything else. If you have a great-looking person you can almost sell them on their looks alone. They don't even need to have a project, or it can be a wimpy project."

Publicists employ personality in the search for the distinctive pitch. Record company publicist Bob Merlis reels off the variety of pitches he tries to develop: when he can't depend on his client's music to be "completely transcendent," he looks for an unusual activity ("You can say, 'This guy races cars in his spare time' or 'He's a rodeo champ' "), an unusual event ("I always ask the managers, 'While the record was being recorded, did the hand brake on the equipment truck disintegrate and did the truck roll into a convent where there was an explosion?' ''), a bit of titillation ("Rod Stewart's many blonde girlfriends and wives—it's great stuff"), or a story about change ("You can always think of something to talk about if you change"). Such personal details allow a publicist to distinguish nearly *any* aspirant. As a cable-television network publicist says simply, "The person doesn't really have to have anything in particular for me to do my job. There's always something you can find to talk about."

Beyond the day-to-day search for pitches, publicists rely on product-improvement and transformation strategies to shape a client to fit the perceived needs of the media market. Personal publicist Michael Levine, who has handled Vanna White, among many others, argues that "what publicists do is analogous to what gift wrappers do in department stores."

They make a gift have a higher perceived value. So, for example, if you were to purchase a gift for someone, and you were to present it to that person in a Tiffany box, and then gave the same gift to someone in a Sears box, the Tiffany box would give it a higher perceived value to the receiver. I think this is metaphorically what entertainment publicists attempt to do for their clients.

Careful packaging involves an assessment of what is of value to the receiver (in this case, media workers) and a development of the performer accordingly.

Transformation activities, especially at the deep level they are advocating, are not nearly as widespread as the *High Visibility* authors would like them to be. They are not, however, uncommon. At times, transformation does approach the pure model. After selecting winners in his I'll-make-you-a-star contest, one entrepreneurial personal manager decided that the female raw material he had chosen was "too tomboyish" and not "organically sexy enough." He "will create the sexiness," his assistant explains, through transformation techniques: "clothes, plastic surgery if he has to, posing, photos, voice, mannerisms; he'll coach and develop her." Like the authors of *High Visibility*, he believes in and embraces "that whole Pygmalion thing." More commonly, publicists transform clients' skills, much like any employment consultant will advise on how to properly "sell yourself." They train their clients to fit the needs of journalists and talk shows for either an interesting subject or an engaging style. "Some people just don't know how to conduct an interview," says Paramount Studios publicist Diana Widdom. "They scratch their heads and smell and wear horrible clothes and answer monosyllabically." So Paramount will bring in someone to "teach the talent how to respond to questions." The celebrities come not only able to respond but often armed with a "good angle." With publicists' help, celebrities become user-friendly and ready-to-use, looking as they need to look, learning to "give good interview," equipped with a suitable narrative.

Celebrity Marketing and the Semifictional

*The last big piece of publicity I did for the film [*Swimming to Cambodia*] was for* People *magazine. They wanted to photograph Laurie Anderson, who did the music for the film, and Jonathan Demme, who directed it, and myself—all of us playing some popular sport that would appeal to our nation at large. . . . The three of us bowled with a heightened theatrical intensity that I'd never experienced while bowling before. It was more than bowling; it was the idealized image of bowling, and we all bowled the better for it. We laughed a little harder, jumped a little higher and smiled a little broader until Laurie had to leave for another appointment. Then Michael, the photographer's assistant, took over for Laurie, and Ken Regan photographed the acted reactions of Jonathan and me to Michael playing Laurie. At last, after Ken got all the photos he needed, he turned out the lights, and he and Michael began to pack up. Suddenly the bowling alley returned to its seedy, everyday fluorescence. . . . "Aren't you going to finish the game?" Jonathan asked. Which game? I wondered. I thought the game was over. Is there really such a thing as just bowling after bowling for* People *magazine?*

Spalding Gray, "The Haul of Fame"

The most common techniques for matching aspirants to markets are publicity strategies—impression management through public appearances—in which only the aspirant's outside coating is developed and transformed. The aspirant is "gift wrapped" in a particular set of images and ideas; the material inside remains the same. Although, as Rein and his colleagues argue, transforming only the surface is riskier than deep-level change (since it can never "guarantee that public image and private behavior will match"[8]), it is also easier, less costly, and more adaptable to changing market requirements. "I think you can have total control of the [visual] image," says performer Nia Peeples, "because you can hire a publicist, you can hire a costumer, you can sit down and sketch everything out for yourself, and you can completely strategize what you want to do. You can pump the public full of an image." Much publicist activity is geared toward controlling both the visual and verbal presentation of the celebrity: providing or approving photos, sitting in on interviews, acting as a spokesperson. "That's part of the art of publicity," says personal publicist Jordan Kamisky.

One of the things you always do with a client is you ask them to keep eye contact with you throughout the interview, so that they can make sure that if they're saying something they shouldn't be saying you let them know. I make it a policy to always be there, so that if the interview is going in a certain direction I would be able to bring it back into another direction. You're always protecting your client and making them look as good as possible.

Control is maintained not only for protection but so that appealing sales pitches can be developed and implemented, narratives based in some truths but publicist-designed for media buyers. Here we begin to see the active production of semifictional information, the day-to-day manufacture of what *High Visibility* calls Dramatic Reality, what Boorstin called human pseudo-events, what Norman Mailer has called "factoids," and what postmodern theorists point to as "simulated" events and selves. Kamisky, for example, tells of discovering that his costume-designer client was giving antique christening gowns to various celebrity couples. "The press loves to hear about that," he says. "So I sit down and talk with [the client]. 'Okay, what can we say? Why don't we say that you're trying to renew a tradition?' We make it up. He didn't see any connection, so I look for the connection." He develops a story line for his client and then advises him to play himself in interviews; he develops a sort of docudrama character "based on a true story."

Similarly, celebrity handlers design publicity campaigns to build particular images to shift or expand the celebrity's marketability. Henry Rogers describes attempts to shift Sylvester Stallone's image from "strictly a dese-dems-and-dose guy."

He has an excellent contemporary art collection, and he has studied, goes to auctions, reads books; he's very knowledgeable about the world of art. One day, *Life* magazine ran six pages on Sylvester Stallone's interest in art. And it didn't happen by accident, because we went to *Life* magazine and said, "Here's a really good story for you. Here's a guy that the whole public thinks is just a dese-dems-and-dose guy, but behind it is an agile brain that thinks in terms other than Rambo."

Amanda Weber had one client who had been "very youth-oriented, so adult editors weren't interested." Her solution: "We adulted him. We did a whole clothing change, a major image change. It's style, maybe picking out certain quotes, building the image through written words." For another client, who wanted to move from comedy into leading-man roles, she "claimed the territory" of an all-black wardrobe as his identifying feature, started to "do relationship stuff, so we had that vulnerable kind of thing." Manager David Spiro has a "ditzy-looking" client whom he prepares for interviews. "You develop a persona," he says.

I'll have her talking about very serious things. We practice. I ask her questions and see how she'll answer. If an interviewer starts talking to you about your sex life, all of a sudden you've changed sex life into talking about the morality of America. When you're asked what you do in your spare time, you want to appear intelligent, introspective. You're reading a lot. Whether you do or not. You have the names of books when they ask you, something that is on the *New York Times* bestseller list but isn't trash.

She is advised and coached on the development of a semireal public personality. It is her, and it is not her. Robin Leach, whose trademark as narrator of "Lifestyles of the Rich and Famous" is a loud, shrill, exaggerated voice, did not begin with that voice, according to a director who has worked closely with him. In the beginning, she says, "Robin talked like a normal person with an accent. Then Dan Ackroyd started doing Robin imitations on 'Saturday Night Live,' and Robin got so much public ity out of it that Robin started doing Dan Ackroyd doing Robin. And now that's how he is, all the time." The personality can be developed from the inside out, but it is safer to work from the outside in.

Why use fiction—and I use the term loosely, to mean anything from embellishment to fabrication—as a sales device? The answer, we have seen, is essentially practical: depending on truth alone may mean losing one's livelihood; fictionalizing frees up the celebrity producer to be competitive. Then why bother with the truth if fiction is more manageable and effective? First of all, truth makes the selling job easier, especially if the product is genuinely outstanding or in demand. If they lie, celebrity teams damage their credibility with media buyers, on whom they depend. Having a basis in truth is insurance against being dismissed as a "wolf"-crier. Second, media buyers in particular are looking for events that really have happened and people who act like people. Having a basis in truth provides the protection of "facts": Stallone really does have an art collection, *Sleeping with the Enemy* really did premiere with flood lights and red carpet, the costumer really did give away antique christening gowns, Spalding Gray really did bowl. The active production of semifictional characters and semifictional events, then, is a practical resolution to the competitive environment in which celebrity producers operate.

The Pessimist's Nightmare?

The celebrity marketing process presented thus far invokes many of the worst nightmares of cultural pessimists and cynical conspiracy theorists. When persons are marketed for profit, say the critics, merit and fame are separated and image overtakes substance.

Celebrity as a business does seem to drive toward these divorces, building and trading on knownness itself. Although there is room for folk heroics, most activity is geared toward a manufacturing process. In that process, manufacturers use the pragmatic strategy of semifiction. These activities are indeed rational: people known for themselves rather than for their achievements are more commercially useful because they can be attached to any number of products. Moreover, divorcing attention from excellence, and merging fiction and reality, serve broad professional interests, opening up the field for both candidates and professional specialists surrounding them.

Like many of the texts that deconstruct image production, both culture critics and enthusiastic marketing advocates display an awed belief in the unified power of entertainment and media industries to impose their will on "the public." Much is missing here, however. The picture painted so far is accurate: celebrity is certainly industrialized, people are certainly commodified. But this is a clean picture of an industry with no seams, no conflict, and no mess—too clean.[9] The picture, to be faithful, must be messed up, complicated.

Chapter Four

The Negotiated Celebration

With Isabel Adjani, I was having the worst time. All of a sudden we're seeing in the gossip columns that Warren Beatty was at the hotel at two in the afternoon, and so and so had come by at three o'clock, and Daniel Day-Lewis was around. It was like, who the hell got paid in that hotel? Someone was getting paid under the table to find out just what was going on. Yes, Beatty was showing up. They're friends. Yes, Daniel Day was there, too, and God knows who else. There's nothing you can do. But you just sit there going crazy trying to stop this from happening, and sometimes you have no control over it. Isabel Adjani is supposed to be a class act, so why would we want to see the National Enquirer *saying all these guys are trudging along in the hotel? We're protecting the image of her as a class act, and that's what she wanted. Then on the night of the big premiere I took her and Warren through a back route just to make it safer, since it was paparazzi out of control. So the car takes off without me, and the next thing I know around the corner come all the paparazzi, screaming at me. I am chased to my car, and stones are being thrown. They were throwing stones because I wouldn't let them have her. To get a Warren Beatty photo with Isabel Adjani, maybe embracing, that's worth some good buckeroonies. And I took away whatever chance they had. Not one photo came out. I was always in the way.*

Janine Rosenblat,
independent film publicist

In real-life journalism you call up the source and you say, "Can you talk?" In celebrity journalism you call up the publicist, you negotiate, you negotiate, set ground rules, negotiate.

Miriam Ross,
entertainment magazine editor

Adjust the picture. Looking closely at the celebrity industry, one sees not the smooth assembly-line manufacture of commodified human sales pieces but intense back-stabbing and back-scratching, negotiations and skirmishes. The language is often not only of sales and industry but also of combat and arbitration. Entertainment journalists—writers, editors,

television producers, and bookers—most commonly describe their relationship with publicists in terms such as "battles" and "bargaining." In
these relationships, intense mutual hostility coexists with intense mutual
buttering-up. Powerful female publicists are on the one hand referred to
by respected journalists as "dragon ladies." Stone throwing is an exaggerated image to summarize the publicist–media worker relationship, but it
works metaphorically. On the other hand, an editor at *Forbes* points out,
it is very difficult to think of another "beat where your sources air-kiss
you."[1] Although the workers in the various celebrity-producing industries
are in many ways tightly allied, the relationships among those actively
producing celebrity representations also pull in a variety of directions.
Understanding these relationships, their tensions, and their resolutions
is critical for understanding precisely what sort of representations they
produce.

Sponsors and Teams: Celebrity versus Spokesperson

In order to most effectively manage the manufacture of celebrity, like the
manufacture of any product, the production process has to have, first
of all, a unified goal. Either through an identity of interests or through
centralized, hierarchical control, those in the production process need to
set out to produce the same product. This was generally the case during
the days of tight studio control, but there is no longer a single organization
in control of the celebrity and the celebrity image. Even if the interests
of all parties were completely aligned (and at times they come close),
coordinating the production process is cumbersome because it is decen-
tralized and nonmonopolistic. In fact, despite a general correspondence
of interests in the production of celebrities, the various parties (the celebrity and her team, the sponsoring entertainment organizations) do not all
have the same particular type of product, and the same particular types
of uses, in mind.

A certain nostalgia for the studio system, along with behaviors that
try to reinstate some of its elements, is heard in discussions with studio and
network publicists. Diana Widdom is senior vice-president for worldwide
special publicity planning at Paramount Studios. "In many respects," she
says, "I wish those days would come back again."

In the good old days, it was, "You report to Stage B and you have your photograph
taken at 2:30." And they did. That's the way to get the most out of your talent

and make sure they'll do what you want them and need them to do to publicize a film. There is no substitute for a star really working for a film. It is terribly, terribly important. And studios now know that going in, and they're sort of backing away from making films with actors who won't do publicity. They're not under any legal obligation, which is a sore point. The Paramount legal department very much wants to introduce back into contracts that the star will have an obligation to promote their film. We have no *real* way of getting an actor to do anything he doesn't want to do.

This last sentence sums up the tensions in the celebrity-production scene: struggles between a variety of parties over what a celebrity should do and be and over the capacity to make him or her do and be.

The question of what a celebrity should be involves more than the constant daily disagreements over what will work (that hairstyle is too young, this role is too much against type); more fundamental disagreements are rooted in different interests. Key players with short-term interests tend to emphasize a performer's vehicles over her career, while players with long-term interests will emphasize career over vehicle. The result is a push in different directions: both toward and away from a celebrity divorced from her particular vehicles and roles, known for her self alone; and both toward and away from interchangeability.

As long as performers are hired on a project-by-project basis, studios, networks, and production companies will want the celebrity to be tightly linked in the short term to a particular project. For one thing, the publicity they sponsor is always geared toward selling the vehicle. "If you went on a talk show and talked mostly about your life and not the film," says Widdom, "that would not be our best case at all. There's a certain way the marketing department is going to sell the film, and we want the talent also to sell the film in that same way." As Bob Merlis of Warner Brothers points out, while the company benefits from a celebrity's notoriety ("the fact that Madonna is written about in a given magazine is good because it raises the consciousness of her as an entity"), fame itself is not enough. "The fact that you're famous is thrilling," he says, "but could we sell something please?" Moreover, to the degree that they do make use of a "personality sell," sponsoring organizations tend to want to use personality to link celebrities to their vehicles (again, as earlier studios did in the blurring of "reel" and "real" lives). Nia Peeples is a recording artist, dancer, actress, and hostess (until its cancellation) of a late-night, youth-oriented, television dance-party program called "The Party Machine with Nia Peeples." Paramount, the studio that produced the show, pushed her to make public appearances and conduct interviews that painted her as a party girl. "Paramount doesn't care about the rest of my career," Peeples said in an interview before the show's cancellation. "They care about 'The Party Machine,' and that's it. So to have me be a hostess out there partying all the time and giving that image is what they would love. But I won't. It's not me. It's just their vision of the ultimate party host." In large part, sponsoring organizations try not only to consistently establish a link between the celebrity and the vehicle but also to line up their celebrity's public personality with the celebrity's character and tone in that vehicle.

Such a strategy can be hazardous for performers and their managing teams. First of all, they may be asked to associate themselves enthusiastically with what turns out to be an ill-received project; the closer the association, the lower drops their market value. Second, being too closely associated with a project may cut off future options. For the celebrity emphasizing "performer" over "star," a commonly cited danger is that of being "typed." As a manager, David Spiro has his eye on what's "good for you long term." For him, this means the ability to diversify.

In the industry they're very short-sighted, and they pigeonhole. It's the only way they can work with you. People have in their head what Eartha Kitt is going to do. It's "Batman" or it's camp. If you're young and put yourself in a position where you're doing lots of slasher movies, it's hard to break out of that. When the industry looks at Joan Collins, they're going to see someone who's beautiful, glamorous, bitchy. Therefore you're not going to see Joan Collins doing *Driving Miss Daisy,* because no one's going to want to invest ten million dollars in a film where Joan Collins is going to play a kindly old woman dressing in rags. They don't think the American public is going to believe it.

Nia Peeples's concerns are both personal ("it's not me") and professional ("the rest of my career"). Paramount's desires, in addition to conflicting with her self-image, may be damaging to her credibility as a more serious and versatile performer and thus harmful to her future value. She runs the risk of giving people in the industry "just that image in their minds of a sexy, energetic, party-going person, that Nia Peeples is a party animal." Not only is that not accurate, she says, but "my goal in life is not to become Downtown Julie Brown or Martha Quinn"—that is, to become locked into the role of "television personality."

For those pursuing bankability based primarily on personality rather than ability, being linked to specific projects and roles carries an even more fundamental risk. The most valuable type of celebrity—commonly referred to as the "real star"—is the one liberated from particular projects and abilities who can gain attention and loyalty for his self, for being "unique" and unprecedented. "It's kind of degrading to think that you're just famous for singing, or just famous for acting, or just famous for dancing, or just famous for being funny," says Los Angeles's Angelyne. "I want to be famous for the magic I possess. I've never happened before." Her assistant, Scott Hennig, even more clearly articulates this notion.

Stars are people whose own personality is so strong, and their own visual image is so strong, that they come across as themselves no matter what they're doing. The people who have been consistent stars throughout time, even after they died, are people who established a certain persona. John Wayne was John Wayne in every movie, no matter what. No matter what Marilyn was in, she was Marilyn.

Angelyne's approach is to "only take projects that allow her to be strictly Angelyne." This strategy severely limits job options, of course, something the vast majority of aspirants aren't willing to do. But to the degree that they and their strategists take this route of developing a transcendent "persona," the constant need to be associated with their particular vehicles gets in the way.

A second set of conflicting interests runs parallel to the conflict between personal promotion and vehicle promotion. Although they clearly want a celebrity with demonstrated attention-getting capacity, entertainment-industry buyers do not necessarily need one with the demonstrated capacity of audience *loyalty*. The ubiquitous term "hot," evoking a temporary, passing condition, captures this short-term interest well. A flash in the pan, as long as it is made use of in its hot period, does no damage to an organization whose use of the performer is temporary. Indeed, a celebrity who is hot and recognizable but not established is easier to come by and less expensive to employ than a major star; the latter, of course, with an established audience, is still a safer form of insurance and can draw a much higher price. A celebrity and his team are obviously damaged by interchangeability; being replaceable is not only a tremendously unstable position but also one that vastly decreases one's value. Relinquishing control of the production process to someone with a short-term interest can damage future prospects in this way as well: those driving toward the safe bet of the formulaic tend to produce imitative celebrities, with a short shelf life. "Your individuality is what sends you to the top and makes you stay there," says Peeples. "Being the most of what I am. Nobody does Tina Turner better than Tina Turner. Nobody is what I am better than

I am." Those who would use her, however, "can only hear the hit that's happening right now."

It would be very simple for me to do that. When I was shopping for a record deal, I had a lot of record companies say, "This is great. You dance. You have a great look. Paula [Abdul] and Janet [Jackson] are happening right now, that's the biggest thing. We could put you in this machine, this formula that already works, and spit you out to the public, and we know that you can perform in front of it."

Peeples fought against this, first of all, because as a born-again Christian she cares about the content of what she's putting out; more revealing, she resisted it because it goes against the individuality she believes is necessary for success. Robbed of the ability to be "wholly Nia" (like many celebrities, she refers to herself periodically in the third person), she believes she is robbed of the chance to become a performer with longevity. The choice to be sponsored, or to appeal to sponsors, often involves a greater risk—being a "one-hit wonder."

We are beginning to see an odd mix of conflicting interests: sponsors are interested in making use of performers as celebrities but want to see them consistently linked to work; the performer who wants to increase his performance marketability often is interested in deemphasizing the particular performance vehicle; the performer who wants to increase her marketability as a celebrity persona is also resistant to the link to work, preferring personality alone; the short-term entertainment-industry interests push toward formulaic, interchangeable performers, while those celebrities and celebrity teams with an eye on the long haul have an interest in resisting that. The relationships pursued between celebrities and their performances and roles (are performances and roles an important part of their public images or not? are roles and lives conflated?), and between celebrities and distinction (are celebrities produced as genres or as individuals?), are not nearly as simple and clean as they first appeared. Indeed, they are disputes built into the celebrity production process.

Publicists, Celebrities, and Outlets: Who Keeps the Gates?

A couple of weeks ago we were going after a big star in a big movie. I thought automatically he would do an interview. I was told, "Well, he's going through a different publicity phase on this." Between the lines, it was, "He's going to try to take the high road on this," go for the cover of Vanity Fair *or* Rolling Stone *rather than "Entertainment Tonight." I was told he wasn't going to do a lot of other things. In the meantime, we were offered three other costars from that film, and we did them, and arranged to do the premiere and all that stuff. Then when it came time to start running them, this actor suddenly started showing up on our competition, on Oprah, Donahue, the morning shows. So I was told by my producers, "Tell them we're not running any of the stuff we've done unless he agrees to an interview." I told the studio and the personal publicist. I was accused of blackmail. It wasn't blackmail, because it was one thing when it started and then all of a sudden the rules changed. So the publicist went to the star, and the star said, "No way," got really mad. So we pulled out of covering the premiere that night. It was a big deal. A day and a half later he agreed to do an interview, and he couldn't have been nicer during the interview. So we aired two pieces, and we reinstated our other ones.*

Pete Hammond, segment producer,
"Entertainment Tonight"

It's a very fine line we have to tread between doing journalism and just being an outlet for whatever a celebrity wants to say. It's very hard to have any integrity and cover Hollywood, because so many people are trying to manipulate image.

Michael Alexander, staff writer,
People magazine

I am my own industry. I am my own commodity.

Elizabeth Taylor

The celebrity industry is the scene of constant battles for control. The most central ones, guided by the variety of interests already described, are struggles for control of the commodification process, the direction and content of the attended-to: Who gets to decide what the celebrity will look like, what she will talk about and with whom? Who, finally, gets to produce the commodity for profit? Because the celebrity has so many producers, the industry so many subindustries, the answer is ambiguous and contested. Parties persuade, cajole, and flatter each other; they barter and trade; when all else fails, they battle. This is the environment in which the celebrity text is created—particularly as it takes form in celebrity-based television "reality" programming and newspaper and magazine reporting. It is, first of all, not a smooth production system. More important, the relationships within it push both toward and away from a pursuit of the "true" celebrity personality. The result, we will see, is most commonly a compromise on the part of entertainment-reporting organizations, and the compromise dovetails with the dominant strategies of celebrity teams: celebrities are reported as semifictional texts.

Journalists in celebrity-based media institutions experience a dilemma in their work lives. Los Angeles bureau chief Stan Meyer hears again and again from members of the entertainment industry that his magazine, a weekly personality-based publication, is "fair with people." For him, the compliment carries an insult. "As a journalist you think, 'Gee, did I not dig deep enough?' " Journalism and public relations, he believes, "should be at odds with each other, not walking hand in hand down the aisle." It is a source of discomfort, therefore, for him to be told by his adversaries that they are happy with his work. If he were doing the job of a "real" journalist, if his work were going "deep enough," his subjects would not be forever thanking him. Like Michael Alexander, quoted above, he's never quite sure if he's "doing journalism" or "being an outlet."

Both the discomfort and the blurry line between serving and reporting on the industry stem from the fact that Meyer's work *does* depend heavily on public relations; if the two are not married, they at least enjoy an unhappy, rocky, but deeply committed and long-standing relationship. As we have seen, they share fundamental commercial interests and are linked institutionally and through day-to-day routines. Publicity professionals, whose careers are plainly dependent on mass-media coverage, also provide services of value to those reporting on the entertainment industry. They suggest angles and stories, provide quotes and art work, offer written and video press releases, arrange and sit in on interviews and photo sessions, train and coach clients to give better interviews. They supply an "information subsidy," usable written and visual information that the reporter would otherwise have to spend valuable time locating and writing up and that the organization would otherwise have to spend money acquiring.[2] They find, mold, and provide precisely what the media covering them need. Television bookers and magazine editors, for example, constantly emphasize their need for celebrities with "name recognition" or "identifiability." Publicists do what they can to provide this. "When I dress a party for video consumption," says Bob Merlis, vice-president of publicity for Warner Brothers Records, "I want to have people who look like who they're supposed to be. You want instantly recognizable people." As Pete Hammond of "Entertainment Tonight" says, "Couldn't do it without them."

At the root of these behaviors is the fundamentally uncertain business environment in which celebrity is developed. Paul Hirsch, providing an organizational model for the analysis of cultural industries, argues that industry workers face first the difficulty of knowing what will succeed in the marketplace; the activities described in the previous chapter are attempts to cope with this difficulty. Here I focus on the second central uncertainty to which Hirsch points: the control of decisions by organizations (primarily mass-media "gatekeepers") "whose actions can block or facilitate communication" and therefore "wield great influence over the access of artist and audience to one another."[3] To ensure that designated persons get a certain amount of attention, that the story lines and images designated as those that will attract and retain consumers get disseminated, and that a consistent and appealing celebrity is produced, decisions regarding coverage must be controlled. As Hirsch argues, legally and normatively these gatekeeping organizations are autonomous, and therefore the vertical integration of a product's manufacture and exposure to consumers is blocked. Producers develop strategies to control this "checkpoint" within these limits, most notably by "co-optation" of mass-media functions.

Although they speak generally of "creating an awareness" and euphemistically of "appropriate exposure," publicists' activities are plainly geared toward control of the gatekeeper role. By preparing their products according to the perceived specifications of the mass media, the publicity industry attempts to increase the likelihood of coverage. "I know how editors think and I come at them from their own angle," says personal publicist Amanda Weber. "I'm talking to them like I'm a writer pitching them a story. I know what they need and we provide it for them before they need to ask for it." By practicing many journalistic tasks (writing press releases, producing electronic press releases into which reporters can insert their own scripted voice, suggesting angles, attending interviews), publicists decrease the uncertainty of coverage content. As Jerome North, a publicist at a large PR firm, says matter-of-factly:

There are certain writers who have reputations for being a hardass or for really getting into areas they shouldn't, or who have a history of writing unflattering portraits. If we get an assignment and it's one of those people, we may go back to the editor and ask for another writer. We want somebody the client's going to be comfortable talking to, to try and get the best piece.

A *Rolling Stone* editor complains that more than twenty writers were approached for a cover story on Tom Cruise and were either vetoed by

Cruise's publicist or opted out rather than work under the publicist's restrictions. "Publicists think of themselves as the editors," complains another magazine editor. "They want to make all the editorial decisions."

In fact, the oft-repeated cliché that "Hollywood is all relationships" contains the reality of informal co-optation. "It's all relationships," says Sarah Tamikian, a cable network publicist, describing a "publicist's nightmare," an interview in which a celebrity bad-mouthed her vehicle to "Entertainment Tonight." Tamikian's response was to call the producer and ask her to remove the quote. "I have a relationship with her," Tamikian says, "and I knew that she would do what she could to make the piece better for me." Jordan Kamisky tells of a client who was asked by a syndicated columnist why he went into acting:

He said, "Because there were a lot of pretty girls I wanted to fuck." My mouth fell open and I kicked him under the table. I thought, what a fucking idiot. It made him seem like an idiot, like he wasn't serious about acting. What he should have said, whether it was true or not, was "I watched Marlon Brando when I was a child and he was so amazing in *On the Waterfront*." He needed an answer like that. Luckily, I had a relationship with this journalist. I said, "Do me a favor, either don't use it or at least tone it down," which he did.

The relationship is used for damage control. Formal co-optation of media decision making is ethically and legally constrained, so informal co-optation via relationships takes on a central and daily importance.

Mutual Co-optation and the Drive toward "Fluff"

Co-optation is neither easy nor complete, and much of the activity involves simple persuasion. Often, when interests overlap, co-optation is unnecessary. In Tamikian's story, for example, the producer who excised the negative quote responded, "it doesn't do us any good as 'Entertainment Tonight' to have an artist who's not really convinced with what she's saying." Both the media and the publicist want the same outcome.

More significantly, co-optation is mutual and two-directional. Celebrity-based media are not simply "bought" through time- and money-saving devices and camera-ready celebrities. Most entertainment media are not in fact "autonomous" gatekeepers. Although they are formally autonomous from commercial culture producers, they are institutionally dependent on them. "We use them, they use us," says a newspaper reporter who covers television. "It's a symbiotic relationship." Whereas the media guard the gates of exposure, the publicists guard the gates of access.

Indeed, since celebrity providers control access to a large degree, it is a professional and institutional necessity for entertainment media to build and maintain successful working relationships with them.[4] "People basically deliver for you," says Ann Sandberg, who books entertainment guests for a national morning show. "I might be close to the head of publicity at a movie studio, and they commit a star to me because they like me and they like the show, and even if we were number two I'd still get it. Those are the things that can really make or break you, your relationships." Here, relationships are used not by the publicist to control media exposure but by the media to control publicist delivery.

The more dependent a magazine or program is on celebrity images for sales, of course, the more powerless they are to make editorial evaluations and control content. "Just to get the face on the cover," complains an *Us* magazine editor, "a lot of times it becomes really secondary what the piece says."

The issues that have the ten hottest men, the ten most beautiful women, the ten most this or that, those are the ones that sell off the stands. Go figure. To me they're insubstantial fluff, these beefcake or cheesecake pieces with big, glamorous photographs and some text about what nice guys they are and what their marital status is. It's nobody's ambition to be generating these kinds of things, but we can't get away from it. They sell.

He pushes for "people who are worth taking a look at," but the answer is usually, "Yes, but they don't sell magazines." *Rolling Stone* senior writer Bill Zehme tells of profiling Albert Brooks, who will never be on *Rolling Stone*'s cover but who, "if you put people on the cover because of merit instead of what will sell, should be on everybody's cover." Instead of subjects such as Brooks, in Zehme's eyes a "comic genius," many of his subjects are like actor Johnny Depp: nice, talented, but attended-to because he is "an image that sells" when "his body of work is almost nonexistent." Editorial control (in this case, the power to cover people who in the opinions of editors "merit" interest, to write stories where content is not "secondary") is trumped by salability and marketing department control.

Fluff writing, these "beefcake or cheesecake pieces," is not so much a result of perceived reader preferences for contentless profiles; the lack of substance comes more from the dependence on celebrity images and the subsequent weak bargaining position against those who regulate access to them. The dependence is clearest and most developed in the relationships between mass-media workers and personal publicists, hired either to facilitate or retain control of coverage. In recent years, both publicists and journalists commonly note, the balance of power has tipped toward the publicists. "As much as we fight it, and we fight it, publicists know that we need the people to sell the magazine," says Zehme. "So they play games with us, they extract things."

Negotiating fills in where relationships are insufficient. One editor demonstrates both the types of demands and the power of publicists to extract them:

When we assigned a staff writer to do a profile of Candice Bergen, PMK [Bergen's publicity firm] said, "While we respect this writer we don't think that she would appreciate Candice Bergen's sense of humor." The image they were trying to create for Candice Bergen was that she was funny, and they didn't think this particular writer would do their bidding on that. The editors basically said, "Screw you. If you want to pick your writers, why don't you start your own magazine?" The epilogue is that shortly after this [a new owner] took over, the editor who said fuck you to PMK was fired, and the new people said, "Okay, who do you want for the piece?"

The answer, presumably, was a writer who would "do their bidding." Even if the media workers *want* to cut themselves off from publicity operatives, it is simply not practical for their professional well-being. Cutting oneself off from publicists means cutting oneself off from the main pipeline to celebrity interviews and information. Perhaps more critical, one risks being blocked from getting the article or segment in process completed as one would like, when one would like. "It's very present-oriented," says entertainment-magazine writer John Rider. "Their power is what they can do or not do then and there." The stronger the journalist's and organization's relationship with publicists, the less can be extracted in these negotiations.

We arrive at one compelling set of celebrity-industry dynamics: the drive against pursuing "truths" and toward celebrity- and entertainment-product promotion. In many cases, developing successful and useful relationships with publicists means developing a reputation for presenting their clients in the desired light. It means avoiding the "hardass" reputation, editing out the complaint about a bad script, replacing "I wanted to fuck pretty girls" with "I wanted to be just like Marlon Brando," granting photo approval, promising a cover. Several large publicity firms handle, in fact, the bulk of the most salable subjects. Therefore if you do "some scathing thing" on a star, says Stan Meyer, "you're not only pissing off an individual, you're pissing off a publicist who has a stable of people that [he] may withhold from you." A publicist who is confident, either because of bargaining or prior relationships, that the outcome will be favorable (the photos will be right, the cover will be theirs, the appropriate areas will be covered, the writer will not write an "unflattering" portrait), is the publicist who will "deliver." This, finally, is the practical, institutional push toward producing promotional fluff, or, in the terms of Stan Meyer's would-be enemies, "fair" reporting.

The Drive toward the "Inside" and the Economy of the Tidbit

The struggles, however, are bitter and the animosity strong. Why isn't the marriage happy? Given all of the overlap in commercial interest, the closeness in informal networks, the interdependent institutional networks, why not simply become a promotional outlet, a fluff factory? Why fight it?

To begin with, there is clearly a genuine sense of threat to many journalists' sense of integrity and professional identity, a resentment of publicists' attempts to do their jobs for them. One overview of studies of journalism distinguishes two types of reporters: "straight reporters," who are "content to collect the facts through recognized channels and to leave to the reader the task of interpreting or evaluating them," and "committed journalists," who "believe more attention should be paid to news-gathering, investigation, to providing background and analysis, even to making judgments on behalf of the reader about the relative worth of different accounts or the implications of particular statements and events."[5] To these a third might be added, the "artistic" journalist, whose professional identity is linked to creative criteria. The identities of the last two are particularly threatened by an alliance with publicity managers.[6] Bill Bruns of *TV Guide,* fighting with a publicist over the assignment of a writer, tells her, "Forget it. You guys are trying to dictate. This is First Amendment kind of stuff." Writer Patrick Goldstein points out the limits set on investigation and depth, both of which he takes to be his job:

Whoever controls the information has a lot of power, and the publicists do control a lot of information. They control your access to it, the way it's disseminated, the timing, the amount. They try to control the image in the sense that they don't want me to get too much of a glimpse of the celebrities' private lives. Then it's just kind of a battle between me and the publicist over how much access I have. The more access you have, the more in-depth, the more texture it's going to have. If you only give somebody an hour to talk, in an office somewhere, you control the environment completely.

Similarly, Stan Meyer's description of a photo shoot with Michael J. Fox points out the limits set on creativity:

The photographer, always wanting to try something different, brought along a very high-powered magnifying glass and for one shot wanted him to just hold it up to his face. I guess the image would be of this really big head and this little body. I don't know what he was after exactly, but he was just messing around. Of course, the publicists were there for this whole thing, and they plotzed when they saw what he was trying to do. They said, "No, no, we're not doing anything like that. Just a regular old shot, the old Michael Fox head shot." And I was trying to help the photographer out so I said, "Michael's trying to stretch in his roles, and we're just trying to get something that will make people stop when they see his picture in the magazine." The publicist looks at me with daggers saying, "People *always* stop when they see his picture."

Giving in to publicists' power undermines the bases of many journalists' professional identities: access to investigation is largely blocked, the possibilities of writing a textured or nuanced story impeded, interpretation and analysis discouraged, the integrity of free and creative expression compromised. These are matters not only of identity, of course, but of interest. Control of defined professional activities as a means of building and protecting status and money is an important force in all lines of work, and here it is clearly threatened.[7]

The push away from allying with publicists goes beyond professional identities and professional control, however, to institutional and commercial requirements. The problem is not only that publicists want to "write the story themselves" but that the story they would like to write is not distinctive enough or "inside" enough to meet the media organization's commercial needs. To be competitive in the marketplace, many programs and publications promise audiences something they cannot get elsewhere: the exclusive, inside story, a look at the "reality" behind the image. "If you are giving your readers a cover story," says Miriam Ross, "you have to deliver. There's an unwritten agreement. If you cheat them, they know, and they're going to remember next time. I think readers know when it's not a real story." When they cannot fulfill that promise, they must at least provide a story that is distinguishable from all the others. The question, says Pete Hammond of "Entertainment Tonight," is always "how can we make this different from ten other interviews he's going to do sitting next to a plant in a hotel room talking about his latest movie? We're going for ratings, and we don't want to put on stories that are unappealing to viewers who've seen them on twelve other shows. We want an audience grabber." When Bill Bruns describes his fight to assign a writer the publicist thought would "ask uncomfortable questions," his description slides immediately from the First Amendment to the practical requirements of the magazine. "The writer is supposed to ask those questions," he says. "We don't want to have someone just talk about being an actress and how she does her role. That's boring." Maintaining control of the story is often demanded not only by professional identity but by competitive viability.

The danger of producing promotional fluff is that it will be seen by audiences as such, dismissed as the same old same old, akin to the ubiquitous and free-of-charge advertisements. Publicist control can get in the way of delivering competitively to the consumer. Publicity workers get in the way of this promise quite literally, first of all, by sitting in on interviews, blocking photos at opportune moments, asking for questions in advance, acting as spokespeople, trying to veto writers and photographers.

Second, with their interests primarily pushing toward safe promotion ("appropriate exposure"), what publicists offer most generally is the celebrity in a standardized, controlled, packaged form. (As we saw earlier, this overriding tendency is supported by the short-term uses of entertainment-industry buyers.) The coached and trained and much-used celebrity works against the promised delivery of "real goods." "Some of these publicists coddle so badly and try to protect their clients," says *TV Guide*'s Bruns, "that they've created a lot of really bland personalities." What to a publicist and celebrity is careful and safe is bland to him; bland does not serve his purposes. What he needs is people who will "open up a little bit with the press"—that is, provide distinctive pieces of personal information. "It's appalling to me," says Stan Meyer, "that as I'm interviewing them I start hearing the quotes I've read a thousand times. The challenge is to get them to get away from their habit of bullshit." *People* writer Michael Alexander underlines the same experience:

For a lot of these celebrities, it's just part of the shtick. You know, "How did it feel doing that scene wrapped in plastic?" "Blah blah blah blah. It was very cold.

I had to drink hot tea. Blah blah blah." They start regurgitating the same answers and they give everybody a very limited idea as to who they are. It's this tug-of-war. You try to get as much stuff out of them as you can, and they try to give you as little as they can.

What the media organization needs is a convincing presentation of "who they are." Alexander tells a story of a *People* reporter's interview with television's Paula Zahn where "the whole thing was, 'Life is just great, life is fabulous.' " For ten minutes the reporter dug, worried that "this story's going to get killed because there's nothing to differentiate this woman from lots of other people." Then, finally, Zahn "started babbling about how her father died of cancer and now her mom has cancer, and the reporter was like, 'Okay, a cancer story.' " The reporter had won the tug-of-war, found the piece of personal information that could distinguish the story and offer more than the publicist-controlled idea of the subject. Competing with the push to present publicist-friendly material that keeps access open, then, there is a strong commercial and organizational push to dig beyond the fluff, to pull the cancer story from the fabulous life. To be competitive, media organizations need access not only to the celebrity image but to unmined pieces of the celebrity personality. For this, they must on some level fight the publicist and the celebrity. They face the dilemma, then, of fighting those on whom their work activities and livelihoods depend.

These battles between publicists and journalists are part of a war in an economy of information—specifically, an economy of tidbits. Bits of personality information, either written, spoken, or photographed, are the primary currency circulating and fought over between those seeking exposure and those providing it. The celebrity is divided up into pieces, and those pieces move between parties, are exchanged, invested, cashed in. Each party wants in some sense to establish usage and ownership rights over the celebrities and their images and information.[8] The celebrity and publicist know the value of the information commodity, and they control its scarcity to maintain its value in extracting exposure. The journalist and media organization try to attain it in order to attract audiences. Significantly, media organizations are motivated to win only the individual battles. If the war were won, it might therefore be lost: the information's value as an audience-attractor, and therefore as a money-maker, depends on its scarcity.

Resistance, Selling Out,
and the Pursuit of the Semitrue

"Dirt" is a term that means all information that stars might not want me to write, which could be just revealing that they're pregnant before they tell anyone, or their secret engagement, or who they're dating, or maybe just an inside, personal story of someone having a tantrum backstage or something. Dirt is not necessarily a negative thing, it's just stuff that for whatever reason they don't want you to know, or don't want to have in print yet. It's my job to get it. I'll pay money to try to get the story before anyone else has it.

Mary Morgan, tabloid gossip columnist

If we asked embarrassing questions, we'd be out of business tomorrow.

Lee Masters, president,
E! Entertainment Television

My theory is that once you sit down with them, everyone is interesting. Sometimes it takes longer than others, but I really do believe that if you sit down with anyone you can get a pretty good story.

Michael Alexander, staff writer,
People magazine

Not all entertainment-media institutions are positioned alike in this economy of information. Some choose sides, either resisting or giving in to the bids by others to control coverage. Those that resist can do so largely because their commercial interests do not coincide with those of the publicity operations; they are genuinely autonomous. Conventional news operations resist where they can; for them, maintaining a reputation as independent pursuers of facts remains more critical for sales than celebrity information and images. Like several other publications, the *Los Angeles Times* is perceived as especially important and thus retains an upper hand facing publicists' demands. Moreover, the *Times* can set terms because "we're not selling newspapers with celebrities, we're not using celebrities to try to build our circulation." The position is thus simple. "If you're going to do these interviews," a *Times* editor says, "you're going to do them on our terms." Speaking to a meeting of the Publicists' Guild, he told them "in as professional and nice a way as I could" not only that they're unwanted but that they're unnecessary:

I said, "If I had my way, receiving your pitches would be zero percent of my job. If you guys never sent me another pitch I'd be happy." And they were shocked to hear that. They think I need it. They're sure that what they do is a service. I had breakfast with a publicist the other day who basically wanted to know how to pitch me. Finally I said, "I know that every time you're given an assignment you've got to get as much as you can, and you have to file a report to someone that says you called the *Los Angeles Times*. Just cut me out of the process. I'll give you a carte blanche rejection. You can say I said no to everything you've got."

The *Los Angeles Times* and publications like it can for the most part dig or skip the story, using some but ignoring much of PR. They can and do, in fact, even investigate and expose those attempts by the publicity industry to control stories.[9]

Ironically, tabloids are also in an autonomous position. "I get my stories *in spite* of publicists, not because of publicists," says gossip columnist Mary Morgan. "I try to avoid them, frankly, because I find when I call them up with a great story to validate it, they'll steal it and turn it over to a daily paper and scoop me. They have no ethics." Morgan's paper is built on "dirt." Inside information—for which the paper pays from $100 to $1000—is the source of its profits.

The activity of "digging" is alive and well, as it is in conventional newspaper reporting, though in a different form. Morgan's column, for example, is made up mostly of information bought from sources. She supplements it by going to events where there may be gossip and gossips to be found.

You'll find some crew member, someone who works in public relations, someone who works as a makeup artist, a hairdresser. I head for those people, and I start talking to them. And if I find out they're gossipy-talkative, I get a feeling for their observational powers, and how open they are about talking. I give them my card. If someone's an extra on the set the day Kirstie Alley walks in and says, "Well, I'm pregnant," that could be a big front page story, it's harmless, and a lot of money. People beat each other up to get to the phones first to call me and get the money. And sometimes I just feel like putting on a wig and I go out and chitchat with people. People will tell you the most amazingly intimate things if you're just a talkative person at a party.

Since it is precisely these intimate tidbits that celebrities and publicists use in the exchange for exposure control, tabloids are their ultimate enemy in the economy of information. "I keep my clients out of the *Globe* and the *Enquirer*," says personal manager Arlene Dayton.

There's outlets and there's outlets. Once they start with you, you become fair game. I tried to explain this to a publicist who does work with them, and he said,

"Wouldn't you rather control?" I said, "What control? There's no control. It's like controlling mad dogs." They don't care about you, they only care about exposing whatever there is about you to expose.

Morgan, however, counters that tabloid coverage can be extremely valuable to celebrities. "I think I'm doing them all a favor," says Morgan, "because I know for a fact that their prices go up. The better their name is known by the public, the more money they get paid." Publicist Kathie Berlin agrees they can be useful: "If I had a movie with a female audience, the best thing I could get would be a color layout in *The Star*."[10] Yet while this mutual *commercial service* still exists, tabloids are structured on an *institutional divorce* from those in the entertainment industry trying to control publicity.

On the other side are those businesses structured from the outset on serving and being served by publicists. *USA Today,* for example, says an entertainment editor who was there at its inception, was "almost designed as an outlet," and publicists love it. "Entertainment Tonight," says a television critic, is "a publicist's dream." At the furthest extreme is "celebrity-friendly" E! Entertainment Television, a twenty-four-hour network devoted to celebrities, with a format described by a *Newsweek* writer as "endlessly rotating plugs, previews, and puff pieces," like "a science-fiction movie in which a Hollywood publicist takes over your brain."[11] Resembling teen-idol magazines, E! profits by providing an outlet for celebrities, gaining easy access to them by relinquishing control of coverage content almost entirely to the industry it covers.

Where E! and businesses like it thrive by providing an ideal venue for the celebrity as a product promoter, glamour-oriented programming such as "Lifestyles of the Rich and Famous" is built on providing an outlet for the celebrity as self-promoter. Designed for viewers who "want glamour, who want a star to be a star and live in an incredible house and have fancy jewelry and drive a Rolls Royce," "Lifestyles" is a safe environment for celebrities, says Robin Smalley, a director for the show. No probing questions are asked, no negatives are allowed. "You don't do anything that's reality-based," says Smalley. " 'Lifestyles' is deliberately 'nice' television. We use every kind of enhancement we can. We use wide-angle lenses to make the rooms look bigger, star filters to make everything look glitzier, fog filters to make people look better and rooms look softer. It's all there to make everyone look wonderful and glamorous and happy and carefree." Thus, although plugging a project is excluded, "it's a good show for somebody who wants to project or foster a certain image."

Although some institutions choose sides, what one analyst has noted of the art/commerce dilemma in cultural production is true in the parallel fluff/dirt conflict as well: "There are more complex adaptations to it than the polar opposites of alienation or acceptance."[12] The bulk of entertainment-media organizations are semiautonomous, and the most common resolution to conflicting pulls is a compromise. Entertainment journalism tends to shy away from criteria of truth and worth. Though not dismissed, they are limited to the pursuit of technical accuracy: facts are tirelessly checked, questions of legality carefully considered. But, faced with a need to deliver inside information where digging for it can threaten essential industry relationships, celebrity-based media work with entertainment criteria that bridge these interests.

Traditional journalistic criteria are here reversed.[13] In coverage decisions, the primary question is not which people are most deserving of examination but which will be most appealing, which are "hottest" and fit current production needs best. Entertainment-media workers, like their counterparts in the entertainment-production fields, categorize celebrities into levels of popularity. "It's a pyramid," says Don Roca, who books guests on a local morning show.

It's like a cumulative knowledge or awareness. We talk with "A-list" and "B-list," "A-minus celebrities," "B-plus celebrities." We have no shame. Everybody's always arguing it out. "Oh, he's hot." "Oh, who gives a shit." Talent as an issue comes into play, but not very much unless it adds to someone's level of hotness. If you're hot *and* talented, then great.

Similarly, in approaching a subject, the primary question is not what is most important to know about them or what will reveal them most truthfully but what about them will be most interesting. The interview is primarily used neither to make a coverage decision (is this person a worthy subject?) nor to search out the depth of a subject (what makes this person worth lavishing attention on?). "It's just any quirk," says Michael Alexander. "It's like, oh, came from a family of twelve kids, started working when you were three." His description of "a great story," on Miguel Ferrer from television's "Twin Peaks," is a revealing summary of typical criteria:

He has famous parents plus he had a lot of family problems. His mom, Rosemary Clooney, was married to Jose Ferrer, they had five kids in a row, split up, then got remarried, then she had a big breakdown, and Miguel was the oldest and was sort of the man of the house at age twelve. These were fabulous details. Now everybody's hunky-dory and he's very successful and so forth. We love people overcoming something. It was the perfect situation. Here was a guy with a high visibility role on at that point a very hot show, and he had a great story to tell.

Once you've selected whom to cover according to the product categories called for by the magazine's format ("big male star, blonde bimbo, rising young ingenue, they fit a niche"), another *People* worker says, "you try and get them to say something real." Investigation provides amusing, distinctive details about a subject dictated by commercial appeal.

The "good story" is thus a narrative resolution somewhere between promotional "puffery" and "serious" investigation, a resolution that balances opposing organizational pulls. Important is the fact that this resolution keeps the economy of information flowing. First, by largely sidestepping criteria of worth for coverage decisions, it allows journalists to pursue commercial appeal and minimize the threat to publicity seekers posed by evaluation. Under entertainment criteria, a critical stance—the evaluation of a celebrity's claim to attention, for example—is bypassed, opening up a nearly endless field of "interesting" candidates. Nearly anyone is an eligible candidate since almost anyone has a good story in them *somewhere*. This is in the interest both of cultural producers, for whom the likelihood of "hitting" is increased as the number of shots increases, and those reporting on the industry, who reduce the risk posed by relying on a small set of subjects.

Second, the good story's deemphasis of authenticity in favor of an engaging narrative relieves the tension brought by zero-sum-game fights accompanying pursuits of "the real goods." "Interesting" is a different informational realm. In daily journalistic practice, investigating-for-interest behaviors are directed toward the "fabulous details" and the "great story," toward narrative elements rather than truth content. As long as the story is deemed sufficiently interesting or amusing—and technically accurate—and enough personal-information "goods" are relinquished to establish an "inside" stance, the purposes of the journalist are served. There are plenty of good stories and interesting tidbits to go around. More fundamentally, investigation, which for institutional reasons must not dig too far, does not need to dig too far to be practically useful. "You as a reporter have some goods, but you don't have the real goods," says personality magazine writer and editor Miriam Ross. "There's a limit to how inside you're going to get. That's the bargain you make." The bargain is a comfortable one: "some goods" are enough. And what is important is that these goods can be easily acquired *within* the bartering network between the media and the entertainment industry without threatening that relationship.

We saw earlier how celebrity producers often use the strategy of Dramatic Reality to increase the chances of selling their celebrity. Outlets that see themselves as amusement are driven toward the same strategy. Clues can be taken from the arena of photographic images, in which the industry–news media alliance works almost without tension. Since the products celebrities appear in and are used to sell are in the visual media of film and television, most in the entertainment industry agree that pictures are the most important component of image making. Publications and programs also depend on an appealing visual image. Questions of "truth" and "integrity" hardly arise in this arena, possibly the most important one, because suppliers and buyers of celebrities are joined here without tension. "When I wrote about Julia Roberts," says Patrick Goldstein, "I said she looked like a librarian. But the picture we ran of her, she had her makeup on, our photographer put up the right lights. His job is to get a nice picture." Because photographic images are widely assumed to "tell the truth," the camera widely assumed to "never lie," there is little need or incentive for the entertainment-news industry to fight the manipulation of visual images. In fact, the industry and journalism together build salable visual images, through both simple techniques such as makeup and touch-ups and more dramatic techniques; *TV Guide,* for example, was caught melding Oprah Winfrey's head with Ann-Margret's body. The obligation to "dig" is erased, questions of what this person looks like in day-to-day life are bypassed. His magazine, Stan Meyer says, is "very photo-oriented" and uses "the cream of the crop of portrait photographers." Thus celebrities and their handlers tend to be attracted to the magazine "because they know they're going to end up looking good." (Compare this to those whose livelihood depends on revealing celebrities as they do *not* like to be seen, the tabloids who are as happy to put a fat Oprah Winfrey on the cover as a svelte one, a strung-out-looking star as a glamorous one. They do not work with celebrities and their handlers to create these photographic images but instead depend on paparazzi to catch them unawares.)

Good-story pursuits effect a similar working alliance. Semifiction becomes a meeting ground for groups with a variety of interests. Focusing on narrative rather than on truth elements also allows *both* parties greater control over the journalistic output. Both sets of commercial enterprises seek to exploit audiences' involvement with celebrities; they do so through a search for a realm between fact and fiction, a realm that, with its dependence on discernible narrative elements and semi-independence from truth, is much more easily controlled than "real life" but looks much like it. The news and entertainment industries often work together day to day to develop and represent a version of celebrity selves that is more explicitly staged than behaved: the actor playing himself for the cameras, writing his life along with the reporter such that both will benefit. It is important to notice that this is rarely a conscious conspiracy to deceive but instead a set of compromises between conflicting but interdependent parties. Staged events, for example, are effective exactly because they are still events: "If Tom Cruise is getting a star on the Walk of Fame," says "Entertainment Tonight" producer Pete Hammond, explaining the program's coverage of events they know are promotional, "Tom Cruise is getting a star on the Walk of Fame." It's a good story. The alliance is not so much around developing lies as developing performances of celebrity selves.

The Talk Show
and Predictable Spontaneity

With television the viewer gets the impression that it's the real person, but it's not. It's acting. Anyone who's done a talk show can tell you that. It's performing. Once a week I'm on a television program, and 80 percent of the time when I finish I feel this sense of incompletion. It's kind of like sex without the orgasm. I wind up automatically saying what they want me to say, not necessarily what I mean to say or what I want to say. It's an unconscious thing. I just do it. I know the medium, I know how it works, so I wind up cute and catchy, the way they want it.

Stuart Stein,
newspaper television critic

Nowhere is the outlets' drive toward semifiction clearer than in the celebrity-based talk show. Talk-show producers perceive their projects as entirely entertainment and thus as exempt from criteria of evaluation other than popularity and amusement. They are not bound by journalistic criteria, only by the need to present amusing people out of their usual fictional roles. Don Roca, a producer and booker for a local celebrity talk show, sums up what he is looking for.

It's my job to bring on the most provocative, intriguing, fascinating, interesting people that the viewership is actually going to want to watch. You want celebrities that have some kind of name recognition, or a celebrity that happens to be so hot at the moment that people are talking about them. If you have to say "Who?" they're almost dead in the water. And you always want a guest who's energetic, vibrant, and is willing to speak freely and openly. That's a great guest, because you're going to watch that person and you're going to see engaging conversation, regardless of what they're talking about. Ultimately, who's really going to care about what celebrities have to say anyways? At least that person, whatever they're talking about, they're doing it in an interesting way. You'll stay tuned, you'll stay with the show. The consideration is how best to entertain the audience and how to have the audience like you and stay with you.

Bob Dolce, who books guests for "The Tonight Show," tells a similar story.

Before we have somebody come in we've done a little bit of research on them to see if we think the potential is there, no matter how much we respect the work, to be an entertaining talk-show guest. And I'm underlining the word "entertaining." That's the primary thing. There are a lot of people whose work we really, really respect who aren't particularly entertaining when it comes to talking. Our primary interest is in people who talk. The primary objective is to get talk time that is light. We're surfacey.

Celebrities on these programs are selected on the basis of their entertainment value, either because they are established figures ("You always want the Pope, the Queen, and the President," says Dolce) or because they can "talk." The quality of a guest's work is irrelevant; under entertainment criteria there is no necessary connection between achievement and exposure.

The guest needs less to have *done* something than to be able to *be* something in the moment. His job is to perform. "This is sort of heightened life," says Dolce. "It all happens in between six and eight minutes. It's forced casual conversation, really more like a performance than a visit, like talking in headlines. It can only look like a conversation. We need someone who can do that, who understands what this is about and is comfortable doing that." Don Roca echoes, "[I'm] almost like a movie director," making sure that the guests each "deliver" in their five-minute performances. The task is not too difficult. "Celebrities are performers, and performers can deliver, if not shtick at least likability. If you're telling them, 'You're really going to have to bring your energy up and have a lot of fun out there,' they'll understand that. It's like a performance. It's a business." Indeed, Roca's program for some time used actual chefs for its cooking segment. Some of them, however, were "real drips on the air," so a change was made to ensure that the segments would be conducted by celebrities who could be "very upbeat, engaging, funny. The recipe is secondary, what they cook is secondary, whether they even know how to cook is secondary. As long as they can fake their way through a recipe in a fun way, we'll have them on." Celebrities are chosen for their ability to perform themselves amusingly.

A performance is clearly more manageable than a spontaneous appearance. To help ensure a predictable performance, talk-show producers conduct a preinterview with the guests and provide the hosts with an interview structure. In the preinterview the booker first pokes around for fresh tidbits or stories that make the guest distinctive. "I look for what I call fingerprints," says Dolce. "Something that applies only to that person, something you haven't heard before or couldn't hear from five other people." The challenge of established icons—worn-out, over-used commodities, in a sense—is that "although you may have a guaranteed audience, you don't have a guaranteed conversation." To find something Jimmy Stewart or George Burns have not "shared before" is "a great accomplishment."

The talent coordinators then try to shape the conversational content into a "successful appearance" by going over "some possible lines of conversation" and making suggestions ("That line, or that thought, might be sort of fun"). Producers also present the host with a "structure." As Dolce describes it, the structure involves

five to eight areas, guidelines, in which you have weeded out anything that is going to be unproductive and removed any area that the guest might consider to be sensitive. [The structure] has questions and a general area of response. I don't punch lines in. I won't reveal where it's going. And the guest basically has also been briefed about what the host might be looking for.

Although the hosts and guests are briefed, spontaneity is part of the show. "Often the hosts will take a completely different tack," says Roca. In looking for conversational skills, a preinterviewer will check for a guest's ability to handle unpredictable moments. The challenge here, says Dolce, is new people. "You don't know what's going to happen, you don't know what their on-air judgment is like. So I have to see how this person handles obstacles, a different direction. What happens if a curve comes in, how fast do they respond, how playful are they, how programmed are they?"

Why *not* script and perform the entire show? If controlling the outcome is desirable, why leave it partially uncontrolled? Why allow curves? The answers are again found in the commercial drive toward pursuing "real" or "honest" moments. Spontaneity is necessary because it provides distinctiveness. A predictable performance can be a dull one. Dolce complains about the new crop of "generic" talent who come into his office "totally prepared."

They're like automatons. I want their real selves. The kids who come in are bright, articulate, attractive, likable—and interchangeable. And that is a problem for me. They don't say anything. They just do everything right. You can't remember whether it was this blonde or that blonde. Was that the redhead? Was this him, or was it that other guy?

Moreover, a performance that is too performed can appear unreal on a program that claims to provide reality. With "civilians," Dolce says, "you get something much more honest. They're unpredictable. They're excited about being here and they're not promoting anything. They're not selling an image, and they're not selling a movie or a record. They're just here. So you get something much more honest, and you don't know what's going to happen." The spontaneity, though, is "terrifying," high-risk. Dolce prefers working with celebrities because, despite the risk that they will appear more canned, "they're going to be anxious to please, anxious to do it right."

The dilemma for talk-show coordinators, then, is that spontaneity and performance are both necessary and risky. The result is practical behaviors aimed at managed spontaneity, a sort of live performance of the semifictional. On one level, like the good story, this set of criteria and behaviors allows the symbiotic supplier–outlet relations to flow relatively smoothly. Besides trading access for promotion, suppliers and outlets reach a compromise on how far into the "real" person the exposure will extend. Taboo subjects, areas the guest and his team feel are "sensitive," are discovered and sidestepped in exchange for a performance that suits the program's needs. As long as "some goods" are offered, image control is left in the hands of the team. On another level, independent of the relationships with publicists, talk shows pursue the middle realm of simulated selves based on their *own* production requirements, the need for safe, structured spontaneity and predictable performances.

The Adjusted Picture

Celebrity is an industry like many others. Celebrities are manufactured as attention-getting bodies, a process complicated but not negated by the fact that celebrities are human beings. Knownness itself is commodified within them. To be more certain of their successful marketability, those producing and profiting from them—they and their team, one set of "authors"—adopt strategies of image management that blur fiction and nonfiction. Celebrity building is a complex task riddled with conflict, and the messiness is telling. In the absence of a single organizational monopoly on the production and distribution networks, various competing interests vie for control. These interests and the relationships that develop from them, when examined, reveal tensions in the process through which celebrities are given meaning. Abstract familiarity, knownness for the self rather than for works or roles, is not something all celebrity-producing parties desire. Celebrities are simultaneously linked to and divorced from the activities for which they are ostensibly famous.

With the introduction of the second set of "authors," mass-media institutions that publicly represent celebrities, an even more developed set of conflicts over control of representation can be seen. Business uncertainties lead both those pitching celebrities and those covering them toward mutual dependence, mutual co-optation, battles, and negotiation. Celebrity-based media organizations, locked to varying degrees into the economy of tidbits, are pulled both toward and away from activities that pursue "truth" or "reality." Although the legal system sets a bottom-line constraint on out-and-out lying and outlets seek accuracy if only for that reason, those whose profits explicitly depend on pleasing celebrities' gatekeepers are not fundamentally pursuing truth, and they make no bones about it. These organizations are concerned with gaining readers and viewers through the exposure of celebrities in nearly *any* form. They serve as promotional outlets for carefully managed and produced publicity; indeed, this is the only institutional arrangement that will allow them such constant access to celebrities. They do not investigate, they publicize. On the other hand, those organizations that do not require celebrity images for sales, and who are thus not highly dependent on cultural producers for subjects, are clearly in a position to investigate. Having less stake in the promotional, they tend to chase what they see as "the facts" or take an evaluative, critical position. These are journalists as investigators in the more traditional sense. Their business depends on a reputation for "seriousness": reporting that seems to be presenting facts rather than advocating, criticism and revelation of their subjects, and a demonstration that their subjects are worthy of attention. There is little in their organizational arrangement to inhibit these activities.

Finally, the most common arrangement—the semiautonomous journalistic organizations caught on the horns of the puff/dirt dilemma—pushes toward a middle ground between artificial image and authentic reality in which the two are difficult to distinguish. The construction of the good story, guided by criteria of amusement, interest, and restricted revelation, characterized by choreographed performances and restricted investigation, largely displaces the pursuit of truth in celebrity writing and programming. It is not so much that pursuing truth is avoided or impossible here but that it becomes largely unnecessary. This, I have argued, has happened because such a displacement is *necessary* for institutional survival.

Perhaps the most revealing arrangement is the tabloid. Institutionally independent in large part, commercially driven to reveal, the *National Enquirer* would seem to be organizationally better equipped for pursuing truth than its counterparts, such as *People,* which are perceived as more legitimate and truth telling. The tabloids are virulently attacked by both those counterparts and entertainment-industry workers not because they *lie* but because they *break the rules* of the information economy, grabbing valued pieces of information without offering the payment of controlled publicity. Why, then, the reputation as the nation's biggest liars? Joined with the organizational freedom to pursue truth is the commercial requirement to provide celebrity "dish." While they are not institutionally bound to serve as promotional outlets, they are commercially bound to amuse through inside information rather than to reveal through it. Rather than "truth," they pursue the "inside scoop" in good-story form—usually the free-wheeling form of rumor and gossip—within the legal limits. "What could be better than that Danny Bonaduce story about picking up a transvestite prostitute and robbing him? I get enough stories that are true," says Mary Morgan. "So I don't have to make up stories." The implication, of course, is that a made-up story does the trick on a bad day—true ones are just less work. Tabloids are, in a sense, commercial-entertainment journalism at its most pure and free: acting in opposition to publicists by pursuing "dirt," they are also liberated from reality by the pursuit of amusement.

What the adjusted picture reveals is a cultural industry in which the creators, the authors of the celebrity text, are far from constituting a monolithic elite manufacturing standard celebrity products. Interests diverge, and the workers actively battle each other throughout the production process; the texts created are filled with the conflicts from which they are born. Yet again and again interests are realigned and conflicts resolved through a central compromise. Either because it is more controllable or because it solves an institutional dilemma, the realm of the semifictional is one in which nearly everyone has a stake. Most roads, however roundabout and bumpy, lead there.

Chapter Five

Props, Cues, and the Advantages of Not Knowing: Audiences in the World of Celebrity Production

I can clap the sound of three people. Attending live television programs and program tapings, I learned the simple technique several times: hold the hands in front of the face, prayer style, and clap in triple time. The first time I did it, at 8:45 one Friday morning, I felt silly. The others in the studio, most also first timers at the superclap, looked around as I did, bemused and embarrassed at their obedience. But we practiced, or rather were made to practice, and soon the fifteen of us, not all of us morning people, were making the sound of at least fifty thrilled-to-be-awake-and-where-we-are people.

There is no preparation, no warning, that attending "AM Los Angeles," a morning celebrity talk show, involves more than simply watching. In fact, the audience waits in an unheated, concrete-floored room with a backstage look: an old piano, a television playing, folding chairs, some inexplicably sitting open on the table tops. No one at that point shows any interest in hosting us, beyond the provision of a large pot of coffee, presumably but not undeniably intended for us. As we are led by a page into the studio, however, the scene suddenly changes. Music is playing, quite loudly, and the room is bright, warm, and cheery. We fill only two and a half of the four rows of numbered folding chairs, but, sitting under the bright filming lights, we are suddenly not just attended to but doted upon.

Almost immediately after we are seated a woman approaches us, telling us how happy they are to have us there and how important we are to the program and its hosts, Steve and Tawny. She speaks, it seems to me, as though to a group of kindergartners, and that tone of voice is adopted by every production staff member who approaches us throughout the hour. "What I need from you today is energy," she says. "When you watch the show, it always sounds like there's hundreds of people in the audience, doesn't it? Well, the first thing I'm going to do is teach you how to sound that way. And we really need you to keep the energy up through the whole show." She tells us that we should scream and yell and lets us in on the "trick" to sounding like more people than we are. She demonstrates the fast clap, holding her hands up in front of her and clapping double time. "Okay, let's practice," she says, and we do. She is right, of course: it does sound like many more people.

We are then instructed to laugh at "appropriate" times. "When Steve or Tawny or the guest say something funny, laugh. When they say something they think is funny, even if you don't think it's funny, laugh. The mikes can pick it up." Another producer later puts it this way: "There are times when something will be really funny, and we want you to let it out. Then there might be times when something is supposed to be funny, and maybe it isn't that funny. This is Hollywood, and what do you do in Hollywood? You pretend. So pretend it's funny." The man in a yellow shirt next to me fakes a laugh, and everyone else laughs. This becomes his routine throughout the whole taping, and the producers, aware of the joke, compliment him on his participation.

Over the next ten minutes, we are deluged with independent requests to perform our clap. "Did they tell you double or triple time?" asks the executive producer. "Do you have the clap down?" another assistant producer asks. We demonstrate. We are starting to enjoy the clapping, silly as it is. She repeats how important our energy is. If we're good, she tells us, we might win a prize. This woman stands next to us for most of the taping, showing us with her hands when to clap, saying things like "just clap first, then cheer when Rose Marie comes on." A male producer comes over and says, "You're not watching a show, okay, this is a workout," which elicits laughter. Yet another producer, a chipper cheerleader, comes over and tells us how wonderful we look and how great it is to have us there.

We open the show with our quick clap and cheer. The male producer is right. There is no time to sit back; we are constantly waiting for cues to laugh, clap, cheer, or be silent. In fact, it is difficult to pay close attention to the content of the show. As Steve and Tawny are guided by cue cards through their cheery banter, as Rose Marie plugs a local production of *Cinderella* and Paul Winfield discusses his bid for an Oscar nomination, as musician Queen Ida "cooks" caramelized popcorn balls ("we have to pretend it's caramelized," says Tawny, after Queen Ida has pretended to cook, and we laugh), I lose track of when we are laughing at the show and when at the constant fake laugh of the man next to me.

During the commercial breaks, it becomes clear that we are not to be left alone. When things get quiet, a production staff member charges over, asking with an exaggerated pout, "Why are you so quiet?" Several people tell us how wonderful we are, how we sound like a much bigger audience than we are, what a "good job" we are doing, to keep it up, to pace ourselves. After the cooking segment, an assistant producer comes over with a plate of popcorn balls: snack time. When the program ends, although still pumped up from flattery and performance, we are cursorily thanked and hustled out of the studio.

The amount of energy consistently poured into "warming up" and monitoring live television audiences is stunning. At a taping of "Into the Night with Rick Dees," a staff member works the crowd like a combination of nightclub performer and cheerleader ("Where are you kids from? Let me hear you cheer!"). After running through the plan for the show and delineating the prizes he will be giving away at the end of the taping, he cajoles two couples into coming up on stage for a dance contest, with audience applause determining the "winners." In between practice clapping and cheering, he gets three volunteers to play air guitar: they wildly pick at plastic blow-up guitars, are applauded, and return to their seats. A short man in a police outfit comes out and does a clown act. Then the whole audience is required to stand, follow cue cards, and sing along to a song called, "I Love LA." Only then does the program taping actually begin. Similarly, the master of ceremonies at the taping of the game show "Match Game" launches immediately into a routine whose one-liners echo vaudeville. (Each day, I am told by a woman with a relative who is a contestant, he uses exactly the same routine.) Gene gets briefly serious, explaining to the audience that "you're not just here to have fun, you have a job to do," that is, to be supportive of the contestants, scream and clap, and be supportive of the celebrities. "You're very important to them," he says, which he repeats twice later. "Don't poop out on the applause. You're very important." He reminds the audience that he will be giving away several fabulous prizes at the end of the show. "You must know by now that you're among friends," Gene says during a break in which audiences ask questions of the celebrities. During this same break, he arranges an elaborate audience-participation game, calling on members of the audience to act out a movie. "We're going to make our own stars," he says as he assigns roles in what amounts to public humiliation: a young woman must do a "lust dance," bumping and grinding while speaking gibberish; a young man imitates several kinds of dogs barking as well as an arrow flying through the air; another woman makes "buffalo patties." In a second break, Gene has a mini talent show, in which the same woman sings a song from a musical, another a piece of an aria, a third a verse from "When You Wish upon a Star," and a young man does his Ronald Reagan impression. Many in the audience escape to the bathrooms during these breaks, avoiding being drafted into the "fun."

Why such elaborate interplay with the audience? Why such infantilizing flattery? Why such abrupt chumminess? Why not simply run the show and let the audience watch and respond? How are audiences used by those building celebrity, and why? How much is known about audiences by celebrity teams and celebrity-based media? How is such knowledge pursued? How much of the behind-the-scenes activities of the celebrity industry do producers allow audiences to see? In short, how much do producers want to know about audiences and how much do they want audiences to know about them?

Audiences as Props and Signals

We have seen how in much of celebrity production the live audience is pushed aside as either irrelevant or bothersome. In celebrity-based programming—talk shows, most notably—the audiences are needed and are given a striking amount of attention. The sort of attention live audiences receive provides clues for one major way the celebrity industry tends to relate to audiences: as a production piece that will cue at-home audiences and create the image of a seamless production system.

The tone on the set of "AM Los Angeles," set by the hosts and among the producers and ultimately the audience, has little to do with the genuine responses of producers to their jobs ("[the job] is a performance," says one, "and we drop [the performance] when the show's done") or with genuine responses of audiences to the celebrities. The producers attempt to control audience behavior, to elicit particular behaviors that are in line with the production needs of the program. As one morning-show producer tells it:

We are the kind of show that's trying to have a lot of energy. The audience brings the host up a level, and it creates a party atmosphere. It's a party. How can you be boring or flat in the middle of a party? So the audience is a production element. When we warm up the audience, we're trying to mold you into our little production element. We want you to have a good time, too, and we don't lose sight of that, but if I have to be brutally candid, you're a prop.

This calls, first of all, for producer behaviors that will "kick start" the audience: a flattering ("you're the best"), temporarily intimate ("you're among friends"), often silly, high-energy "performance for the audience," often bolstered by the incentive of a prize. Second, producers must direct the performance of the audience as an audience. Since, unlike celebrity guests, they are not already trained in their "job," audience members require a good deal of attention to ensure that they do it right. Thus, for example, they practice cheering and clapping and may be pounced upon if they become silent. "We worry about silence," explains the producer, "because once people become flat and listless we worry they're not going to respond the next time we need them to respond." The attention and flattery last, of course, only as long as the production requires.

Moreover, behaviors that are in line with the actual responses of the audience member may or may not fit the need for "energy." Genuine response is uncertain and difficult to control. Thus artifice is called for and explicitly coached. "We want people to react naturally," says Don Roca, "but people don't always feel that they have the license or the freedom to do so. Let's say a host tries to be funny, and if you were left to your own emotions you might just stay stone-faced. Well, stone-faced does not fit our purposes. We would just as soon have you fake a laugh." A group of people laughing at the false, even mocking response of an audience member is as effective or more effective than a group laughing at actual conversational events. As long as the laughter does not cross the line into "inappropriate" situations, it is consistent and predictable. The behavior, not the motivation, is what's important.

Producers mold the audience as a "production element" not only to create a "party atmosphere for the hosts" but also to elicit behaviors that will serve as suggestive signals to those viewing at home. The perception is fostered that people onscreen are enjoying themselves and that therefore those flipping across the channels might also enjoy themselves at this particular stop. The result is a celebrity environment that appears seamless and in which producers appear to present exactly what audiences desire.

On other shows relying on celebrity-based reality programming, one finds less activity geared toward controlling audience behavior and less apparent fear of authentic response. In contrast to local morning programs and shows such as "Match Game," which make extensive use of minor celebrities, "The Tonight Show" depends mostly on its capacity to provide an exciting show with "A list" stars. The audience is still a production element, cued to respond through applause signs, and there is still an audience warm-up. The warm-up, however, is more of a pre-show show: there is no applause training, no flattery, just introductions and some talk. The experience for an audience member is of watching rather than performing. Audience responses work during the taping much the way they do at paid live performances, in which people laugh, for example, when they think something is funny, without the nervous coaching of producers. Even at this level, though, audiences in television production tend to be used to represent and model an enthusiastic response to the viewing audience.

The Medium Is the Audience: Publicists and Audiences

"We don't even think about them," says long-time publicist Henry Rogers of audiences. Despite having highly developed marketing and sales strategies, celebrity PR workers do not have much precise information about audiences, and the lack of knowledge is not considered problematic. "Research" in the celebrity industry is pursued haphazardly or, in the eyes of participants, intuitively. As personal publicist Michael Levine puts it, "You touch it, you feel it, you sense it." In other words, you don't try to know "scientifically" or directly what audiences think or feel. Although film studios and television networks do conduct serious audience research, testing and adapting their products, celebrity teams do not. Most commonly, they scan the general and entertainment media to stay on top of what's "hot"—adopting an odd naiveté by assuming, despite their intimate experience to the contrary, that media coverage directly reflects audience tastes.

Why not learn more? Why not depend on more than the gut? To begin with, as Todd Gitlin has pointed out in his analysis of the "problem of knowing" in the television industry, there are general professional reasons, particularly in an industry with "so little firm grounding in ethics, aesthetics, or rationality."

The professional's deeper claim to privileged status—deeper than any general knowledge—is prowess, or wisdom, or "feel," a personal quality gained from experience and grafted onto the principles and practices of the profession, a mystery that permits him or her to make right judgments under difficult practical circumstances.[1]

To the degree that "any publicity is good publicity," moreover, publicists have no reason to gain knowledge about an audience beyond its broad outlines. As HBO publicist Richard Rothenstein describes it, he may want a star to be glamorous, but most coverage opportunities can trump that strategy.

So what if in *People* you see her at home in jeans? Who cares? They spell her name right. To get the movie out there, if she's in jeans and a fucking shmata on her head baking lasagna, I don't care, because the movie gets represented in *People* magazine. It's really just getting the attention, getting the word out, trying to hit as many places as possible in just some way.

Building one-way communications to "get the word out" does not require a deep understanding of audiences.[2]

As we have seen, however, celebrity teams with longer-term agendas (personal publicists, managers, performers) are concerned with more than getting the name spelled right. They employ marketing activities to link the performer to audiences and presumably would stand to benefit from finding out about audience tastes. Yet they too guess and feel and mediascan their way toward the audience. Why, in an industry seemingly so dependent on audiences, is knowledge about them pursued in such cavalier fashion? Most centrally and simply, the primary market for their product is a different one from the mass audience. As Rogers says, "most of our target audience is the industry." Although considerations of mass market and mass-market segment characteristics certainly affect presentation, most activities are undertaken to communicate to those most immediately "consuming" a celebrity. "You can't leave it up to the audience because they're not the ones doing the hiring," says personal manager Gene Yusem. "I don't think about the audience. You can't second guess that far ahead." Broader audiences are only superficially relevant to the sales work.

Broader publics do, however, take a place here, one similar to their place in live television. Rather than depending on the actual evaluation or generation of audience interest, publicists use the *perception* of audience interest as a signal to industry buyers that their client has a reliable market. They do so by bypassing audiences, using the more controllable media coverage as a proxy for audience interest. "The public doesn't really enter into it," says film production company publicist Jack Emilio. "The publicists and the outlets, we're almost in a hermetic system. That's the direct nexus." The important information to be acquired by celebrity teams is not about the mass audience or its segments but about the needs and tastes of the media communicating about and to the entertainment industry. The audience thus remains a broad abstraction in the work lives of publicists, more important as an idea than as an actuality. Plenty of theories circulate about what "people" want and like, but they are never backed up by research beyond buying patterns and media attention. The working assumption is that media institutions are in touch with and reflect audience interest. As long as that assumption is maintained by entertainment-industry buyers, publicity workers can operate without requiring more knowledge about audiences. The news media provide all the necessary information: the fodder for pitching the entertainment industry. How much, then, do celebrity-disseminating media outlets in fact know about celebrity-watching audiences?

"We Don't Know Shit": Media Outlets and Knowledge about Audiences

It's always a big guess. Ultimately, we don't know shit. . . . Why should we know? Where is it written that we should really know this stuff? It's such an intangible. It's fickle. Just when you think you've figured it out, the audience proves you wrong. Nobody really knows. So nobody takes it that seriously.

Don Roca,
celebrity talk-show producer

Around Don Roca's office there is a running joke. Whenever someone claims to know what the audience wants or thinks, someone else always responds with, "I know, that's why we're doing a twelve"—an unattainably high rating for the time slot. The idea that one can understand audiences is itself a joke, punished with ridicule. Journalists, editors, and producers confirm this constantly, describing their own activity as a guessing game in which the outcome is unknowable. One movie critic tells the story of a producer ignoring adult guests and pouncing on the critics' kids at a social event: What do they like? Whom do they like? What's their favorite movie? Such desperation in encounters with "the public" is common. Like publicists and managers, editors and journalists most commonly claim that their knowledge about audience desires and interests comes from talking with each other and with industry sources, imagining "my aunt in Texas" or some such "typical" audience member, and from reading and viewing other media coverage. Audience research is uncommon and untrusted. Beyond the broad cues of the market, media workers tend to take their cues for coverage decisions mostly from each other. The central link between the celebrity industry and the consuming publics operates with very tenuous knowledge about those publics.[3]

Other studies of media organizations have found similar dynamics, providing some hints into what lies behind this resistance to approaching audience tastes, needs, and desires more systematically. Herbert Gans, in his study of "CBS Evening News," "NBC Nightly News," *Newsweek,* and *Time,* found that journalists rarely "take the audience directly into account when selecting and producing stories." Not only did journalists have little knowledge about the audience, they rejected feedback from it. "Although they had a vague image of the audience," as Gans describes it, "they paid little attention to it." Even those "top producers and editors" who keep up with ratings and circulation studies "pay only cursory attention to the audience studies that come across their desks, and the remaining journalists never see them." One producer explained, " 'You do the show for a cell of people—the office staff, the wife, and the kids. These are the only known audience. I know we have twenty million viewers, but I don't know who they are. I don't know what the audience wants, and I don't care. I can't know, so I don't care.' "[4]

Gans suggests several reasons for this state of affairs: the audience is simply too big to keep in mind; journalists do not believe audiences to be capable of determining their news needs; they come from backgrounds suspicious of statistics; they act out of "fear of the audience and its potential power"; they are wary of audience research because it is conducted by nonjournalists. Journalists, Gans argues, "are reluctant to accept any procedure which casts doubt on their news judgment and their professional autonomy."[5]

Celebrity-based news organizations share this general profile in varying degrees. Some outlets deliberately resist what they see as "pandering" to audience desires. "Newsier" organizations, particularly those whose sales depend more on their credibility as in-depth information providers than on celebrity images, resist any pressure to assess audience tastes. "The pandering I consider almost maintenance," says daily newspaper editor John Martin. "You throw the want-to-knows in there to make it interesting. I'm a purist about the idea that newspapers give you what you need to know, not what you want to know." These journalists and editors tend to take the traditional stance of leading or informing the audience, either through the "discovery" of talent or through a critical analysis of an entertainment product, person, or thing, uncovering its merits or revealing its deficiencies. Patrick Goldstein of the *Los Angeles Times,* for example, experiences that "certain thrill that you can discover something, whether it's discovering a talent, a trend, whatever." What concerns these journalists most is their *own* "curiosity," their own "visceral response," their own search for the outstanding. They attempt to lead rather than follow the audience. To the degree that they consider themselves news as well as entertainment organizations, informers as well as amusers, entertainment media are pushed away from the pursuit of audience desires.

Most outlets, however, are not commercially detached from either the celebrity industry or a celebrity sell; they are not in a position to take journalistic high roads. "We're not in an ivory tower here," says the editor-in-chief of a weekly entertainment guide. "My sense of the editor's job is that you carefully read the public's interests and curiosities. You don't preach to them." Editorial decisions at magazines like his, he explains, most fundamentally involve (and have always involved) evaluations of potential sales. His job is to follow trends and audience desires, not to influence them. To do this he depends on his "gut," market gauges such as ratings and box office figures, the familiarity and likability indicator called TVQ, and the week-to-week sales figures at his own magazine. When yellow backgrounds for covers seemed to do well for a while at *TV Guide,* says editor Bill Bruns, the publisher suggested running them every week; if the majority want yellow, or more young faces, or more Delta Burke stories, give them Delta Burke and a child on a yellow background. Trend chasing is seen as a safer bet than discovery, and sales figures and other media are scanned for signs of trends.

That yellow backgrounds were seriously considered the key to sales gives some indication of the odd relationship to the audience commonly found in entertainment media. Even among those media organizations built on following rather than leading audiences, understanding those audiences is literally a joke. Despite their search for audience fulfillment, they know what fulfills through only indirect or very broad input. They want to know what appeals and why but don't think they can know; they try to find out what audiences want, discuss it with each other, make constant claims to that knowledge, but only rarely take the step of asking audience members directly.[6]

In-depth audience input is avoided because it has certain disadvantages: it is expensive, since it must be ongoing; it poses a potential threat to decision-making professionals, since it eliminates their claim to be able to "feel" public tastes; and it is not entirely necessary, since enough broad information about what sells is available. In addition, although it would make decision making easier, it is not necessary to know, while working on a project-by-project basis, *why* certain performers appeal, only *that* they do, for the moment.

There is more, however, to the reluctance to systematically approach the sought-after audience. Most outlets, however dependent on audience approval, still operate according to conventions of professional journalism. "It may be fluff news," says Pete Hammond of his infotainment program "Entertainment Tonight," "but it's treated and approached exactly like a news show." The more seriously an organization and its workers take themselves as news providers, the more dissonance is raised by activities perceived as "bowing" or "caving in" to audience desires.[7] "If somebody had told me twenty years ago that in twenty years newspapers would be trying to assess what their readers want to read and give them that," complains newspaperman John Martin, "I would have gotten out of the business that day." Journalists continually complain of threats to their integrity not only from publicists but from the pressure to produce the popular. For a celebrity-based outlet, pursuing extensive audience research amounts to relinquishing more editorial control—already threatened by publicists—to audiences.

One set of resolutions to the conflict between offering audiences too much or too little power takes place narratively. Issues of audience control are incorporated into the reporting, attracting the audience through information about its own power to make or break careers. "It's the William Morrisization of America," says Pete Hammond about his program's reporting. "Out in Iowa they're concerned about grosses now." The growth of reporting on the *business* of entertainment and celebrity, the "infotainment" phenomenon, can be seen in part as a response by entertainment journalists to their dual roles as audience pleasers and audience leaders. Reporting about box office grosses and ratings—popularized largely by "Entertainment Tonight," and now standard fare—serves partially to bridge the two requirements. On the one hand, journalists edify by taking audiences into the business of show business; here, they are traditional reporters in control of the story. On the other hand, the stories themselves tend to affirm the audience's power to set the terms of the rest of show business coverage, by suggesting that coverage is determined not by editorial staffs and cultural producers but by popularity at the "polls" of consumption.

A smaller set of journalists, particularly those committed to artistic criteria, use irony to bring out what they see as the absurd results of audience-driven celebrity making and audience-driven journalism. Bill Zehme is senior writer at *Rolling Stone,* a magazine he jokingly says "has always had a patina of integrity going for it." He is serious about his task as a writer: to take a subject and "try to elevate it," to "take it a little bit farther and make it something else" through "a voice and a style." He must find a way to elevate "mediocre," generally undeserving subjects in an industry he finds "repugnant, ridiculous, stupid." In this effort he differs from the magazine with which *Rolling Stone* shares an owner and an office, *Us.* "They're about flat-out, bubble-gum, feel-good celebrity worship," he says. Most celebrity journalists just "report the comings and goings of a celebrity and give you what you want," but the expectations for his organization, and for himself, are for something slightly different. He must both amuse and educate the audience.

Publications such as *Rolling Stone* are not in a position to directly attack the industry and its audiences, dependent as they are on the approval of both; indeed, Zehme argues that he and *Rolling Stone* are active participants "in the process of building celebrities." Yet he is expected not to write "bullshit." Irony and parody—what Zehme calls "the antidote to the times"—fulfill these needs, calling attention to the production of stupidities without quite undermining it. Zehme's resolution is what he calls an "edge," a "new irony." Thus Zehme wrote a "tongue in cheek" cover story on a best-selling issue featuring the women of "Twin Peaks," parodying their reason for making it to the cover of *Rolling Stone* ("They're on the cover," he says, "because they're extraordinarily attractive girls"). And he took a "mock reverential" approach to profiling actor Johnny Depp, an ironic, worshipful blow-by-blow of mundane activities intended to reveal the absurdity of a "kid with his qualities becoming such a celebrity." In that piece, he says, "I'm making fun of the whole celebrity journalism process. It's my most passive-aggressive act." He calls attention to the celebrity journalist's celebration of idols he does not idolize, suggesting that the dependence on the popular elevates many of the unworthy. In doing so, he reclaims the traditional role of the journalist as informer and educator, taking the reader to new understandings. The blatant fact remains, however, that this is a profile of Johnny Depp; his photo on the cover draws paying customers. The choice of subject itself is a bow to the power of the audience, while the treatment of it expresses distaste for that power. Populism and elitism thus live together. Given the institutional needs of the organizations from which it emanates, the passive aggression of ironic laughter may be the only acceptable aggression.[8]

The middle ground, however, remains not in the narrative but in the work life. By embracing the unknowability and fickleness of audience tastes, these media workers sidestep the sticky question of their relationship to those audiences. Do audience desires need to be understood? Neither a yes (because content is dictated by their desires) nor a no (because content is dictated by their needs as perceived by media professionals) is entirely acceptable. If they are incapable of being understood, the question need not be confronted.

Dupes or Accomplices: How Much Should Audiences Know?

The best campaigns are the campaigns that don't look like campaigns at all. I think it's damaging for them to be revealed as campaigns; it mitigates the ability to do it. Certain things grow well in lots of light, and certain things don't. The petri dish in which romance grows is maybe not always so clinically dissected, and I also wonder if what has to be done in war to achieve its strategic ends is something that is assisted by massive knowledge of the most minute detail by everyone. Maybe there's some moderate analogy to public relations.

Michael Levine, personal publicist

I don't think it matters if people find out more about publicity. It might just make more people want to go into the profession. I don't think they'd be cynical and horrified by it. I think they'd say, "What a great job. I want to learn how to do that."

Marsha Robertson,
film studio market coordinator

> *What happens as the audience gets savvier is you write savvier stories.*
> *You write stories in which you incorporate the publicity machinery into*
> *the story. You write about how the star didn't show up and the publicist*
> *was biting their nails or you write about the negotiating process to get*
> *the star.*
>
> Miriam Ross,
> entertainment magazine
> writer and editor

Turn the question of what producers know about audiences on its side: How much do celebrity-industry workers want audiences to know about their activities? As we have seen in the discussion of celebrity texts, the artificial, manipulative elements of the commercial celebrity system have become increasingly common in texts. It would seem that revealing to the audience a celebrity industry that, while claiming to be in audiences' control, in many ways excludes them, would be a threat to producers. As Michael Levine indicates above, the revelation of the publicity activity as a publicity activity threatens to render it ineffective.

Many publicists object to reporting that makes their activity visible, advocating against "lots of light" and "massive knowledge of the most minute detail" and being "clinically dissected." Having finally reached personal publicist Charlotte Parker (who handles, among others, Arnold Schwarzenegger) to request an interview, I myself was subjected to a lengthy grilling by Parker and her husband/partner (where am I studying? what do I intend to do with the interview? what exactly do I want to talk about?) and an immediate attempt to "set some terms" for discussion. Offered anonymity, the Parkers were nonetheless wary and immediately assumed a defensive posture. They are uncomfortable with the topic area—as it was put to them, how they do what they do—Joel Parker explained, because they like to stay "behind the scenes." They are reticent to talk about their work because that is precisely the most threatening kind of revelation. Paramount publicist Diana Widdom is less defensive but no less adamant.

Periodicals like the *LA Times* are always wanting to do marketing stories, which Paramount never, never wants to do, because they don't want to give away what their marketing tools and resources are. We don't want the public to know. It's nobody's business how we do what we do. People will learn our inside secrets. That's nobody's business. What happens when you want to do it again next week?

Widdom argues further that people do not want to know. "They don't want their image destroyed," she says. "I think everybody likes to dream, likes to fantasize, and likes to imagine." One hears a similar argument from entertainment-news workers talking about their resistance to revealing the mechanisms of celebrity production. "Sure, you're carrying on the myths of Hollywood," says Pete Hammond of "Entertainment Tonight." "Why burst people's bubbles, you know? People need something to believe in." Although he does not shy away from showing them, writer Patrick Goldstein believes that "people don't want to know about the warts, the flaws of their celebrities. They really want to be able to dream a little bit." If people knew that they were getting "one blow-job story after the next," that everything in a magazine was "sanitized by the star, by their publicist," says an entertainment magazine writer, it "might turn readers off." (He was speaking, of course, of a competing magazine, not his own, which he claimed had "resisted that kind of manipulation so far.") People don't know, the argument goes, they don't want to know, and nobody wants them to know. Each, for his or her own reasons, prefers the illusion, which is best left alone. Those celebrity-industry participants who do not want to see the industry mechanisms exposed justify themselves with audience desires (about which, of course, they actually know very little for certain).

Running hand in hand with this argument—which, it should be noted, takes for granted that the celebrity industry involves activities that, known about, would spoil its effects—is a perception of the audience as not only bored and fantasy-driven but also gullible at best and stupid at worst. "I don't think the general public has a clue," says publicist Sarah Tamikian. "The public is ill-informed," says manager David Spiro. "The *National Enquirer* does not sell two million copies a week to smart people. The people in this world want to believe certain things, and they will always believe certain things." Performer Nia Peeples suggests that celebrity carries a "huge social responsibility" precisely because people are gullible.

I think the majority of people don't know that a lot of these celebrities are manufactured. I forget until I get out there in middle America that Hollywood is like another planet to them, and they believe everything. I think there's a group of people smart enough to know that they have to read things in, that nothing is as it is perceived, but that the mass of people don't. I think the majority of people want to be led.

Indeed, many argue, the job of the celebrity team would be much more difficult if this were not the case. "The audience accepts what they read as gospel," argues publicist Henry Rogers. "PR really wouldn't work if people were skeptical."

For many others in the celebrity industry, revealing the publicity machinery is not threatening, because there is nothing to hide except the dull mechanisms of an industry. People know, they say, and they don't care, or they don't know and don't care. "I don't think the demystifying process is going to turn anybody off," says film production company publicist Jack Emilio.

> Even if you do demystify it, it's quickly forgotten. Just like you forget that when you go to McDonald's there's a guy who drove up there with all the hamburgers in the morning. I'm sure you know that somewhere some guy had to kill that cow, some guy had to grind it up, some guy drove it up there frozen, but that's longhand. You don't need it. It's the same thing with what we do. We're the longhand behind the scenes. You forget about us.

Visibility is not a threat, it's just pointless. The publicist should not be seen, says film studio publicist Linda Fox, not because "if you're visible you're revealing the magic," but simply because she isn't relevant. This point of view remains agnostic on the gullibility or insight of celebrity watchers and assumes a lack of manipulation and artificiality in the celebrity-rise process.

For some celebrity teams and outlets, however, behind-the-scenes machinations are not threatening *because* audiences already know: either because they are inherently incapable of being fooled or because they have become increasingly astute. In one variation, articulated by those who stake a claim to "real" stardom and "magic," the visible machinery and marketing is unthreatening because it bolsters the real. "The viewer finds you out eventually," says television programmer Susan Rice. "If you put a newsperson on and this person's an asshole, if you really work at it and they really work at it you can fool the viewers for about a year or so. Eventually people begin to feed back to you exactly what this person's like." Since being found out is inevitable, she prefers to put a likable person on the air. In fact, the more tools they have for discerning, the more capable audiences are of distinguishing true from fake celebrities and of trusting their own loyalty. "You can only fool some of the people for so long," says Scott Hennig, Angelyne's assistant. "They wouldn't relate to Angelyne the way they do, and she wouldn't have made it the way she has if it was fake or if there wasn't that underlying current of truth or reality to it. People know when they're being conned. Even the stupidest people know when you're songing and dancing them." For those who claim to be offering some "underlying current of truth or reality,"

increased audience abilities to recognize a con are a boon rather than a
threat.

Perhaps the most interesting perception of what celebrity audiences do
and should know, though, comes from those who do not believe in magic.
Magazine editor and writer Miriam Ross speaks with a cynical edge:
many of the people she writes about are "fools," "products," "generic,"
"the fourth Jeff Bridges lookalike on the left." She is less cynical, in fact,
about the magazine's readers than about its subjects. "Our readers are
smart," she says. "People are very savvy." The fact that people see the
publicity machinery does not mean they will feel cheated. On the contrary,
given that they already know it exists, the more they see of it, the less
likely they are to distrust the information they receive. They know the
deal and expect to see evidence of it.

I think readers know Sandra Dee is on the cover because she's telling us about
all these terrible things that happened to her. They know Michael Fox is on the
cover because he's selling a movie. However, they are interested in the fact that
he recently got married and became a father. Therefore, it's almost as if there's
complicity. Okay, if he's willing to talk about getting married and becoming a
father, I'm willing to buy it knowing that what he's also going to do is plug the
movie. It's an agreement you make.

Seeing evidence of the publicity machinery and marketing behaviors,
rather than scaring readers off, increases their confidence in the fairness
of their tacit "agreement" with the celebrity industry.

Knowledge and Visibility

In the world of celebrity production one finds a vagueness and openness
in the approach to audiences. Beyond the obvious direct sales information
(what are they buying? what are they watching?), little information is
sought about them. There is a certain utility in having knowledge about
audiences unsystematic and unanchored. Even when not being used directly as live production elements, audiences tend to be as important for
their internal industry uses as for their actual responses and behaviors.
Fuzzy understandings of "what the audience wants" render notions of
audience desires very malleable. Audience tastes, in such loose form, more
easily justify a wide array of coverage decisions and more easily serve a
wide array of sales pitches. They threaten no one and allow media institutions to more comfortably bridge entertainment and journalistic norms.

Audience knowledge is approached with a similar lack of consensus. Industry professionals respond differently to the possibility of increased audience exposure to celebrity-production activities; they are not uniformly threatened. The view that publicity operations should be kept invisible lest they "spoil the magic" or enlighten a gullible audience does not clearly dominate; many publicity operatives do not expend much energy keeping themselves and their activities hidden. Here a range of ideas about the audience, again rarely grounded, informs a range of activities: from deliberately refusing to show celebrity production and marketing, to weakly recommending against it on the grounds of lack of interest, to deliberately incorporating it into the celebrity story.

Populist and elite tendencies once again appear simultaneously, here not in texts but in daily work lives. The audience is at once pandered to and bypassed in the service of internal organizational needs. Respect for audiences runs alongside confidence in their gullibility, secrecy alongside openness, restricted access alongside the offer to audiences to participate more actively in the commodification and management of celebrities—that is, to become the producers.

Part Three

Celebrity-Watching Audiences

Chapter Six

Hunting, Sporting, and the Willing Audience: The Celebrity-Watching Tourist Circuit

The young woman in the purple evening gown in the lobby of the Beverly Hilton is an oddity. She has flown in from Omaha specifically to wait outside the Golden Globe Awards for actor Richard Gere to arrive. Gere has cancelled, she found out from the camera crews gathering earlier in the day, but she is giving up neither hope nor fantasy nor excitement. She keeps up a steady stream of comments during the celebrity arrivals, both general (this actress is from Nebraska, that one had her hair done by someone she knows) and Gere-specific. "If he shows up and I faint," she says, "just catch me." She, like everyone else in the crowd around us, has heard the rumor about Gere having a gerbil surgically removed from his anus, but it does not bother her. "He has a house in Long Beach," she informs us. "I'd really like to find out where it is." When I leave, after the program has begun and the watching crowd has thinned out, she is still there, all dressed up and waiting.

This is perhaps the strongest stereotype of the celebrity watcher: the obsessive fan, devoted to a fantasy of meeting and winning over the object of her adoration, out of touch with and resistant to reality, undaunted by negative information, governed by an overwhelming desire to be close to a star, willing to travel great distances and to seek out his house. No one around this particular fan, however, shares those characteristics. In fact, she is treated as amusing, perhaps pathetic, and certainly different. No one else in the crowd of Golden Globe onlookers has dressed to attract attention or as if they are going to a special event. They have dressed comfortably, to watch. In addition to tourists, there are some locals and hotel guests, all in casual attire. Most have small, inexpensive cameras. Although they often express excitement at particular celebrity arrivals, they have not come to see anyone in particular. These celebrity watchers are very different from the fan devoted to a single person or a small set of performers.

The spectators fall into two detectable groups: hobbyists, ranging from the serious to the casual, and tourists. Both are mixed in terms of age, gender, and race. The hobbyists tend to be more serious about celebrity watching; they are regulars at such events. The activity of the tourists differs from the hobbyists' less in kind as in the degree of its seriousness. Near my position in the crowd of some two hundred people, two young women, who switch between English and Spanish, tell me they come every year; two Asian men, also annual attendees, plan to stay for the after-program scene because they "just love them"; a white man nearby refuses to take certain people's pictures because they are "just too far away," and besides, he says, gesturing dismissively to the tourists, he can get better pictures afterward, when all "these people" are gone. These seasoned observers tend to claim "insider" knowledge. When Robin Williams arrives, the tourist next to me asks if his wife is Meg Tilly; no, says one of the hobbyists (patiently, but clearly amused at the ignorance), he is married to a woman who used to babysit his children. When Sally Kirkland gets out of her limo, another man warns those around him about her reputation as a publicity hound: "Oh, boy, here comes another scene stealer."

As we watch celebrities arrive, two main activities occur. In the first, the spectators mimic the photographers: they call out the names of stars and try to get them to look over, pose, and interact with them. Some celebrities evoke much more excitement and a bit of cheering. Spectators may try to attract a star's attention so they can tell them something: "You look wonderful," "We love you," and "We've seen your movie hundreds of times," they shout to Shirley MacLaine. Mostly, though, onlookers attempt to be noticed and acknowledged by the celebrity. (The celebrities, however, rarely make movements toward the audience beyond a wave, as they are occupied with walking through the series of posing stops.) To a large degree, the name calling arises from a genuine personal excitement about the moment of the encounter, about being in the same place at the same time with celebrities.

Yet name calling is as often a practical act directed toward the photographs, which, I am told by several people, they collect in albums and show to their friends. "Get Kirk Cameron," a girl calls out frantically to her sister. "I got so-and-so" is a constant refrain: the language and feeling is of a hunt. The competition with the paparazzi is fierce and difficult, driven by the spectators' sense that they are being given fewer opportunities than they deserve. At one point, a woman in the crowd yells to a star, "James, your fans are over here. Those are the tabloids. Your fans are over here. We have a right."

Attention and energy are focused equally on getting the attention and photographic documentation of celebrities and on joining the other spectators in a continuous game of identify the star. As celebrities walk in, everyone wants to know who they are, from where they do or ought to recognize them. Identify the star is a game that can be played alone—an elderly man with a cane, alone by the window, announces "that's Brenda Fricker" to no one but himself—but is best played with others. Rather than competing for a celebrity's glance or a good photo position, spectators join together in the game; by the end of the event, there is a feeling of camaraderie. With the big stars, the game is simple: there are many cues, in the form of extra light flashes and people calling out the name. The smaller stars create discussion among the spectators: one commonly hears, "Who's that? Do you know who that is?" Occasionally, no one can figure out who the celebrity is or what they are famous for; more frequent are claims such as, "She's Katey Sagal from 'Married with Children' "; or "She's on 'China Beach,' or maybe she's from 'Twin Peaks,' " or "He's the one that replaced Ken Wahl on 'Wiseguy.' " The word then spreads. Often people know the name but not the work, or the work but not the name. The most successful and valued player can also provide a bit of extra information. The specific answers themselves are less important than finding someone who has an answer, who can fit the incoming celebrity into a category (name, work, level of celebrity).

Observation and participation in in-person celebrity watching begins to raise questions and provide clues about widespread involvement with fame and famous people. Any insight into *why* audiences are drawn to celebrity "texts" (in this case, as they are enacted live) starts with the audiences themselves, with *what* they are doing and *how* they go about it. What are their central activities? To what are they paying attention?

The Golden Globe Awards experience offers immediate suggestions. Live celebrity watching typically has more in common with whale or bird watching, spectator sports, or stamp collecting than with the well-established images of weeping, swooning young women or aggressive autograph hounds waiting at the stage door. Certainly such people exist, often in strong and active subcultures, but in live celebrity-encounter settings (awards shows, television tapings, book signings) they are relatively rare.[1]

Although among the collectors, hobbyists, tourists, and spectators there is ample evidence of excitement, satisfaction is garnered not so much from recognition by a particular star but from acknowledgment by any celebrity. The pull between hierarchy and equality, seen earlier both in texts and production settings, is evident here as well. The celebrities are treated, if not as a traditional power elite, as an elite with the power to anoint, however briefly. In a formal democracy, personal distinction, self-importance, glory, and honor are ideologically problematic and hard to achieve. Celebrities as an elite mediate this problem: they have been legitimated by popularity, distinguished by the fact that millions of eyes have dwelled on them, by the glamour of envy.[2] To be acknowledged by them—to meet their eyes—is to briefly feel their power. It is, literally, a rush, a charge.

The excitement of the celebrity encounter is perhaps expected. What is remarkable in celebrity tourist settings, however, is how consumed spectators are with activities that neither revere celebrities nor pursue recognition from them: the game of identify the star, for example. Paying attention to celebrities is, first of all, as much a social activity as a personal one. Although there are certainly important processes of psychological identification and projection at work, visible celebrity-watching activities are focused mostly on collective experience.[3] (Neither do they necessarily express personal admiration; indeed, they are occasionally quite irreverent.) Instead, much of the activity is laterally or horizontally focused: rather than looking "up" at celebrities, people are looking "over" at each other. Watchers are connecting with each other through the "sport" of sighting, identifying and categorizing celebrities, exchanging bits of information, or through their common experience of and role in the spectacle. A closer look at these activities is telling.

Hunts and Games

The tourist celebrity-watching circuit in Los Angeles generally operates like a hunt for rare game. The tourist always has his or her eyes open for a celebrity, and stories of "sightings" circulate bountifully. As in a hunt, the relationship between chaser and chased is both structured and mediated: audiences, who want as much as they can get, pursue celebrities in a controlled environment, but if they are too widely available and easily gotten, the celebrities are not worth having.

The ubiquitous tours and maps of stars' homes—which take you to various landmarks and past the homes of celebrities both dead and living—capture this well. "I hope you're more enthusiastic than my last group," driver Kenny tells his noon group of tourists. "With the last group we saw three stars: Jay Leno, Tom Bosley, and George Burns. And that group didn't even get excited." A middle-aged woman from Wisconsin with her two grown children says, "Oh, we'll get excited." She asks where they saw George Burns. "He had just left his house. He was, you know, going to have a martini and play cards with the fellas. Maybe you'll see some stars, you never know," Kenny says. As we drive down Hollywood Boulevard, he tells us that it is all a matter of being in the right place at the right time. He offers tips. "You've got to keep your eyes on those cars, the fancy ones. Jay Leno was driving one of those antique cars, he had on some glasses. He took them off, and I said, 'Hey, that's Jay Leno.' Honked my horn, he waved. It was great." As we pass by cafés on Sunset Boulevard, he suggests that we might want to come sit here. "You never know who you'll see. You come in here and sit down, you never know who you might be sitting next to."

Our first house is the former home of Marilyn Monroe and Joe Dimaggio during the "very short six months that they were together." From here, the tour consists of an hour and a half of driving by people's homes, looking at them from a distance, occasionally pausing. The litany is the same the whole time, once again taking the form of a game: "How many of you are familiar with Dinah Shore? This is where she resides," or "This is the house of the man who wore a long raincoat and a cigar, he played a detective on TV," and when we guess correctly, "Yes, this is Colombo, Mr. Peter Falk." He fills in with little details: Morrie Amsterdam usually has a gold Rolls Royce in the driveway, so if it's not there he must be out with his wife, who drives him everywhere; Danny Thomas built a chapel onto his house for the wedding of daughter Marlo and Phil Donahue; Prince painted his house purple, but the neighbors didn't like it and the fans were all over it, so he sold it to Eddie Murphy, who painted it pink and sold it to Warner Brothers pictures; Dean Martin sold his house after his son died in a plane crash and also has a home in Vegas; Johnny

Carson stays in Bungalow number 10 at the Beverly Hills Hotel between marriages; Ed McMahon has a license plate that says "Heeere's Ed"; W. C. Fields used to sit behind his entrance and shoot a BB gun at tour buses; Bonnie Franklin would give us the finger if she encountered us, as would Barbra Streisand; the Reagans' address had been a satanic 666 but, on the advice of Nancy's astrologer, they traded numbers with a neighbor so that they could be 668 instead.

The watchers often appear bored but nonetheless participate in the guessing games, shoot photographs, and occasionally ask questions. Some groups just don't get excited, Kenny explains later. To him it is clear that a celebrity sighting ought to be the highlight of the tour, perhaps the whole point. At Dinah Shore's house, a woman is getting out of her car, carrying groceries and some balloons. Kenny honks. "Who's that? Are you anybody? Wave at me." It turns out to be a false alarm. Later, we do see Jimmy Stewart and his wife pulling out of the driveway; they wave. The group becomes very excited and animated. Then we see television producer Aaron Spelling, a smaller fish, since he is not in front of the camera, but still a somebody. Kenny says this is his record for a day, five sightings. "See if we can get one more," he says, "that'd be nice." In these sightings, the cameras pop up as if automatically. The photograph not only records but caps the experience.

Events such as awards shows are draws, of course, precisely because game is plentiful: the experience is like fishing on a trout farm or hunting at a zoo. At the Academy Awards, most spectators begin arriving in the morning—some even camp out the day before—many hours before the first famous person will walk the red carpet. The seating arrangement is drawn from sports: bleachers overlook the "field" onto which celebrities arrive. The crowd's behaviors also ape sporting events. There is the rowdiness—loud calling out to friends, boisterous joking, milling around, chatting with strangers, collective complaining chants (in this case about the need for drinking water in the stands). There is the camaraderie born of waiting together and of focusing on the same event and of being identified together as spectators (media workers circulate among us, filming and interviewing "the fans"). In years past, a veteran tells me, before the new security restrictions, fans would arrive two days early and camp out on the bleachers with hibachis and beer. "It was like a big tailgate party," he says. People seem to be there as much for the event of waiting as for the event of watching; as much for the spectacle as for the celebrities.

When I and a friend arrive we see the Wisconsin family from the tour of the stars' homes. We greet each other happily, comrades in celebrity tourism. The mother reports in a hushed, reverent tone, knowing that it will impress greatly, "We saw Barbra Streisand." They plan to make this an annual event. "By next year," they say, "we'll have forgotten the rain, the cold, the sitting around. All you remember is how great it is when the stars come by." They are seated near the front, the spot for the more devoted who arrived, as they did, at dawn. The rest of us sit farther away, and there is little reverent talk around me about stars and Oscars. Even if it doesn't impress you, a young Latino who brought his girlfriend here for her birthday tells me, it can impress other people that you were there, that you saw so-and-so. He complains about how much money celebrities make and then spend on themselves. "Anybody could look like that," he says. "My girlfriend don't need that to look good." A man arrives with his preteen cousin. "Celebrities are no big deal," he says. "It's just fun. We're doing this as a touristy thing." Next to us is a young Australian couple. They see some of this on Australian television, but not much of the arrivals, they explain, and are very excited about seeing stars. Why? "I've never really thought about it," the man says.

As part of the spectacle, the spectators eagerly play their roles, like fans doing "the wave" or playing to cameras at a ball game. Various television reporters, along with some print journalists, make their way through the bleachers interviewing people over the course of the next few hours. The interviews become mini-events that attract a small crowd of listeners. People wishing to be interviewed call out "Over here!" When the cameras periodically pan the fans, the crowd cheers and waves. "You ready to be on TV, homey?" the young man near me asks. He says proudly that he has already been interviewed once, by an E! Entertainment TV reporter who asked him how he felt about the restrictions imposed on the fans this year (apparently in response to security concerns stemming from the Persian Gulf war). The interviewers focus on a group conducting what appears to be a mini-rebellion against these restrictions: the petition they are circulating on yellow legal-sized paper states that "the fans feel the need to eat and drink during their five-and-a-half hour wait." The petition contains no demands. In fact, one organizer tells a TV interviewer, they are not planning to do anything with it now; instead, they will send it to the Academy for consideration for next year. Rather than an expression of them-versus-us displeasure, the petition is a gesture of temporary "fan" identity and consumer loyalty and involvement (how can we, fans and the Academy, improve this event?).

There is, however, one very unwelcome restriction this year: no cameras are allowed in the stands. The spectators complain loudly about this, as getting photos is one of their primary objectives and activities. However, the ban is a boon for several people selling celebrity snapshots at two dollars apiece or three for five dollars. A woman nearby has bought two photos of Tom Selleck, for a friend, and one of Kevin Costner and his wife that she will put "on my bathroom wall, on the mirror, you know, so I can look at it, and pretend." She laughs; it is silly and she knows it. If we could just cut that wife out of there, she jokes. One of the photosellers describes his business. He and his wife, both avid fans, go to a wide variety of events and shoot photos of celebrities of all levels; they sell directly to customers at events like these, to magazines and tabloids, and by mail order through advertisements in soap and teen magazines. They have many regular mail-order customers and write to them all personally, often sending bits of gossip along with the photos. "If someone really likes Johnny Depp," he says, "we might tell them, 'Hey, we saw Johnny and Winona going to this premiere the other day, and they went in the back door so nobody would bother them,' and so we give them something a little extra that nobody else knows about. Then they can tell their friends about it." Customers put the photos on mirrors, give them to friends, put them in photo albums. He thumbs through the photos with familiarity and sits and looks at them with people. He is no cynical businessman but a devoted celebrity watcher (with greater access to the celebrities) who enjoys sitting around with others like him.

Finally, in the late afternoon, the area below begins to fill with guests milling around. These are noncelebrity guests, however, and those around me agree that they are an irritation, since they will make it much more difficult to pick out a celebrity. When emcee Army Archerd asks the guests to please move inside, the crowd cheers with a sort of "get those glorified nobodies out of the way" glee. When Whoopi Goldberg arrives, the first big star, she creates a stir, and the excitement level picks up palpably as spectators strain to get a good glimpse. Now the crowd is focused, conversation is reduced to "Who?" and "Where?" and identify-the-star games take over: scan and locate a star, with cues from people around you, make sure your companions see them too, make some small comment, applaud, watch, cheer, then look for the next celebrity. When the college kids nearby call "Amanda! Amanda! Amanda!," a woman in front of them turns and asks, with some excitement, "Amanda who?" Amanda, she is told, is just a friend of theirs who is somewhere in the crowd below.

The woman is a bit embarrassed, disappointed. The man who had claimed it was just a no-big-deal touristy thing is busily craning his neck and identifying celebrities. The watching becomes a game—party, hunt, spectacle, sporting event—as much about connecting watcher to watcher (on the site and later with photographs) as watcher to celebrity.

Enthusiastic Role Playing and the Search for Documentation

The watchers do not necessarily admire or construct fantasies around the objects of their surveillance, yet they will pay twenty-five dollars to drive by other people's homes, or spend a whole day waiting to crane their necks to see a person walk a hundred yards. Why? What are we to make of such activities?

Turning for the beginnings of an answer to another audience, the studio audience, we return to an earlier question: Why are people willing to set aside genuine responses and to clap and laugh instead according to the instructions of producers? Why do people do what producers tell them to do? The commonly noted draw of the spectacular, and especially of the mass-media spectacle, explains a good deal. Many celebrity-watching events differ little in experience and in appeal from other spectacular mass events such as football games, fireworks displays, and parades.

Answering even more directly, the attraction of many celebrity-based events is not so much the celebrities as the opportunity to witness moments in the continued creation of celebrity and to participate in the media of celebrity. As one essayist describes it, studio audiences "don't come to hear the visiting guest, perhaps not even to be near the star, but to touch the medium, to have their faces on the screen in that instant when the camera pans the audience, to be on."[4] At talk-show and sitcom tapings, as we have seen, audiences are enthusiastic about "playing themselves," adopting stylized, hyper-upbeat selves, performing as instructed regardless of genuine response, and enjoying their own performances. Audiences in these situations embrace their place in the celebrity system and in mass commercial culture more generally. The draw is not only to witness but to help create the spectacle. Producers recognize this: they are not afraid to make the performance aspects of an audience's "job" explicit.

The position audiences embrace includes the roles of simultaneous voyeurs of and performers in commercial culture. The recognition of oneself as a production element is hard to avoid as an audience member. The point is that no one seems to mind since that is largely what they are there for. At the game show "Match Game," for example, a good portion of the audience even chants "double, double!" (when the contestant spins the big wheel, which, if it lands on certain spots, will mean she is playing for double the amount of money) without any producer prompting whatsoever. On "AM Los Angeles," when the woman in seat 113 wins the prize (a weekend local hotel getaway), she instinctively jumps up, knowing her role. Signaled by a producer to wave as the camera pans them tightly, most audience members do so. They know their role and they play it to the hilt, dwelling in it.

The general experience of spectacles is very much in the *present* tense. The past, importantly, is backgrounded—so, for example, *how* or *why* some celebrity came to be parading in front of you and commanding attention is irrelevant. Exposure to "the way it works" can of course at times be disillusioning, even in the present tense. "I used to really like Arsenio Hall," a woman tells me in a TV-show taping line, "then when we went I saw he was reading. He read everything, and I liked him much less after that. I used to think he was a really talented, really funny guy. But he's just reading. I mean, anybody could go up there and read stuff." She is still going to tapings, however. For the most part even such disillusioning knowledge is translated into "insider knowledge" rather than a reason to turn away.

Disillusionment hardly takes away from involvement because enjoyment is both momentary and derived from the celebration spectacle rather than from the qualities, admirable or not, of the celebrity. Disdain, humor at celebrities' expense, and only a vague knowledge of celebrities' claims to fame are quite common at these events. At the Academy Awards, a college student jokes about throwing an umbrella into the crowd of celebrities and then explaining in interviews, "I just wanted to be noticed, is that so wrong?" A group of people waiting in line to attend "Match Game" for the second day in a row tell me which six celebrities were on yesterday. They can name the people and their work with only partial clarity: Vicki Lawrence used to be on "The Carol Burnett Show," this guy (name forgotten) is an "up-and-coming comedian," some other woman (name also forgotten) used to be on a sitcom. "They're mostly used-up people," explains one. At a Joan Collins book signing, along with sweetly shy book bearers and admiring fans who "wanted to see her in real life," a couple of affluent women are comparing Collins's physique to their own. "She has a wonderful figure, but she's very, very short," says one. "Do you think she's had a face lift?" responds her friend. "Many times," the first answers with certainty. "What, you think it's magic?" Behind them, two young men and a woman in their early twenties, who did not stumble onto but sought out this book signing, are making fun of Collins: as she says things, they repeat them to each other, embellishing, adding, exaggerating, laughing. Moments of fame celebration do not require any particular reverence for celebrities.

The draw of the spectacular, however, does not explain the particular forms and characteristics of celebrity-encounter "games." The superficiality of these games offers deeper explanation. If we look, first of all, at the rhythm and end-point of much of the play: simply *identifying* a person is enough. One simply sees them and finds out who and what they are, and then one moves on to the next. There is little attempt to go further, to make some sort of connection with the person or to dwell on them at length. No depth is required. Second, there is genuine *excitement* in this game, even when it is recognized as superficial, as it often is. Finally, the activity is rarely complete unless the encounter is somehow *documented*, primarily with photographs, trophies from the hunt.

It is this last piece that threads these activities together: the pursuit of documentation. A quick see-and-identify move is enough to satisfy exactly because the excitement is in *confirming* the existence of celebrities in "real life." The excitement derives from the simple *fact* of Dana Delaney or Andy Garcia or Robin Leach actually being physically there. One young white woman, for example, describes her response to being at a San Francisco 49ers game:

It's so stupid, right, twenty-six years old, college-educated person, and I was excited to be breathing the same air as Joe Montana. I go to my mother, "Mom, we're breathing the same air that Joe Montana's breathing." I just couldn't believe that he was right there. He's a person. I guess you realize that they're a person, and they walk like a person and talk like a person.

Another describes working at Harrah's resort in Lake Tahoe and finding that Bill Cosby had checked out and left his "bathroom things" in his villa room. "We just stood there and stared at Bill Cosby's bathroom stuff going, 'Whoa, isn't this cool?' " This is the excitement of proof.

"The question of the star's authenticity can be referred back to her/his existence in the real world," Richard Dyer has pointed out. "Stars appear before us in media texts . . . but unlike other forms of representation stars do not only exist in media texts. To say that stars exist outside of media texts in real life would be misleading, but stars are carried in the person of people who do go on living away from their appearances in the media."[5] Much in-person celebrity watching centers on affirming, by seeing them do it, however briefly, that in fact celebrities do exist outside of media texts, do "breathe the same air" as everyone else. At times other evidence (Cosby's toiletries, indirect proof that he brushes his teeth and perspires) serves nearly as well. At Grauman's Chinese Theater in Hollywood, handprints, footprints, and signatures of movie stars (most of them dead) are set in concrete. The typical snapshot taken there is of the tourist with his own hand in one of the handprints. "Here I am with Marilyn," the snapshots seem to say. She actually stood on this spot at a moment in time, her hand like this, and here is the evidence. For tourists of the stars' homes, although it would be interesting to see *how* they live, it is enough just to see their houses: it is enough to see *that* they live.

The photograph thus takes its central place at many of these events not just as an item of future social exchange (this is when we went to the Grand Canyon, and this is the Academy Awards) but as concrete proof of celebrities' authenticity. "A photograph," as Dyer puts it, "is always a photograph *of* something or somebody who had to have been there in order for the photograph to be taken."[6] The hunt, the excitement of the moment, the identify-and-move-on game, and the often manic "getting" of celebrity photographs all take place as a means of nailing down for oneself the real-world existence of what is typically encountered only in the other-world existence of the mass media. What one observer has written of spectacles applies here: "Great numbers of men and women are highly reflective, even reflexive, about their own loss of consensus about 'what is real and what is not.' And they are active agents in the creation of events and performances that, however much they deepen the quandary, stand also as public forms of condensing, displaying, and thinking it out."[7]

The live encounter and the attempts to capture it suggest a crucial instability that I will explicate further as we proceed: that authenticity is always potentially in question, always in need of confirmation. Indeed, attempts at these events to take the authentication process further, to go beyond the fact of existence to the details of character, quickly and easily meet obstacles. "We just came to check her out," a man at the Joan Collins book signing tells me, "to see her in real life." His friend came because she likes her books, thinks she's pretty, and likes that "she's bitchy." I comment that she seemed nice while she was signing books. "Yeah, well, she's on display," the woman explains. "She's an actress. She can be any way she wants. She's on display. Anyone will be nice when they're on display."

Both popular and critical wisdom on celebrity often disparage not only the phenomenon's superficiality but also its audiences. Celebrity watchers are accused of a long list of weaknesses: needing people to look up to and believe in and imitate, mistaking appealing manufactured images for appealing reality, leading unfulfilled lives from which they require constant distraction, desiring attention and fortune they cannot attain, needing reassurance that the success ladder is still open to anyone, or simply being addicts hooked on fame's "contact high."[8] Most critics typically assume that "needs," first of all, are being met by the relationship to the celebrities themselves, by means of fantasy, imitation, diversion, or learning. Most also assume that the superficiality of the activity is a sign of the participant's superficiality or even stupidity.

Examining celebrity watchers in person brings into question many of the assumptions built into these arguments. As we have noted, much of the action takes place between spectators rather than between the watcher and the watched. Moreover, if watching is recognized as a form of game rather than a form of psychological identification, its superficiality seems not only unremarkable but in many ways crucial. First, audiences often enjoy witnessing and dwelling in moments of media image creation; they exhibit, in other words, an interest in the superficial. Second, the celebrity encounter is used to confirm and reconfirm that surfaces have something, in this case someone, beneath them. When we watch the audiences, what we see challenges the stereotypical. If we listen to celebrity watchers talk, the challenges deepen and clarify.

Chapter Seven

Can't Beat the Real Thing:
Production Awareness
and the Problem of Authenticity

*For manipulation to be most effective, evidence of its presence should
be nonexistent. When the manipulated believe things are the way they
are naturally and inevitably, manipulation is successful. In short, manipulation requires a false reality that is a continuous denial of its existence.
It is essential, therefore, that people who are manipulated believe in
the neutrality of their key social institutions. They must believe that
government, the media, education, and science are beyond the clash of
conflicting social interests.*

Herbert Schiller, *The Mind Managers*

Celebrities are usually heavily rewarded. They exhibit all the trappings
of prestige, not only wealth but signs of "the esteem, respect, or approval
that is granted by an individual or a collectivity for performances they
consider above the average."[1] That definition of prestige, from William
J. Goode's *The Celebration of Heroes*, once again calls attention to one
of the central dynamics of contemporary celebrity. The rationalization
of public relations and the celebrity system has turned on an actively
created ambiguity: often the indicators of prestige are mimicked or massaged, reflecting commercial interests and production needs rather than
collective estimations of the above average. Public-relations techniques,
Goode argues, "subvert the processes by which groups seek to reward
the deserving, since thereby some people are being rewarded for their
skill in affecting others' responses or decisions, rather than for their merit
whether achieved or ascribed."[2] In one of the only other sociological
analyses of celebrity, Francesco Alberoni echoes this: "The problem," he
argues, "is to demonstrate that such a great improvement of status has
been obtained not by illicit means but thanks to meritorious conduct
and to exceptional or charismatic qualities."[3] From the point of view of
celebrity production, the utter disappearance of a merited claim to fame

ought to be disastrous. Indeed, the visibility of artificial techniques for celebrity manufacture and marketing would seem to undermine the system's operation by challenging its sustaining myth.

Joshua Meyrowitz, drawing on both Erving Goffman and Marshall McLuhan, notices a parallel problem: the loss of an isolated "backstage" arena in which social performers can learn and practice their "onstage" roles, brought about by the development of electronic media, which break down and "bypass the once strong relationship between high status and territory." By moving "the dividing line between traditional back and front region behaviors," they have problematized performance, particularly for public figures, whose roles "rely heavily on mystification and on the aura of greatness." Audiences see a "sidestage" or "middle region" view, "parts of the traditional backstage area along with parts of the traditional onstage area; they see the performer move from backstage to onstage to backstage." This shifts the content of the drama, such that rehearsal, staging, and self-conscious performance become central aspects of the text. It also creates a crisis for public performers, who must integrate the rehearsal into the performance, convert the backstage into an onstage performance, control their images by appearing not to control them. High-status social roles are thus much more difficult to pull off.

Hierarchal roles often demand a metaphysical dimension; that is, they require an *appearance* of innate qualities that transcend humanity and mortality. . . . The high status person can maintain his or her status only by carefully controlling information and by hiding the need for, and the techniques of, control. Yet if one's strategies for appearing important are exposed, one loses one's image of importance. All techniques of creating awe, therefore, bring with them the danger of shame—shame caused by the potential revelation of the need for technique.[4]

The celebrity system would seem to depend on avoiding the shame of revealing technique.

The story of celebrity manufacture poses a threat not only because it suggests that status may be technique- rather than merit-based. The artificial-manufacture story gives rise to a question (is this a true celebrity or one without what it takes?) and offers glimpses behind the scenes as an opportunity to answer (here is what they are really like, judge for yourself). But the story potentially undermines the code of authenticity on which it depends, casting doubts on the very judgments it invites. The problem for textual representation of celebrity, as Richard Dyer points out, is to negotiate authenticity, to make the image be "something more—truer, more real—than an image." The behaviors of audiences in live celebrity-based settings suggest outlines of the problem: a lack of confidence in realness, a need to see for oneself, to verify and document the very existence of celebrities. The "rhetoric of authenticity" sets a bottom to the pit of suspicions raised by the awareness of artifice. Its power to do so rests in a final confidence that the markers of authenticity can be trusted, that they cannot be faked. When markers indicating authenticity—signs of lack of control, lack of premeditation, and privacy—are revealed as techniques, they can lose their intended meaning, as "yesterday's markers of sincerity and authenticity are today's signs of hype and artifice."

Corroboration that a star is really like she/he appears to be *may* work, but may be read as further manipulation; showing that the star is not really like she/he appears to be *may* itself be taken up into the image, its further construction and rereading, but it could also shatter the illusion altogether.[5]

The story of celebrity manipulation and manufacture, by potentially undermining the ability to decode the text as anything *but* artifice, can potentially be mobilized to subvert rather than support the story of deserved, internally derived fame.

The mystery is that none of this appears to be especially problematic. Manipulation, machinery, marketing, illicit means, public-relations techniques, false sincerity, manufactured spontaneity, backstage rehearsals, and the staging of the self are all very present in the celebrity text, alongside the dominant myth of celebrity as merited by exceptional conduct or internal qualities. Yet there is no evidence of malaise in the celebrity system, no evidence of audience disengagement. Why such widespread interest and consumption in the face of what ought to be extremely damaging, even shameful, revelations of technique? How does the celebrity system survive, even thrive, under these conditions?

Talking with Celebrity Watchers

These questions seemed remote and abstract until I actually sat down to talk with people about celebrity. Over the course of several months I met with sixteen groups of three to eight people recruited through flyers, advertising, newspaper briefs, friendship circles, and contacts through prior participants. These were celebrity watchers in a middle range of involvement. As opposed to fans with an exclusive interest in one or two performers, or nonconsumers with no interest at all in the phenomenon, they were people who consistently but casually paid attention to a range of celebrities and regularly read or watched celebrity-based publications or programs (they watched variety talk shows once a week or more, for example, or read an entertainment magazine once a month or more).

The discussions drew from "the middle" in another way. Almost all the adult participants were middle-class people working in service professions, ranging in jobs from office workers to salespeople to homemakers to administrators. They were otherwise diverse: more than a third male; about two-fifths people of color; about one-quarter high school youth, a third in their thirties and early forties; half with higher-education degrees; about two-fifths urban dwellers and the rest suburban; evenly split between those who consider themselves religious and those who do not; about one-seventh openly gay men.[6]

The discussions were designed to re-create the typical way people watch, discuss, and make sense of celebrities and the celebrity process. These were not one-on-one interviews but focused group discussions (in some cases groups of friends, in others groups of strangers) in informal settings (participants' homes, my home, an office space, their own school). I arrived with cookies or donuts and a bag full of copies of *People, Vanity Fair,* and the *National Enquirer* for perusal and conversation-provocation. Conversations were often rambunctious, gossipy, and thoughtful.

The topics and questions were consistent across the groups but were raised in broad terms and in an order directed more by the flow of conversations than by my protocol. We discussed favorite celebrities, what it was about the favorites that participants liked, and in-person encounters with celebrities; we talked about participants' interest in celebrities, what they wanted to find out or hear about and what tended to bore them, and their theories about their own involvement; we discussed how participants read and viewed, where they got their information, with whom they discussed it. We then spent the bulk of the conversation on their theories about how and why people rise to celebrity status, how and why they stay there. (For more on the focus-group method, the participants, and the discussion questions, see the Appendix.) From the concrete stuff of these conversations, illuminating patterns emerge.[7]

Producers' Theories and Audience Realities

Celebrity producers, when questioned about their own visibility, took four basic positions on whether publicity activities should be kept hidden,

TABLE 1. *Celebrity-watching Audiences: Interpretive Strategies*

Audience Type	Text (Realistic vs. Fictional)	Dominant Story (Natural Merit vs. Artificial Creation)	Level of Production Awareness	Mode of Engagement
Traditional	Realistic	Natural merit	Low	Modeling, fantasy, identification
Second-order traditional	Layered but realistic	Artificial discernible from merited	Medium to high	Modeling, fantasy, identification
Postmodernist	Fictional	Artificial creation	High	Deconstruction of techniques
Game player: gossiper	Semifictional	Irrelevant	Medium to high	Evaluation, interpretation
Game player: detective	Semifictional	Both, but not distinguishable	Medium to high	Movement between image and reality

with corresponding images of audience sophistication: first, that revealing campaigns as campaigns (and artifice as artifice) mitigates the ability to conduct them since the audience is made up of people who are and should be ill-informed and gullible; second, that increased visibility of celebrity machinery is helpful because audiences, who are increasingly capable, can better discern a con job from a genuine article and because withholding information about the production system insults and alienates them and encourages disbelief; third, an opinion less frequently voiced, that audiences are interested in and knowledgeable about celebrity production itself, and signs of its existence contain their own thrill; and fourth, that the audience, gullible or not, knowledgeable about the publicity system or not, does not care about that system, and revealing it has no effect. Each of these answers the question of the system's continued survival and presents itself, in varying strength, in audience conversations. Each, we will see, corresponds to a different audience position or interpretive strategy. (See table 1.)

First, it may be that the celebrity system survives through the not-seeing of the artificial-manufacture story, through a mystified and believing audience. Celebrity watchers swallow only the simplest story and accept their admired as deserving of admiration, as having attained high status naturally. Celebrity watchers approach the text in which the natural-rise story dominates and accept its messages. They are ignorant of its production, passive in encountering it, and powerless in the face of its ideas and effects. Call them the *traditionals* or the *believers*.

Or, second, the system may survive through a more complex compromise, similar to the textual one, in which merit is preserved despite a revelation of artificial techniques. The dominant textual coping strategy is a process of

infinite regress by which one more authentic image displaces another. But then they are all part of the star image, each one anchoring the whole thing in an essential, uncovered authenticity, which can then be read back into the performances, the roles, the pin-ups. . . . The basic paradigm is just this—that what is behind or below the surface is, unquestionably and virtually by definition, the truth. Thus features on stars which tell us that the star is *not* like he or she appears to be on screen serve to reinforce the authenticity of the star image as a whole.[8]

"Inside stories" of the "real lives" of celebrities and opportunities to see them "as themselves" may be mobilized to anchor truth and merit and weed out impostors. Audiences see a more complex narrative in which publicity mechanisms play a part but do not pose an obstacle to esteem. Their belief is not based on ignorance of the production system but takes it into account; nonetheless, it is a belief in both discernible authenticity and the deserving celebrity. Call them the *second-order traditionals*.

Or, third, audiences may be entirely skeptical but in fact interested in the techniques of artifice in and of themselves. They know about celebrity manufacture and seek out its evidence and its details, rejecting or ignoring the story of the naturally rising celebrity as naive and false; the text is read as essentially fictional. Theirs is an engaged disbelief, and the revelation of technique feeds rather than damages their interest. Call these the *postmodernists* or the *antibelievers*.

Or, finally, it may be that the system survives because it does not require the demonstration of deserving conduct or qualities for survival. Audiences glean both narrative challenges to and support for admiration, but they do not turn away because celebrity is not for them a prestige system. Their involvement may be based on pleasures that simply bypass the question of claims to fame or that even make use of both the stories and the ambiguity they together create. These audiences use celebrities not as models or fantasies but as opportunities: to play freely with the issues they embody (the construction of the self in public, for example). Call them the *game players*.

At issue here is the relationship between awareness of production processes (the activities through which meaning is encoded), belief in the veracity of the celebrity text (essential to audience decoding), and engagement with the text (the pleasures derived from celebrity watching). How do audiences position themselves in relation to the two claims-to-fame stories and in relation to the rhetoric of authenticity? How aware are audiences of the production system and its attending artifice, and how does awareness affect readings of authenticity? Are these texts in fact read as realistic representations, fictional tales, or in the middle range in which they are developed? To what degree is the distinction between fact and fiction useful and meaningful to celebrity watchers? What in their activities might explain different patterns of interpretation?

Imagine two axes on which audience members are located: one runs from a low level of awareness about celebrity-production activities to a high level, the other from a low level of belief in the veracity or realism of texts to a high one. At one point are those whose belief is high and whose knowledge is low; these people come closest to the stereotype of celebrity involvement. This is the audience of traditionals or believers, who believe that what they read is a realistic representation of the celebrity. Exposed to more knowledge, they often ignore or resist it. At the opposite extreme are those whose belief is low and whose awareness and knowledge of production are high. They make up an audience position fitting an image popular in academic cultural criticism: the postmodern audience, opposing the possibility of arriving at truth as hopelessly naive, reading the celebrity text as a fictional one, undisturbed by evidence of manipulation.

These two audience strategies are in fact the least common by far. The traditional position is essentially a gullible one, in which audiences want to be presented with believable illusions and, as long as image-making activities are effectively hidden, will believe what they read. It ought to be uncontroversial to suggest that gullible people exist, perhaps even in frighteningly large numbers. When one talks with celebrity watchers, however, it is extremely difficult to hold onto gullibility as the *explanation* for the survival of the celebrity phenomenon. It is similar with the postmodern position, in which audiences are more interested in celebrity making than in celebrities and view celebrities with a high level of self-conscious disbelief. Disbelief rarely floats endlessly since, even when the celebrity is seen as a character, the fact that he or she is "played" by an actual human being is difficult to ignore.

Neither of these audience positions takes strong, pure form in discussions, and this ought not be surprising since neither naiveté nor deconstruction is favored by the text's narratives. (The audience strategies I describe are only analytically distinct, of course; in practice, people may actually take overlapping positions.) Most celebrity watchers fall between these two extremes. Indeed, most seem to actively travel the axis of belief and disbelief in their everyday celebrity-watching activities. The traditional and postmodern positions nonetheless are good starting points, both because elements of each weave through all discussions and, more important, because they set the outer limits of audience decodings.

Driven from Without:
Production Awareness and
Celebrity-Watcher Cynicism

They're just basically people who if you see them on the street might not have anything to them. It is a lot of fabrication. There are just media personalities that are put together piece by piece for us to admire. And they just keep bombarding us with all this imagery. I think most personalities are very much fabricated. There's many, many people who we think are the greatest and they're not. They're just images that are presented to us, and we don't go beyond that. All we see is this picture or this image, and everything's being directed or construed in some way.

Abatto, accountant,
Latino, 46

People get noticed, and so this is where they end up. Anybody can be noticed. It's money. My mom would put me through acting school and modeling if she had money. She would. I think it's awful that so many of us have so much talent that is so developed and so great, and because we don't have cash we can't expand it and be noticed and be appreciated by people. Anybody could be made up as beautiful as her if they had money. Anybody could be an actor or an actress just as good as Jodie Foster if they had money. If I was on the cover of every magazine and was in two really productive films people would look up to me. If I was made up to look really beautiful people would look up to me, too.

Holly, high school student,
white, 17

They say, "Let's put that you went down to this restaurant. So-and-so was seen dining at such-and-such with such-and-such." Everything's marketing. It's all a big marketing campaign.

                                                    Peter, salesman, Latino, 32

"Let's say I am a mediocre sort of person," I inevitably brought up in discussions, "not especially talented, not especially good-looking, not particularly dynamic, just somewhere in the middle range. I come to you and tell you I want to become a celebrity, and I want your advice. What do you say?" Once or twice I was told to go study, to work hard to improve myself and my craft, to overcome my mediocrity. In the most frequent response, though, groups suggested in a variety of ways that I find routes to fame that do not require extraordinary internal qualities of any kind, by using the publicity system to my advantage. "I'd set you up in situations," said Rudy, a 39-year-old Latino living in a suburb.

Be there at the right time at the right place, where celebrity people are walking by, somebody takes a picture and you're there with them. It's really dirty work when it comes down to it. You know, run in front of a car. You get hit, then all of a sudden it's a big thing in the paper, "Promising young star almost gets run over." It's in the paper, your name gets used a lot, it gets tossed around. That's how you do it.

"Have a gimmick," said Marsha, a white homemaker and student, in another suburban group. "That's it," agreed Gina, an unemployed Latina 43-year-old. "It's true, you've got to have a gimmick. You've got to have something to sell yourself. Something different." A white urban group of mixed educational backgrounds expanded on this:

SANDY (human resources assistant, 41): It's getting publicity, getting your name out there, getting your face all over the place so people know who you are.

RON (customer service coordinator, 41): Anywhere there's a lot of paparazzi, be there.

BOB (writer, 44): I'd suggest you create a look for yourself, you know, like package yourself a certain way. That if you're just an average-looking guy with so-so talents and you want to make it big, there's nothing to distinguish you from the next average-looking guy who wants to make it big. So you should then, like Boy George or like Tiny Tim or like Madonna or like whoever, naturally or artificially you create a personality. You change your hair or you change your look. You might create a new history for yourself, create a new look. Have something to sell.

RON: Sure, what you lack in talent you make up for with a creative manager or agent. [laughter]

Another urban group, of mixed races and educational backgrounds, also went into detail:

TORI (legal worker, African-American, 33): I'd advise you to go to a publicist, get the agent that you needed. Or you needed to change your image, grow your hair out, get a bigger earring, get tattoos. I'd say, "Hey, look, this is what's hot. This is the genre of entertainment you're in, and this is what people who are already successful are doing. They're wearing the leather so you've got to wear the leather too, and you've got to have a little longer and greasier hair."

HELEN (sales manager, African-American, 50): I would tell you if you need to change your image.

TORI: There are the people that do research. They're always taking polls, they do analysis of what people like. What do men like? What do men in this age group like? What do women in this age group like? Do they like blonde hair? Do they like guys with long hair and look like bikers? So they come up with these quotas and the guys have to fit in the range. If you look at heavy metal rockers, they fit in that small range. The skinnier, the tighter the pants, the longer the hair, the more hair they have, and the raunchier guitar playing they're playing, fine, they're going to make a success. These polls and the agents, they have all these statistics and they try to find what this person comes across as initially and what the closest thing that they're going to be associated with. Boom. You try to find what the public likes, what image they like, what you feel that person comes across as, and then you go on that and you exaggerate it.

ED (self-employed, white, 31): Like Madonna, when she first came out, she wasn't wearing nighties out on stage, she was wearing normal clothing. And then as times went along and she wanted to shock people more and more, she used it to grab attention, and somebody had to be there to teach her how to do those things. Most likely she probably had help in what to wear, how to dress. Like New Kids on the Block. They really weren't anybody and their manager just took them and dressed them a certain way, had them singing certain songs, and built up this image of New Kids. Modern day Osmond boys. They really weren't anything until that guy created them to do that. So in that way they can be created.

A suburban high school group had similar ideas:

ELIZA (white): Say if you were like nobody, I'd have you get a new wardrobe or something, dress you all up so you're like with the newest fashions. Then you'd have to do something controversial. Say you were going to be a rock star or something, like Ozzy Osbourne or something, like biting off a rat's head or something like that. Then you're all over, it's in all the papers. And I'd put this one article about you, and I'd write about all this crazy stuff that you do, and then that your music is really cool and really good to listen to, and it makes you wild and stuff.

ERICA (Latina): You could just do a lot of promotion. Going to charities or having your own. You can do good things, too. Like how the Lakers do things for the McDonald's House, and stuff like that. It gets around, 'cause people like that.

STEPHANIE (white): I'd have you jump off a bridge and video record it.

I was told to jump off a bridge, run in front of a car, bite off a rat's head, hit a reporter, get tattoos, find a gimmick; I was told to adopt a charity; to create a personality; to find a good publicist, market researcher, and marketing strategy.

In fact, the artificial-celebrity story line almost always arose *spontaneously* in discussions, without an advice-seeking probe. Often, consciously manipulative activities aimed at retaining notoriety were described along with those aimed at initially gaining it. "The TV, the magazines, they make you think that they're something when most of the time they're really not," a white high school girl explained. Her friend Nikki elaborated:

They make them seem perfect. You know, it's like, they make them seem, "That's the kind of person that I want to be." 'Cause they make them seem beautiful. If you put enough makeup on anyone, anyone can look beautiful. The characters that they play are perfect. Basically, they're the characters that we want to be. Like, I wish I had as much money as that, I wish I had that boyfriend, I wish I could have those clothes. In magazines they look good, too. In magazines they're not going to show them after they just woke up in the morning, like how we all look right now. They're going to show them with like tons of makeup.

A group of white suburban women of mixed educational backgrounds explained multiple manipulations:

KATHY (recreation supervisor, 42): The hard work is staying on the covers and keeping your name in the mill.

NORMA (retired secretary, 57): That's why they do some outrageous things. They publicize themselves, they behave outlandishly, they do strange things.

KATHY: And they pay big bucks to their agents and publicists to keep that stuff churning. If they don't make a movie or don't do the talk shows or don't write the book, and they're out of circulation for a while, they know that people are going to forget them. I think they need to make a real conscious effort to constantly be in the public eye. They need to go to those parties. You have to be seen and you have to have your name in print. And be photographed.

NORMA: Wear strange clothes, like Cher.

KATHY: This whole business of celebrities kind of adopting their own personal causes and speaking to them, it's definitely another way to keep themselves in the news, and some of these people are not qualified to speak at all on their particular topic.

NORMA: You don't know how sincere they are.

CHRIS (switchboard operator, 35): They tell you to go to this party, they tell you, "You date this girl. Okay, I'm going to fix you up with the little cutie that's on that Beverly Hills show because she's real hot right now, and you're not that hot." Then if you're seen dating her it's, "Oh, he's that guy dating Sarah Snotgrass, oh yeah, he's cute, oh yeah, isn't he on Channel 4?" or whatever. Be with the right people at the right time, and be seen. I think a lot of it is set up. You know, you be at this restaurant 'cause he's going to be there.

"You have to be creative as a promoter, as a seller, as a marketer," a woman in another white suburban group said. "They'll make the public want it. I think a marketer can channel it. It's all marketing." Her sister agreed. "You use difference. They need good PR, somebody pushing them. They'll shove that person down your throat and you want to say, 'Get the hell out of here.' " Another participant joined in: "It's a person who's a product and they're selling it to us via the television, via the Hollywood screen, via the magazine. Hollywood says that this man, Patrick Swayze, is the handsomest man alive. He's become the product." A man in another group complained that

it's like we're told. Who voted that Julia Roberts was the most beautiful woman in the world? Ten editors that she's on covers for? No one asked me. There's like a million people who are nicer looking. But yet her publicity department's going full speed ahead. It's not as though we were all polled and we were given the chance to decide is she the most beautiful woman celebrity or not. We're told that everyone already declared it. It was just her PR people doing that.

An exchange between two men in an urban gay group further echoed these ideas:

FRANK (retail sales manager, Latino, 29): They just pick them because they have that quality that they were looking for in someone, and then just publicize it and make it a big thing and the next thing you know they become stars. A lot of it also depends upon what kind of people you want to target. Someone could just have researchers out there finding out what is it that people want, what is it that people want to hear, what is it that they want to see. They just try to saturate the market into believing that this is good, this is good, buy it. A label. This is new and fresh. And everybody likes that. Even if I particularly am not a big fan of all these things, it's so saturated that I just finally give in and say, "Okay, so what is this all about?"

PAT (restaurant worker, white, 25): They fill a need. They're products.

The key elements of the story of manufactured celebrity are all over the place: people as commercial products, market saturation, market research, image manipulation by both celebrities and their hired hands and by the media reporting on them.

This story line is bolstered by a number of other routes open to a person who may be undeserving of celebrity. First of all, as a few of the participants quoted above suggested, money can buy fame regardless of the characteristics of the aspirant. More generally, finding a rich or powerful sponsor, or a key inside connection, can move nearly anyone into the spotlight. Michelangelo became the best-known sculptor from the Renaissance, said Alex, an unemployed white man with a college education, "not because he was the best one but because he had patrons who paid for his room and board and bought his marble for him. There could have been some schmuck who was better who didn't have the wherewithal to conduct his business visibly. It's the same thing here." A group of urban high school boys, Latino and African-Americans, captured the same idea, emphasizing that easy fame is a privilege of race and class.

JAVIER (Latino): Most of the time, these are all just straight white people, right, and their families they come from—

LUIS (Latino): —rich white families.

THOMAS (African-American): Maybe their parents started the business up, or maybe they had connections with Hollywood or certain things like that. They just got their kids right into position, now they become famous.

JAVIER: People in San Francisco, they have to go through everything to be actors. They have to go through all the schools. Do you think all these actors on these magazines go through all the schools? I don't think so. I think they're just, "Hey, you look good, you can act, let's see what you can do." If someone from this school wanted to be an actor, they just wouldn't get looked at. They would have to go to some school, pay hella money, buy all this stuff. The bottom line is you just got to know the people. Connections.

LUIS: Yeah, like, "I know a agent's cousin's girlfriend's aunt."

The more that participants knew of the production system, of course, the more they offered connections and nepotism as commonplace explanations of celebrities' rise. "I think it all has to do with agents," said a young gay white man, an operations supervisor. "It has to do with the power of your agent. If your agent is in with those people and can work it, if they have a relationship with Johnny Carson or Joan Rivers or the producers of those shows or the writers of those shows, then they can get you on the show." Sex was also occasionally debated as another possible means to advancement, particularly for women. One white suburban woman quoted something she had recently heard on television: "If you want to get anywhere, screw everybody."

In this cynical interpretation, the notion of celebrities as ordinary or similar to audiences was mobilized to demonstrate that celebrity has no clear internal prerequisites. With enough money, or with careful packaging, with a proper marketing campaign, anyone can make it. The drive comes from outside, and that these people turn out to seem unexceptional in "real life" simply underlines that fact.

Postmodern Skepticism and the Pleasures of Deconstruction

The fact that a good portion of audiences notices the publicity system ought not be especially surprising, given the hype-heaviness of the entertainment industry. Different audiences integrate and use their awareness differently; their decodings are inflected by the varying pleasures they derive from celebrity watching. What distinguishes the postmodern audience position is that, equipped with this high awareness of commercial-cultural techniques, it *embraces* the second story as its primary truth. Celebrity is nearly always the result of machinery, money, manipulation. The awareness of systematic activities for creating celebrity and loyalty dominates, leading to the notion that *all* public personality is consciously constructed for gain. As Eric, a white 29-year-old social worker, described it,

> You read about stars having a staff of twenty people, and they just kind of tick off all these people with inscrutable roles. It just seems like what they're able to do, in addition to kind of selling the idea that the person is talented and successful, that they're able to sell a personality that goes along with it that people really want to like or people want to sort of get behind, like I want to support this person because they've had an underdog experience. There's something that sort of strikes a chord, and that's packaged and sold.

Made up of profit-driven packages, celebrity from the postmodern position is a fictional realm, and all information is assumed to be inauthentic, regardless of the source. Even when celebrities appear in person or are quoted directly, what they put out cannot be accepted as real. In a group of urban gay men, for example, Pat argued a more traditional line, distin-

guishing between performers who are always "on" and those who are
only on when playing a fictional role: with someone such as Roseanne
Arnold, "who has a persona on all the time," the true self is impossible
to discern, but with actors such as Kevin Costner, who can be seen out
of role "acting like a normal person," the real self is visible. Eric, who
had described personality packaging, disagreed. He articulated the skeptical, "it's all image" perspective.

> But I think Costner is just as constructed. He's one of those actors that come
> across as the sensitive actor, you know, like he's not into the publicity machine.
> But he has so worked his not being in the publicity machine, so that it's like,
> Kevin Costner being sort of doddering and absent-minded and not really the big
> star is like a cliché. When he did the Academy Awards and he was reading off
> his fucking cue cards and scratching his head, it just seemed like total construction.
> Maybe some of that's real, but then that becomes the image, of the sensitive nice
> guy, and that becomes to me sort of unbelievable.

Even when they appear not to be, celebrities are "on." Everything, this
position posits, is self-conscious performance aimed primarily at sales.
Celebrities are decoded as manufactured and marketed characters, read
more as fiction than as real people.[9]

   This is a position clearly outside of the range preferred by the text but
not outside of what the text contains. The everpresent story of artificial
celebrity is interpreted in a way that opposes the text's claims that celebrity is, at least in some cases, the result of a discernible, deserving self.
The position is found, remember, among those who consider themselves
celebrity watchers: although such an oppositional reading may very well
push people away from celebrity watching, it turns up here without being
translated into lack of interest, dismissal, or nonparticipation. That the
sense that "it's all bullshit" does not disturb involvement needs to be
explained.

   From the antibeliever position, the text's inauthenticity is precisely
what is interesting. The activity that engages audiences in this reading
position is the pleasure that comes from recognizing manipulation, from
deconstructing the encoding process, from dwelling on the visible machinery itself and on the play of images. Indeed, given that celebrity is seen
as a marketing phenomenon, the most interesting celebrities are the ones
who make manipulation explicit. This is clearest in discussions of Madonna, a favorite of both postmodernist critics and antibelieving audiences, who see Madonna as consciously taking control of and calling
attention to her own manufacture.[10] She "makes a point as part of her

image being, 'I always wanted to be a celebrity and I knew how to do it,' " said a receptionist in an urban white group. The others agreed: she "repackages herself every six months," said one; "she's as much aware that we're aware, that we know what's going on here," said another. In another urban white group, a man in his mid-twenties explained that "it makes it more interesting to figure that they manipulated it."

That's what I think is interesting about Madonna. When I read about Julia Roberts, someone about whom I care very little, I think how some PR company tells her what to say, decides what she's going to say this week, decides what she's done for the last month, decides what's interesting about her, how to market her. I may be naive about Madonna, but I get the distinct impression that she's marketing herself. And I find that fascinating. At some level I have to think this woman is a genius because she came from absolutely nowhere to the point where she can manipulate the media as well as people who make their livings doing nothing but manipulating the media. It's curious to me how she does that, irrespective of what she says, the substance of what she has to say.

A man in another group, a white high-school-educated bar worker, sounded remarkably similar. "She's my megastar," David said, "because she manipulates everything. It's so orchestrated. I love it." Madonna reincarnates Barnum, her knowing audience consumed with the "operational aesthetic."

It is important to notice that this sensibility does not always constitute a rejection of merited celebrity. Often, it simply translates it into a media-conscious language: admiration goes to the "genius" who can "manipulate the media," who can master the celebrity system. Nonetheless, in many cases it pushes toward self-explosion, toward the impossibility of a hierarchy of the deserving. David, for example, took his interest in Madonna to its logical extreme: even the self-revealing hypester is just another package. Even as he is drawn in by Madonna's orchestration, David pointed out, the image of a calculating, manipulative, work-the-system performer cannot be believed.

The whole thing—your, my, his, our attitudes that Madonna is in control—that's part of the package. There's no way that I can think that Madonna is in control of her career and know that it's true. I listen to you say it and I hear myself saying it, and it's just part of the whole thing. We state it like we know it, but we can't know it. To me that's such a key thing.

Nothing is certain except machinery, manipulation, and commercial packaging, themselves the primary intrigue in this reading position. Surfaces are the point, "endlessly referring to, ricocheting from, reverberating onto other surfaces."[11] Celebrity is a never-ending series of images to be read, so that even those whose truth appears to be that they are in control of their own manufacture cannot be known to be so and must also be read as essentially fictional. Reading the celebrity text from this angle is like encountering mirrors facing one another: there is no end-point, no final ground.

Driven from Within: Traditional Belief

In the "traditional" decoding position final ground is believed to be found, and most information is taken as a literal representation of real people. It is certainly rare to find people with pure seeing-is-believing naiveté, people without some form of critical reading and viewing skills. In the most "gullible" version, these skills take the form of a hierarchy of source credibility: information acquired through personal networks is at the top, then "news"-style publications and programs such as *People* and "Entertainment Tonight," and finally tabloids, which are rarely trusted. So, for example, a white high-school-educated suburban woman said that she knows "what really, really happened" to Natalie Wood because she has a remote studio contact.

It was a horrible thing that happened, and it was really quite stupid. She got drunk, she accused Robert Wagner and Christopher Walken of wanting to get rid of her so they could be together, they pooh-poohed her, sent her away, and she went and drowned. This is sixth party down. The guy who told me ran the Firestone shop that supplied all the automotive to "Hart to Hart." It all funneled down, and I got it. I believe this to be what really happened.

The perception of tabloids as unreliable bolsters confidence in the reliability of other sorts of reporting. Carolyn, a white college-educated researcher in her late twenties, captured the common stance: "I don't believe the tabloids, but I believe *People. People* to me does not lie. They don't seem as exploitive. The tabloids are out to like freak you out." Her friend Joe, a white law student also living in the city, agreed: "Nobody ever sues these magazines. And they don't have things on the cover like 'Elvis looked like cave man.' " As long as a source is quoted directly, information is accepted. Tabloids are not believable, said a participant in a group of white suburban women, because "they don't have anything to substantiate their claims." "They say, 'This friend told a friend' and 'This person said.' I mean, if you're going to state something, give a name. *People* generally backs up their information with sources. It's coming directly from the source, the individual who they're talking about, so it's believable." An African-American urban high school student spoke the same way, explaining that "some of the stuff about these people is phony." Instead of "actual quotes in there, it always says 'a close friend' or 'a source' or something like that. I'll believe what the person said, and say if it was like the girl's mother or something."

When the level of knowledge about the workings of the celebrity system remains low, however, critical reading stops at this point. Pushed to explain how the system operates, people in this position answer without an answer. "However Hollywood does that," said a white suburban saleswoman. "Whatever channels they use in Hollywood." A young white school teacher with a professional degree simply admitted that "Actually I have no idea how it works." Information that challenges the text's realism is often screened out. "I don't like to think about it," said an African-American legal secretary. "I hate thinking that they were artificialized and mass-produced in some way, so I guess I sort of short-circuit it off in my own mind." The only form of manipulation from this angle is lying, and that activity is limited to tabloids. Indeed, appearances by and interviews with celebrities provide direct access to the real self. Once the publication or program has been deemed to be reputable, and whenever the celebrity is heard from directly, the information presented is not examined for authenticity but simply assumed to be authentic. The text is read as realistic and swallowed more or less whole.

Not surprisingly, the traditionalist audience reading strategy embraces the natural-rise story of celebrity, devoid of or avoiding an awareness of techniques of celebrity production. The pattern of interpretation here is heroic: merit and notoriety are necessarily linked, and celebrity is the result of outstanding talents or extraordinary personality gifts. Fame is a process in which natural merits are recognized and rewarded. Here, discussants sounded much like hyperbolic fan literature. "Next to Jesus I think Elvis was one of the greatest people that ever lived," said a white suburban insurance saleswoman, because "he was so incredibly talented," there will "never be another entertainer like Elvis Presley," and "he was wonderful, he was handsome, he was the nicest person." Talent and creativity, seen as natural, inborn differences, set celebrities apart, stars above; their natural uniqueness justifies their fame. "I think most Hollywood stars and would-be stars are very different and have very different personalities," said the Elvis admirer, "because they're very creative people. We're all born with something." Sammy Davis, Jr., was "so great," said a white retired secretary, because "all he was was a performer, it was in his blood and bones, like second nature." Two urban high school students, one white and the other African-American, put it simply. "They're good actors and actresses," Valerie said. "There isn't one person that we mentioned that isn't a celebrity because they do what they do good. Every movie they were in, everything." Tonya agreed: "They're always on newspapers and always on television shows, see, because it's an honor that those television hosts and hostesses want to let them know that they're great at what they do." "Yeah," Valerie continued. "Because the ones that are more of a celebrity are because they're more. They just do more and they're good at what they do." Celebrities command attention because they are good at, great at, more.

The natural gift need not be for performing, of course, but can also be charisma, star quality, outstanding personality. A fifty-three-year-old Latina secretary living in the suburbs spoke about Elizabeth Taylor. "What a woman," she said. "I've always found her very gutsy. I've always thought she's been a very, very beautiful woman, one of the most beautiful women in the world. And still a beautiful, right-on woman who can have anything she wants. I found her very charismatic. Liz is Liz. There's only one Liz in this world." Their uniqueness, the fact that they're unlike the audience, is the whole point. "They're not ordinary, and I don't want them to be ordinary," said Norma. "If they were like me, they wouldn't be interesting. These are regular folks? Do you have a complexion like Doris Day? Are you as virginal as Doris Day?" In another discussion, two white, college-educated bank workers articulated the notion that an indescribable something sets certain people apart.

DEBORAH: In your life you meet certain people that just sort of like have a star quality. They probably eventually get publicists and they work really hard, but there's something about them that gets them there. I don't know. Charisma maybe.

DEBBIE: If you read about some of the stars and their brothers or sisters or whatever, and if you ever see one of them interviewed, there is kind of an aura around that one and not the others.

DEBORAH: Yeah. Sometimes people just have a certain something, something that makes them stand out.

When the aura is discovered—when, as participants often pointed out, someone is "in the right place at the right time"—the celebrity begins her rise. The standard discovery narrative, in which a person is discovered while just doing her thing, is picked up and retold by traditional believers, demonstrated through anecdotes, either imagined or once heard. A suburban white woman suggested that "they chose the field they were in and they were in it for a long, long time, and all of a sudden they were discovered." An urban African-American high school student speculated that one of his favorites, rapper Too Short, "just probably started rapping with his friends in high school and then made his way up and somebody noticed him one day," and he "makes his demo and takes it in, and somebody likes his music, and then from there he just makes it famous." Martha, a white homemaker and teacher's aide, told the story of a friend's grandson who moved to Los Angeles, accompanied his mother's boyfriend to an emergency dentist call, and wound up in three major movies. "The little boy was sitting in the dentist's office, in the waiting room, and this agent walked in and saw this little boy playing, like reading to himself. And this agent goes, 'That child's so talented.' He had no background in that, and he just got discovered." These are, of course, the familiar elements of the traditional celebrity story, in which fame is the recognition of internal gifts.

Second-Order Traditionals

When Martha told her waiting-room story, there was laughter. "I'm serious," she said a bit defensively, "he got discovered in a dentist's office." It's quite clear that the idea of Lana Turner–style discovery is usually perceived as atypical, unlikely, mythical. Indeed, the question of whether celebrities as a group are the most talented, cream rising to the top, rarely fails to draw laughter. More commonly than not, the awareness of commercial interests and manipulative behaviors is quite developed; yet they are believed by second-order traditionals to be discernible, obstacles to finding the real goods but fundamentally harmless. In many groups, the term "grain of salt" comes up, sometimes self-consciously exaggerated to "box of salt" or "pound of salt." To the traditionals' notion that tabloids are not trustworthy is added the more developed awareness of other parties (celebrities and their handlers, production teams in nontab-

loid media) who may be interested in or required to manufacture inauthentic images. As a white urban man in his twenties put it, "In these
tabloids you assume that the reporters are all lying, and in these magazines
you assume that the reporters are telling the truth but if anybody's lying
it's only the people who are speaking to the reporters." A white suburban
woman in her late fifties argued that "we get a lot of distorted information, and we get not a lot of full information." She pointed out that "years
ago they manufactured information constantly so that we would go to
the movies"—"they" being the studios and celebrities. Raymond Burr,
she said, "had put out publicity that he had been married and that his
wife and child had been killed in an automobile accident" but "was
strictly covering for the fact that he was gay." Self-interested cover-ups
and overt lying are not the only problems. Celebrities are both performers
and salespeople, professional impression managers. Lee, a 43-year-old
white suburban saleswoman, articulated the problem in her discussion
of Elizabeth Taylor.

We might label Liz Taylor as not a nice person, but she probably is. I work for
an insurance company where I have to be constantly taking care of people and
their needs. I'm on stage, too, not literally, but from the moment I walk in the
office I'm on stage. I was a nurse, and it was the same thing. You're performing.
Well, Liz Taylor was at Macy's promoting her fragrance, and she had her producer
or whoever telling her what to say. People are telling them what to say because
they're an image, they're in public. It's like the president. Somebody, his press
secretary, tells him what to say. She went off on a tangent and was just forming
her own opinion, Liz Taylor's opinion, and her producer, he didn't want it. I
guess he didn't want her to expose Liz Taylor the person. She was there to sell
the product and shut up.

Kay, a 22-year-old white legal secretary living in the suburbs, said that
"sometimes I feel as though it's really, really fake."

You want to get a feel for what these people are like, but they could essentially
be acting while they're in their interviews. They could be putting on just as much
of a show as if their sitcom was on at the same time. And it's like, was that just
an act, and if so, how many people do that, totally mislead, knowing that half
the country's watching the show? You just got to wonder. That's their life, is
acting. You just never know what is the real them.

Artifice creation is expanded from simple lying to image control and management, massaging of information, performance.

   From the news-production side, not only are tabloids suspect, but so

are entertainment-news programs and entertainment reporting magazines. On "Entertainment Tonight," said Bob, a gay white real-estate
appraiser, "it's just all sort of put out there, whatever's being fed to them
by their PR people." His friend Billy agreed: "It's really flowery shit.
Because I think that's what these guys think we want to hear and see."
A group of white suburban women (a flight attendant, a mail carrier, an
unemployed woman, an administrative assistant) wound up reversing the
typical take on tabloids versus others.

JOY: Actually, I would believe the *Enquirer* before I would believe *Vanity Fair*.
Because *Vanity Fair* has all the publicists.

KELLY: Yeah, that's true. First of all, the editor. Tina Brown is in with them. It's
a whole hook-up and they're not going to have anybody that's going to step on
anybody else's toes.

JOY: It's going to be all whitewashed in there.

DEBORAH: Streisand's publicist calls Tina and says, "Let's do a story on *The Prince
of Tides* that's coming up. I'll give you the story." And it's, "We're grateful to
get Streisand. Thank you. We'll do it, and we'll do it your way."

JOY: And we'll write something really nice.

MICHELLE: It's to get the person. Because Streisand doesn't do interviews. In order
to get her then you do it my way or you don't get my interview at all. I will give
it to you but I'm not going to give it to *People*, but you have to do it my way.
They could be out of jobs. They could be out of business after a while. I trust
Vanity Fair to not lie, but I would say they're going to put in there what the
person wants them to put in there, and they're not going to go in depth.

Like those in the postmodernist position with a high degree of knowledge about celebrity production, these audiences read the celebrity text
as a series of commercially motivated, managed performances. Unlike in
the postmodern position, though, the text is decoded not as fictional but
as layered. Audiences in this position decode the text with intervening
steps, translating it into their own language, reading through fiction to
realism. Interests are taken into account. "I don't sit there thinking 'Linda
Evans is in love with Yanni,' " said Alex, a college-educated white man
in his thirties, pointing to a *People* cover. "I sit there thinking, 'Linda
Evans wants us to believe she's in love with Yanni.' " Phyllis, a 55-year-
old white secretary with a high school education, described a similar way
of reading.

I don't accept it as gospel. With "Entertainment Tonight," I think that when
they're interviewing these people, they say, "Well, what did you think of John

So-and-so," and of course they're not going to say he was a horse's ass. But they might say, "You know, we really didn't get along that well." They wouldn't say he was a horse's ass. Your career's on the line. Am I going to sit there and say that Liz Taylor is a horse's ass? I mean, after all, I've got fifty million people watching. You say, "We didn't get along too well."

With a theory of how the performance works, the image is decoded for a real or hidden meaning. Linda Evans "doesn't want us to know what we really want to know," said Alex. "We didn't get along" translates for Phyllis into "he was a horse's ass." Rather than reading texts as either realistic (a gullible position that is difficult to maintain given the visibility of publicity activities) or as endless images (a cynical position difficult to maintain given the physical existence of the celebrity), they move in each case from disbelief toward belief, from fiction to reality. Knowledge about the production system provides a sort of road map and code key, making the traveling easier.

This is, of course, the code of authenticity favored by the text: genuineness is supported by authors who provide the tools for weeding out the inauthentic. Rather than dismissing authenticity as a hopeless or uninteresting concept, as the postmodern readers do, audiences with this decoding strategy maintain a second-order belief: in order to get to the real stuff, the text is deciphered for signs of artificiality and manipulation. When "inside stories" are suspect as further performances, the search simply continues for more believable stories that go further inside. The "real" may be difficult to find, but the more you know, the easier it is to sift through the false and recognize the true. "I'm thinking more and more these days what is a stunt, what is a publicity plot, and what isn't," said Kirsten, a suburban white woman. "I'm thinking more that these things don't just happen by sheer coincidence. It's just trying not to be duped." From this position, one must *guard* against falsehoods and find sources likely to get behind the artifice; one must always *translate* the text into the language of realism.

The traditional story is hard to hold onto, given an awareness of the production system. Second-order believers, rather than settling on one or the other, use their knowledge to integrate the two stories. The centerpiece of this reading is the distinction between "true" or "real" stars and "fake" ones. Manufacture and manipulation are deemed harmless because they are believed to be transparent. Second-order traditionals interpret with a constant confidence that the "real" celebrities can be distinguished from the pretenders, the wannabes, the impostors. "You can count the number of the people that really last on one hand," said a salesman in an urban group, "because they have some kind of special talent or charisma or something." In a group of otherwise quite cynical gay men, Sedric, an Asian-American, argued that "longevity has to come with talent. You can have beauty and all that, but you're not going to maintain interest if you don't have the talent to keep you going. The ones that will rise to the top are the ones that are really talented." Others challenged Sedric but Mark agreed, arguing that Paula Abdul was very successful and talented as a choreographer but mistakenly tried to "change her career to make a lot of money and become a big fat star." It can't work, he said, because she can't really sing, which will inevitably be revealed. "She doesn't have the talent to take her through. She'll have to go back to her roots, to what she's good at."

Participants in this position tend not only to see longevity as evidence of merit but also to see celebrity operating on parallel tracks. A white suburban group represented this well:

KELLY (flight attendant, 44): There's so many on the peripheral edge, the Marla Maples or the whatever. There's just so many of them. Lisa Hartman, Audrey Landers. All of these people come to mind. [laughter] There's probably many more of those types than there are the real true, talented stars.

DEBORAH (unemployed, 31): I hate those people. I really hate those people.

MICHELLE (mail clerk, 36): They are conniving.

KELLY: Those people to me are just disgusting. And there's so many of them. They want to be stars, they want to be famous. They're not really talented, but they might be attractive. Known somebody. A woman gets her boobs done, has some stuff here and there. And they're just there and I don't know how. Some of them are laughable. They must know somebody, or they get a good agent. And it's really sad, because there are so many talented people who won't make it because they don't have the look.

JOY (secretary, 40): They'll always be grade B.

KELLY: And they either have a man like Donald Trump, or maybe they've had to sleep with somebody, or somehow they've just gotten to be in a lot of TV movies. They're just always on the outside trying to get in, and I just can't stand them.

JOY: It's like they don't deserve to, you know. They should pack up and go home.

The strength of the disdain toward the "peripherals" (as the women in the group took to calling them) is not especially typical, but the other conversational elements are common.

Celebrities who don't deserve to be celebrities are easily picked out. They fit into the story line of externally derived fame and can be distinguished from the real, true stars, who fit into the story line of internally derived fame. Armed with evidence of both stories, audiences tend to use artificiality and the undeserving to reinforce the deserving and the natural. Second-order believers thus interpret the text very much in line with its preferred meaning. The two stories are bridged by the acknowledgment, rather than the suppression, of celebrity artifice: the story of artificiality is read as a limited one that only goes to prove the value of those celebrities whose claim is internal qualities. The essential element of merit is thus protected, nurtured, maintained.

Second-Order Believers and the Self-made Celebrity

One success model is particularly critical to the protection by second-order believers of naturally merited claims to fame: the Horatio Alger story of individual effort. Obsessive love of the job, a calling and drive, along with dedication, hard work, and perseverance dominate as explanations of the rise of some rather than others to a position of celebration. Rather than being the uniquely *qualified* self—the claim articulated by traditional believers—the celebrity in this decoding is the uniquely *driven* self, who chooses his fate rather than is chosen by it. A white writer in a city discussion group suggested that "voracious hunger" may be the answer: "You put the will and the vision together, and it's like that willingness to do anything and then really holding to it, always believing really positive about it." A college-educated suburban white woman in her mid-twenties working for a charity organization: "They have a drive to be something, to be somebody. Madonna said she didn't want to die without everybody knowing who she was by the time she died. Now that's a drive." A 31-year-old white suburban woman with a high school education: "I'd like to tap into that chemical that allows them that kind of focused drive, that drive that allows you to say, 'My life is fucked up, all of these things are going wrong, but you know what, too bad. I want this and I'm going to do whatever it takes.' " A self-employed urban white man began arguing that "they're the best at what they're doing" because they "have the most talent." As he explained, it became clear that the talent is for loving the work and being willing to risk for it.

I always look at it like this. Whatever you enjoy doing, if that's what you enjoy a hundred percent, completely, totally, and you have the ability to pursue those goals, then I think that's what these people have found. The things that they love doing more than any other profession in life, they pursue it. They're not afraid to take chances that they think will pay off. They seem to really love what they've chosen to do, and that's what makes them the best.

A group of people of color in a suburb began in some disagreement over the relative weights of chance and drive and wound up in agreement:

MELINDA (African-American): They believe where they're going with unequivocal dedication. I believe every single one of them has seen at some point in their life where they are right now. They've visualized it, and I think that, whether consciously or unconsciously, they have pursued it with total, absolute dedication. I guess it could be summed up for me in what my mother always says: "Find something you love to do and do it, and everything else will follow." I think that's how they get where they are. They absolutely love to the point of obsession what they do. It's total focus.

RUDY (Latino): I disagree. At first things happen by error, by chance. Rock Hudson was driving a truck.

MELINDA: I think it's deeper than that. People who want to be something tend to hang out with other people who are either doing that or on their way to doing that.

RUDY: Maybe so. Maybe it's not conscious. Maybe because it's your calling you're going to go for it and you're going to be focused and maybe that is ultimately your life's work.

MELINDA: I think they do what they love and they pursue it relentlessly. They want to be in front of the camera. It's a drive, it's a need, it's almost like you're filling a void.

THELMA (African-American): You got to have the drive, you got to have the determination, you got to have the want to. Otherwise you'll never make it.

RUDY: You get turned down a lot, but it's that instinct that drives you.

MELINDA: It's that instinct, it's your need, it's your high, it's your life, it's you. There are a lot of people who never made it who are better at some of these roles that these people are getting paid millions and millions of dollars for. You'll never hear from them. You'll see them out on the streets smoking crack. Because they did not have that absolute total need to be in the top, not even in the top, but to be out there, to be relentless about being out there, to totally be consumed by being out there. It's like a drug. It's like a fix. It's a high. You're out there, and the minute it stops you're planning on how to get that next moment. And that's what I think it is. I don't think it has to do with talent, I don't think it necessarily has to do with brains. I think it has to do with total consuming need.

RUDY: You have to have talent, too. [laughter] I think these people have talent.

MELINDA: I don't think you do. I really don't think you do.

Drive and need and calling take the central place here; talent has a questionable role, even a laughable one.

Along with drive runs the component of determined hard work, the relentless fulfillment of ambition. Norma, a 57-year-old suburban white woman: "When you read about these people, a lot of them went through a lot of hardship and privation. They paid their dues and really struggled and stuff. There are very few people who get there that don't work hard." A 35-year-old white medical group administrator echoed Norma: "You really have to want it and be really willing to work really hard. You sort of have to forsake everything." A high-school-educated man in his early thirties quoted cosmetics marketer Mary Kay: "The person who's the most successful has the bloodiest knees." Celebrities are not necessarily the best, not even especially good, not necessarily the people most appealing or deserving of attention. They are the ones that work hardest to get it, and in that sense they are deserving.

The common perception of celebrities as ordinary people ("without the makeup and the clothing and the jewelry," said a mail clerk, "they're just like everybody else") links up with and supports the notion of hard work as a means to fame. Ordinariness is mobilized here as evidence that stars are regular folks who simply wanted something badly enough and made different choices. Ordinariness is taken as proof not only of merit (they must have worked hard to transform themselves from a regular person to a star) but of the openness of celebrity (anyone can want, choose, and work). Deborah, a white woman in the suburbs, underlined this as she described "looking through the keyhole" and seeing "that they can be successful, and they can be living these great lavish lives, but they are in fact human."

And that if they can do it, I can do it, if I so choose to do it. I don't choose to do it, but there's that secret part in the back of my mind that says, "Yeah, if you really wanted it, look at what this person overcame to get there. It's just that you have to want it badly enough, and you obviously don't want it badly enough, Deborah, or you'd be out there doing it."

The ordinariness of celebrities keeps the door to success, measured as fame, always somewhat ajar; interested and determined individuals can always kick it open. "I consider them equals," said one white man. "Just in their life pursuits they solved problems differently. Sometimes you can use the information they had used to help you." With the proper individual effort, anybody can be a star. As a white suburban high school student put it, "We could probably do it if we wanted to, but most of us don't really want to be like this and have our faces all over the place and have all these people wondering what we're thinking." A star is not born but self-made. Celebrities are attended to not because they are born with outstanding talents or personalities (the traditional claim to fame), and not because they are taken up by effective image managers (the postmodern claim to fame), but because they take control of themselves, because they have heightened drives and work styles.[12] It is important to notice, though, that the claim to fame is still located *within* the celebrated self.

Believers and the Destination of the True Self

Despite their different levels of production-system awareness, first-order and second-order traditionals share the belief that an authentic celebrity self is presented and knowable. More to the point, they share the *requirement* of authenticity for the activities that engage them. Theirs are the activities conventionally associated with star watching, those in which pleasure is derived from a feeling of connection with the celebrity: admiration, identification, modeling, and fantasizing.

These are activities that, it should be noted, themselves push in somewhat different directions. Escape, fantasy, and often admiration are damaged by decreasing the distance between watcher and watched, whereas identification and modeling are enhanced by it. "The more I know about Garth Brooks, the farther off his pedestal he comes, the more like a person he becomes," said a young white Garth Brooks fan, "and I kind of like having him on the pedestal." Such fantasies must be maintained in spite of "inside" information.[13] A white suburban high school girl articulated this resistance, the advantages of not finding out that celebrities are not as they appear. "Why know?" she asked.

I think if they showed the way that they really are, like in the morning or whatever, I think it would totally ruin everyone's view of them and then they'd be equals to us, and then we wouldn't have them up on a pedestal anymore. If we saw them normal we'd think, "Oh, they're equal as us. Why pay?" We know it exists, but as long as it stays behind the closet everything goes on. We know they're normal people but we don't want them to be normal people on the magazine covers or in the movies or else we wouldn't have them to look up to. It's sort of like you want to know but if you find out it might be disappointing. So why know?

Finding similarities is essential for the more commonly articulated identification and modeling activities, however, as an urban African-American woman captured.

You think, if they're on the magazine they must have something together, so you're going to follow them. It's like we try to draw a parallel, to see that, yeah, okay, you're rich, you're famous, but you're not isolated from pain and problems. I like to see that, hey, these people aren't perfect. Not in a mean or cruel sense, but it's like I can identify with that. You're not going to be in a sacred ivory tower, you're approachable, you're real, shit happens to you. So I draw a parallel there, too, that in spite of what's happened to these women they've still made it. So it's encouraging for me. It gives me strength to go on.

Identification-driven audiences want to know what these celebrities are "really" like, a desire driven by a perceived gap between the celebrities and their screen images (the traditional reading position) or the celebrities and both their screen and media images (the second-order belief position). "I want to know what makes them tick," said Marlene, a white elementary school teacher, in a typical comment. "I want to know what their philosophy on life is. I want to know what kind of person they are, their empathy, their compassion if there is any. I want to know the deep inner working of their psyche." Digging inside celebrities is part of a pursuit of their success secrets. "What I've always wanted to know is how it is that they got to be where they got," said a Latino suburban man. "Were they always like this? Did they always have this talent? What were their childhoods like? I've always wondered what kind of belief system they had." A white woman in another suburban group was an admirer of Oprah Winfrey because

I'm curious about how she got to be who she is. I'm very curious about her background, which was checkered. She's a bright woman, she's a warm woman, she's a multimillionaire, she's a business woman. Very accomplished for a poor black gal from the South. And that fascinates me. I like to look and see how they got where they are, or what made them what they are, or what influences were on them, or why they've chosen to do what they do.

Clearly, if authenticity is an unresolvable issue, these activities are threatened, the pleasure gone.

Despite their different approaches to star/audience distance, in fact, both fantasy and identification activities require a resolution of the question of truth. In order to get pleasure from the activity, these audiences need to be reasonably certain that what they are getting in each particular case is the real thing. The questions of who and what celebrities really are must be answerable. Certainly one can identify with and fantasize about a fictional entity; the actual existence of celebrities as living humans, the fact that they are somewhere now, speaking or kissing or brushing their teeth, gives celebrity fantasy and celebrity identification their power. They require not only pursuing but arriving at a real self, whether taken from texts as-is (first order believers) or in artifice-savvy translation (second-order believers). That self is *the destination.* For production-aware, second-order believers, then, as for less knowledgeable traditional audiences, both the overall backdrop of authenticity and specific truths are essential to pleasure.

Far from inhibiting the system, production awareness clearly sustains it, by allowing a radically diverse range of interpretation. For antibelievers, it confirms and makes pleasurable the dance of appearances: celebrity as a system of performance rather than of prestige. For true believers, second-order ones in particular, "It is always a question of proving the real by the imaginary; proving truth by scandal. . . . Everything is metamorphosed into its inverse in order to be perpetuated in its purged form."[14] Celebrity as a prestige system, as a hierarchy, depends on the continual exposure of its inverse: the system that transforms ordinary people by blatant artifice. "Once the techniques of establishing awe and mystification are opened to the public," one might reasonably expect, "the mystification is undermined."[15] Yet quite the opposite is true.

Chapter Eight

Believing Games

The real Marilyn Monroe is a proper appreciation of her fictions, even if they are facts; or her facts, as long as you're not sure they cannot serve as fictions.

David T. Bazelon, social critic

Audiences are continually offered, and gladly accept, tidbits of the "private" selves of public figures, are approached by and seek out celebrities as first-name familiars; yet audience-celebrity relationships are of course not reciprocal or close at all. There is no question that what is actively created by the celebrity industry is an "illusion of intimacy" in texts. As analysts noticed already in the 1950s, "the persona's image, while partial, contrived, and penetrated by illusion, is no fantasy or dream; his performance is an objectively perceptible action in which the viewer is implicated imaginatively, but which he does not imagine."[1]

Celebrity personas are in a practical sense constructed such that distinctions between fact and fiction break down, the blend of truths and fictions settling dilemmas in the production setting. In fact, over the course of this century the balance has shifted, with changes in the production system, from fabrication activities (the fictional creation of celebrity images, stories, and personas) to blurring activities (the molding, manipulation, and management of celebrity images, stories, and personas). The production setting encourages, furthermore, a dwelling on the superficial: an economy of tidbits, an emphasis on the available and controllable trivial pieces of celebrity information.

Celebrities take on their own middle-range reality in which selves are simultaneously spontaneous and simulated and staged, doled out in bits and pieces that are simultaneously composed and authentic. Like advertising, which speaks in its own peculiar language (Michael Schudson calls it "capitalist realism"[2]), celebrity texts represent neither a fully counterfeit world nor a fully authentic one.

Unlike the true believers (who read celebrities realistically) or the anti-belief hipsters (who read them as fiction), a good chunk of the audience reads the celebrity text in its own language, recognizing and often playing with the blurriness of its vocabulary. They leave open the question of authenticity and along with it the question of merit. For them, celebrity is not a prestige system, nor a postmodern hall of mirrors, but, much as it is in the celebrity-watching tourist circuit, a game.

Gossipers: It's the Same Difference

You can't decide these things. Roseanne now has accused her parents of incest, and who the fuck knows? I mean, how do you tell between Anita Hill and Clarence Thomas? It's the same difference. You say, "Well, this is juicy, so let's pretend that it's true." I'll tell my friend and we'll giggle and have a good time with it, even though it's probably BS.

Bob, writer, white, 44

For one large segment of the celebrity-watching audience, textual authenticity and celebrities' claims to fame are unproblematic simply because they are moot. Rather than dwelling on either the inauthentic or the real, audiences simply go about the business of gossip without an overall concern for questions of authenticity. A young white receptionist explained her position:

I love things that are like none of my business. I have no right to know this, and that's what's fun. You love to talk about people in your office or stuff like that, but the information in their lives isn't available to you. It's sort of a matter of just knowing things about people. I know so much of it is not true. You take it all with a grain of salt. I want to read the dirt on Julia Roberts or whoever, it's just fun to read about, but if she was here I can't think of ten questions I would care to know her answers to. My larger curiosity is about things that are just none of my business. You know, everybody goes into other people's houses and looks in the medicine cabinet. It's sort of an extension of that. Nosiness. Things you're not supposed to know about, just trivial little things that are fun to know. We know most of it's not true or exaggerated, and you can read it and know it can be interpreted in a million different ways, but it's just sort of fun knowing about people.

The fact that "most of it is not true," that "it can be interpreted in a million different ways," is acknowledged but irrelevant. "You don't go into a discussion with a friend going, 'Oh, this is what I heard but it's probably not true,'" the receptionist continued. "You go, 'Oh, this is what I heard.' In terms of discussion and stuff it is true, even though you know it may not be." Discussion takes place with an assumption of an indeterminable level of fictionality but operates *as if* "real people" are being encountered. Although they see gaps between performed and lived celebrity selves, and to varying degrees of sophistication can articulate a process by which these gaps are established, gossiping audiences quite simply do not care. Their strategy decodes by a continual suspension of disbelief—and, for that matter, of belief.

Belief is unnecessary for the pleasure of gossip. The "real self," so central in traditional decoding positions, is not critical to the activity.

CHRIS (switchboard operator, white, 35): It's kind of exciting to flip through and say, "Well, what are they going to say about them now?" You really don't in your heart believe it, but it keeps the lie going I guess.

NORMA (retired secretary, white, 57): I know that I can't believe everything I read. I don't know how to sift it. I read it and I take it in and I enjoy reading and that's it.

CHRIS: Like with Oprah and Stedman, I am enjoying waiting to see when she gets married and look at the dress and who's going to be in her wedding. So it's the anticipation of knowing what the next thing is. Maybe it's real, maybe it's not. I don't even know if that's really her boyfriend, maybe it's just like I was saying, he's cute, she's popular, so put them together. It's just, what's going to happen next?

JUANA (self-employed, Latina, forties): Whether we believe it or not is secondary. In the moment we don't care whether it's real or it's not real.

NORMA: I don't think whether it's real or not is significant. What difference does it make if it's real? It's like you go to the movies. It doesn't have to be real. You are using what's given you, and you don't have to delve or to look behind the scenes.

Not believing in your heart, the knowledge that it may be real or it may be fabricated, is not at all disturbing. The celebrity text is analogous to a movie based loosely on a true story, or a soap opera: you wait to see "what's going to happen next," the next plot element to develop, the next tidbit to be offered up; you use "what's given you." As long as the performance is an interesting one, the story an amusing one, the fact that selves are performed is undisturbing. "Zsa Zsa Gabor was total comedy," said a young suburban white woman of the coverage of Gabor's arrest and trial for slapping a policeman. "Because you never know what she's going to say next. And you really don't believe her, but it's not that you think she's lying." You do not believe her and you do not disbelieve her; you simply let her perform herself for your enjoyment.

Gossip, moreover, bypasses questions of merit through its emphasis on the present. It does not matter for gossip how celebrities got there, or even how they manage to stay there, but how they behave once they're there. "It's who they are and what they are once they're celebrities," said a white urban gossiper, "and unless there's some dishy story about how they got that way, it really doesn't matter." Gossip consumption, like much in-person celebrity watching, takes place in the moment. Deborah, a white suburban gossiper, was articulate and savvy about "the machine." "I'm aware of it, I know it's there, I know how it's going down. But I don't think about the publicity machine, the publicist machine, when I'm actually doing the read, or watching. I'm in it, I'm in the moment, I'm absorbing it, 'Oh, this is good stuff,' whatever." In the *moment* of pleasurable activity, knowledge about celebrity manufacture simply does not apply.

An "as if" position is adopted and story lines trump truth pursuits because what is important here is a process rather than an end-point, a game rather than an outcome, and relationships between players rather than with celebrities. In gossip, pleasure comes from the activity of circulating information and forming evaluations. The suburban women above, discussing Ted Turner and Jane Fonda, captured a typical gossip session.

JUANA: Someone made the comment that both of them are high achievers and that the reason that they are both such high achievers is that they're basically both insecure people.

CHRIS: Interesting how they ever got together. I can't see the two of them together.

JUANA: But I have a certain admiration for both of them. They're very high-powered people.

NORMA: I read something recently which said that she always goes to the power. She did it with Vadim and she did it with Tom Hayden, and now she's going to the top in her own field.

CHRIS: Because she can't stand to be alone and raise her children and stay at home and go to PTA meetings.

NORMA: I don't know about that, but she also wants to be important, I think, and be with either a celebrity or a politician or somebody with a lot of money or clout. I mean, this is a need she has.

CHRIS: But take Jane Fonda or any mother or father, their children are in and out of rehab centers and going from this person to this person, they have a nanny, they don't really have a mother figure. Princess Diana, she has a nanny and she has a butler and all that, but I think she's a very giving, caring, loving mother and I hope that her sons know that and appreciate that. I don't think Jane Fonda's kids have that love. Maybe I'm wrong, but I just think, you know, she's shoving them off to Switzerland.

It is not necessary for the gossip game that the information be demonstrably true; in fact, too much truth can stop the game.

What's important is not only the opportunity to "know" things about people but the activities of discussion, story telling, interpretation, judgment. It is not the truth about Fonda and Turner that is being pursued but the active trying on of various interpretations and evaluations: insecurity lies behind their high achievement, they are a bad match, she has a need to be with important men, she's an irresponsible mother. "It's just fun to sit and dish," said an Asian-American gay male participant. "Whether I believe it or not is a different question." As Patricia Spacks describes it,

the relationship such gossip expresses and sustains matters more than the information it promulgates; and in the sustaining of that relationship, interpretation counts more than the facts or pseudo-facts on which it works. . . . Gossip involves exchange not merely, not even mainly, of information, and not solely of understanding, but of point of view.

The trivial details in which gossip delights, Spacks points out, are used as a means for gossipers to "construct a new oral artifact" of their own.[3] The pleasure is in the exchange, in the development of new story lines. "You're talking about other people, period," said an African-American suburban woman. "So the parameters that you would use to talk about your neighbor are the parameters that are used to talk about these same people."

Celebrities are actually in many ways better objects for this game than neighbors. "They're up there and you can know all this stuff about them," as one woman said simply. Celebrities are like neighbors whom nearly everyone knows, in nearly every social setting, and "stuff" about them is easier to find and share than information about friends or colleagues. More important, celebrity gossip is a much *freer* realm, much more game-like than acquaintance gossip: there are no repercussions and there is no accountability. A white woman in a suburban group described herself as "a pretty serious person, a heavy reader," who likes "to absorb information, know what's going on in the world." She described gossip as a form of freedom.

The whole field of gossip and that kind of stuff is relaxing. If I were to say to her right now, and you heard me, "That guy is funny looking," God, I can be in big trouble. But I can say Debbie Reynolds is a lesbian, which I understand she is, and no one's going to yell at me for it. This is the whole thing of gossip as far as I'm concerned, because it's totally irresponsible. I don't have any responsibility. I can enjoy myself with no culpability whatsoever. You can't do that in everyday life. I mean, you can, but there could be repercussions. And even if I knew something terrible about somebody I mightn't say it because I wouldn't want to circulate it, or I wouldn't want it ascribed to me, or maybe I'm not right about it. But I can say it about Debbie Reynolds because who gives a damn? Now, I'd rather not see Oprah marry this guy. I don't like him. That's her business, but I have an opinion, and I'm free to have an opinion, what the hell. It's total freedom. Which you don't have in a lot of other things you do in this world. That to me is what gossip is.

The pleasurable freedom of celebrity gossip is built precisely on its freedom from but resemblance to truth.

Knowledge of the machinery of celebrity production thus does little to hamper gossip; indeed, by providing more tidbits and more opportunities to reveal secrets, it often feeds the game. A challenge to authenticity is neither here nor there. Of course it's manipulative, gossipers tend to say, but it's good stuff. Or, they say, here's a juicy bit of manipulative, artificial behavior. The commercial nature of the celebrity enterprise, for example, is seen from other positions as something that needs to be taken into account in decoding since it provides motivation and opportunity for image manipulation. For gossipers, it raises no such problems. One white urban participant compared it to redeeming a coupon. "You know they're there to sell something. That's what they're there for, and I'm here because I like gossip, and it's sort of an understood relationship. It's like I've got this twenty-cent-off coupon, and it'll make me buy their product, but I'll get the hair spray, and everyone's happy. It's a give and take." For gossipers, who are not after the real self, the fact that information is bought and sold, and thus is likely to be managed and massaged, is an acceptable part of the bargain.

The gossiper reading strategy is, on the one hand, fundamentally a refusal since, from its view, none of this is serious. It refuses, or at least can readily do without, the text's assertions of authenticity; true or false, it's the same difference. It refuses the text's conventional integration of the production system into the story line of earned prestige, usually acknowledging artifice and manipulation with indifference. Gossip refuses, in essence, the prestige and admiration system offered by the text, the vertical relationship offered between celebrity and watcher, opting instead for a system of collective evaluation and horizontal relationships between gossipers. White suburbanites Joy and Kelly, for example, placed bets on the longevity of celebrity romances. Joy laughingly gave newlyweds Clint Black and Lisa Hartman two years.

I have a certain disdain for those people. I mean, I'm taking bets on these ridiculous relationships. They get together and you know they're not going to last. It's fun to see what kind of games are being played out. As much as we're fascinated by them, we really don't respect them. And it doesn't matter if I don't respect them, I'm still interested.

On the other hand, the irrelevance of truth and merit grants the same freedoms to the celebrity system as it does to gossip. In particular, it makes it possible for the emphasis on the "good story" to engage even under the threat of revelation of information-management and celebrity-manufacturing techniques. The gossipers' refusals lend an important piece of support to the celebrity system.

Artifice Detectives:
Will the Real Julia Roberts Please Stand Up?

A final segment of the audience shares the gossip position's gamelike activities and its agnosticism about the genuineness of the celebrity text. What distinguishes this position, though, is that, rather than ignoring the authenticity problematic, it transforms it into the basis and end-point of activity. These celebrity watchers continually *ride* the belief/disbelief and fiction/reality axes but with no particular destination. Three white suburban friends captured the texture of this game:

KIRSTEN (social service coordinator, 26): That interview with Julia Roberts on Barbara Walters, she was like honestly affected by being there. She was very shy, she told like her innermost secrets.

KAY (secretary, 22): Yeah, but then again she looks right in the camera and says, "I love Kiefer. He's the only one." Next week, ba-dah-dum, he's out of there. She was like, "I love him. He's the one." You know? So what's the truth? That's a pretty bold statement to make on national TV.

LUANN (teacher, 26): How much do you really care about the statement, though? At some point, I kind of like decide whether I like the person or not like the person, and then I just choose to overlook and excuse them for whatever happens to go their way. And it's really easy to do, because things get magnified as they go through publications. So if you see here that Patrick Swayze did something awful, you can just say, "Oh, it was probably something that was 10 percent of what they really said." And you excuse him and that's that. I don't trouble myself with those things.

"So what's the truth?" is the constant refrain. Production knowledge brings up the question. "Like when you have two movie stars together," a white man in an urban group asked himself, for example, "is it publicity or do they like each other and want to go out?" Knowledge of publicity activities, however, is neither viewed as nor mobilized as any guarantee of the ability to discern the truth. Gaps between image and reality cannot be confidently bridged because, as the legal secretary above argued, "I don't think I'll see any of these people in my entire life, so whatever image I get is on the TV, it's through media."

Most of them I really believe that's them talking. But sometimes I wonder. I was a nanny for a boy who watched this one show, and the star was like this little boy's idol. All of a sudden, this guy's in jail because he beat the heck out of his wife. Now I'm sure you didn't get that through the interviews, that you didn't come out of this special going, "God, I bet that guy beats his wife." I bet he came off like a prince.

The most production knowledge can do is provide one with reasons for taking a position on the answer: if you want to believe in the person, Luann said, the media exaggerated; if you want to disbelieve the person, they were making a publicity maneuver.

Belief here is self-consciously perceived as a matter of choice since the text itself has no particular authority. "There's all this buzz about Natalie Wood," said Alex, "and we'll never know what happened there." (Compare this to the confidence with which a believing participant quoted earlier related the story of Wood's death.) "So I believe what I want to believe," he continued, "what suits my needs. Ultimately it doesn't really matter." A discussion of Madonna's film *Truth or Dare* in a group of urban gay men ended in a similar place.

ABATTO (accountant, Latino, 46): That movie completely changed my perception of her. I didn't buy it all, but something came from that movie that was very genuine or natural about her.

BILLY (landscape architect, white, 30): The thing is, she said it wasn't natural.

PETER (salesman, Latino, 32): She said after the movie was out it was all script. A lot of that was worked in to make sure that it came out that way.

TROY (operations supervisor, white, 25): It was all editing, that's what I think.

BILLY: The first thing you see when it ends is, "Executive Producer, Madonna." I really enjoyed the movie, and when I saw that I thought, my God. I saw that flash up there on the screen and I realized that this was basically put together by her and whoever else and to make it look a certain way, to make money, you know. It doesn't really make that much difference if it's true or not, because it was fun, and she's great.

As with traditional believers, authenticity and sincerity are central discussion issues for artifice detectives. But the question has a different tense, one more complicated, less certain of answers. The impulse is not so much to find out "who she *really* is" but rather "who she had seemed to be but might not be."

For detectives, as for postmodern readers, truth and reality are indeterminable. Belief, however, is not dismissed but freely chosen in each specific case, not bound by the so-called facts, which cannot be trusted to reveal truth. This is an in-between code in which the real self beneath the surface both exists and cannot be found. The text is decoded as composed of a mush of truths, half-truths, and nontruths, all of which look quite similar: that is, like semifiction.

If truth is simultaneously sought after and unattainable, why don't these belief-travelers exhibit frustration or anger? Why don't they take the more extreme postmodern position, opposing all textual claims to authenticity? Why in fact do they stay engaged? The tourist-circuit celebrity-watching activities suggest important clues: audiences there tend to be involved largely with game playing (identifying, categorizing, "getting" celebrities) rooted in questions of authenticity. This belief-traveling audience is involved in a similar activity, a game of detection, like an ongoing version of television's "To Tell the Truth" ("will the real so-and-so please stand up"), or what one critic has called "the tenacious problematic of Memorex (is it real or is it . . .)."[4] Although sincerity and authenticity are pivotal issues, it is not especially important to nail them down: the discussion among celebrity watchers is more important than their felt relationship with the celebrity. Whereas with believing strategies the awareness that celebrities are rarely what they seem poses obstacles, here it is embraced. "That's kind of the whole mystery of the thing," said Kay, after a rowdy argument about Julia Roberts, "is you really don't know."

As in any game, the outcome is less important than the process. A discussion between two white, college-educated friends captured the love of questions regarding truth in the detection game and hinted at its indifference to answers.

CAROLYN: I think that actually makes it more interesting to me that we have these theories about whether or not it's true. It sort of adds to this whole debate. It's not just, "Is she married and is she getting divorced and does she have another boyfriend?" It's, "Is it true and are they lying? They just wanted to fabricate it." It adds a whole other layer of interest.

JOE: It adds a whole other layer to the discussion of celebrities. First of all what the hell are they doing, and second of all is it true and why are they doing it?

Knowledge of machinery and marketing and manipulation, without which the game would not exist, is used less as a means for determining authenticity than as a useful tool in the game. Knowledge greases the discussion game. These audiences get more pleasure from the game of searching together for authenticity than from finding and dwelling on the "real self," more from the act of playing detective than from the truth content that detection reveals.

Compare, for example, descriptions of seeing celebrities in person. One common refrain ran through them—"They're always shorter"—essentially a concrete instance of "They're never what they seem to be." A traditionalist's response to encountering famous people, whatever the level of celebrity-manufacturing awareness, is either disappointment for the fantasy-driven or, for the identification-driven, increased closeness to the more humanized and real-seeming celebrity. From the detective-game position, there is neither a disturbed fantasy nor a heightened intimacy: the enjoyment is in the comparison itself, in the back-and-forth revelation and reporting of gaps between reality and image, in the traveling. "It's like there's the celebrity and then there's the person," said Joy. She and her friend presented some details to their suburban discussion group: actor Jimmy Smits, Joy reported, "has bad skin and he was wearing brown"; Madonna, with whom Kelly shared an elevator in Portland, is "a little thing" with "the greasiest, yuckiest hair" who was "not anything you would look twice at." They expressed neither wonder nor disappointment but offered their tidbits with distanced but gleeful interest and humor. In an urban white group, Lara offered her Liza Minelli story in a similar fashion, demonstrating that the comparison need not always demonstrate difference in order to be satisfying.

She came in and she ordered her stuff, she was with a friend, and she was sitting at the window drinking a soda and stuff, and she was just like very Liza Minelli, just like laughing and throwing up her arms and "darling" this and "darling" that. And it was like, oh my God, Liza, you really act like that. I cannot believe it. It was so funny just watching her. It was just hysterical. She was totally Sally

Bowles sitting in the window, just laughing really loud and throwing her head back. That was like, my God, is that really really really, under it all, she really is like that. She really is this glamorous cackling thing.

The surprise and enjoyment comes in finding that the celebrity in this case is as she had appeared to be; "public" persona and "private" behavior match unexpectedly. The pleasure in this reading position derives not so much from finding out the answer to the question of "what is she really like?" but from lining up the various possible selves—screen persona, offscreen public self, private self—and seeing how they match and mismatch. "It's comparing their public image persona versus what they really feel like," said a man in Lara's group, "if you just stumbled across them in a little bar where they had no sense of being on." The code of semifictionality, an awareness of artifice and simulated reality, authenticity destabilized, are not simply acknowledged and accommodated by this game. They are absolutely essential for it. Like many gossipers, artifice detectives read the celebrity text in a code that subverts the text's authority but are no less engaged by it, using it for their own purposeful activity.

Game Playing and the Importance of Triviality

What can be gleaned from audiences who read the celebrity text knowledgeably and without tremendous mystification but who read and use it as a semifictional text? What can be learned from those who recognize the difficulty of distinguishing the real from the unreal but accept and enjoy it? What can be taken from behaviors that recognize but thrill to the trivial? First of all, they explode the notion that commercial culture blunts audience members' "imaginations and their critical judgments" and diminishes "their taste for intelligent public and private discourse."[5] These game players are neither necessarily uncritical nor inaccurate in their reading of textual authenticity, yet they are wholly involved. Artifice, inauthenticity, and manipulation are muted here not because audiences are unaware of them or because they buy into them as affirmations of reality, genuineness, and merit. Instead, the celebrity text is approached as a part of games in which "realness" is unnecessary—even at times an inhibition. The hybrid truth-fiction form of the celebrity persona is here read in its own language, and the gamelike pleasures depend on that mix.

Gossips and detectives also make clear how viewing celebrities as rehearsed and performed selves, acknowledging backstage manipulation and construction, can pose a challenge to the status of *celebrities* without posing a challenge to the celebrity *system*. These celebrity watchers refuse to see celebrities as a popular elite or celebrity as a prestige system. Disdain is as likely as reverence since for both games an undeserving, artificial celebrity is as useful and interesting as a deserving, natural one; admiration, learning processes, modeling, and fantasy may be there as well, but they are not necessary. As in the activities on the celebrity tourist circuit, celebrity watching as a game is a social activity in which relationships between players, more than relationships with celebrities, are being established and reestablished. Moreover, players are enjoying the collective process of making their own meanings, choosing their own beliefs, building their own temporarily as-if-authentic texts. Knowing the tricks of the trade in fact invites audiences to play games with meaning, to experience "the pleasure in the process of making meanings, that is, over and above any pleasure in the meanings that are made."[6]

The celebrity text, *because* it makes visible and available its own encoding processes, is particularly suited to games of audience meaning creation. Game players are more likely to express frustration with the *way* a particular celebrity text is being put together than with the fact that its truth cannot be trusted. One young white woman, for example, complained about her "latest beef," the breakup and final tour of a mother-daughter country music duo.

This end-of-the-Judds thing, I thought it was almost over with three months ago. They're still playing out the end of the Judds. I can't believe how long this thing has gone on, and now there's a pay-for-TV concert. I feel like they've pushed it way too far. They had my sympathies about three months ago, when it was like a two-month drawn out thing, but now that it's a five-month drawn out thing, I'm like, this is not right. I just think they should be a little more respectful. This is totally taking advantage. I'm used to the general overprogramming, but this to me is like pushing the limits of decency.

She takes a "producerly" stance, similar to the enthusiastic participatory stance of live audiences encountered earlier.[7] Literacy about the commercial production process is mobilized not as criticism, nor to see through to a deeper reality, but as a means to further involvement, in which the producer's position is imagined and improved upon. The "general over-programming," the manufacturing and performance of celebrity lives, is accepted; the problem arises when the stories aren't properly programmed, when they become *too* unbelievable and the "as if" position can no longer be maintained.

Why hold onto semifiction? For the game of gossip, information and evaluation exchange can be conducted most easily without the constraint of truth, and for the game of detective, riding between truths and fictions can be conducted most enjoyably without the obligation to reach a final truth. But too much falsehood also detracts. If no underlying truths are out there, the game of detection is meaningless; if the behaviors being evaluated have not at least potentially been enacted, the game of gossip loses its meaning. The games being played are thus well served by a middle range in which the real and the unreal are known to be blurred.

These celebrity-watching games require of celebrities another characteristic that is often disparaged: triviality. Why dwell in the trivial and the superficial? The critical piece is the fact that people are playing, that these are games. Play, Johan Huizinga argued, is a "free activity standing quite self-consciously outside 'ordinary' life as being 'not serious.' " "Deep play," Clifford Geertz argues in a similar vein in his classic discussion of the Balinese cockfight, "renders ordinary, everyday experience comprehensible by presenting it in terms of acts and objects which have had their practical consequences removed and been reduced (or, if you prefer, raised) to the level of sheer appearances, where their meaning can be more powerfully articulated and more exactly perceived." It is the fact that game-playing celebrity watchers don't really care about the celebrities—contrary to the stereotypical image of the fan who cares so much and so deeply—that makes the games possible and enjoyable. Celebrities are what Francesco Alberoni has called a "powerless elite," with high status and visibility but limited institutional power.[8] They literally have no power of any kind over audiences. If they did, the "freedom" of the games would be dampened. What matters to celebrity-watching play is that celebrities do not matter.

The superficial and blurring aspects of the celebrity phenomenon are thus not necessarily indicators of increasingly superficial audiences, and the development of a semifictional realm does not necessarily erode audiences' abilities to discern substance from surface. Superficiality and semifiction take a very different place, as prerequisites for the game playing that is so central for these celebrity watchers.

The dependence of play on the inconsequential does not mean that it has no depth, however. Games have content. They are opportunities for interpretation, for people to build and witness, as Geertz puts it, "a story they tell themselves about themselves."[9] Playing with culture offers participants the chance to work through in a free realm everyday life experiences that typically appear in arenas of consequence. Celebrities are particularly suited to these games precisely because they are encoded in a semifictional language: audiences can easily play evaluation and judgment games "as if" with real people but without an ultimate authority (gossips), or they can play at the borders between real and not real (detectives).

Gossip contains its own built-in ambivalence about hierarchy. Even as it dwells in surfaces and semifiction, gossip continually sizes up, interprets, judges, and exchanges judgments on personal behavior in general. Going after the most central shared figures, it maintains the hierarchy as it is: whoever is popular at the moment is accepted as a discussion topic. But in its impulse to apply the same standards of behavior to all, to level differences, and in its insistence that celebrities do not matter, it simultaneously undercuts celebrity as prestige.

The game of detection delights in a different cultural strain: the distrust of the public self, the experience of role playing and performance in everyday social interaction. It makes these central experiences visible and comprehensible, takes them out to look at, play with, consider, practice, and master. In a new publicity-seeped tongue it tells an old story, again and again: of opaque, mysterious people who, for their power and for their survival, wear masks covering only parts of them, masks that look like faces; and of others, also part face and part mask, peering upward and sideways and sometimes even downward at them, catching elusive, exciting glimpses of a face.

Conclusion

Celebrity, Democracy, Power, and Play

In the film *Reversal of Fortune,* the character of Klaus von Bulow, about to go on trial for attempting to murder his own wife, is offered the best table in an elegant Newport restaurant. In America, he dryly notes to the character of lawyer Alan Dershowitz, fame rather than class gets one such privileges. He overstates the case, of course, but the point is undeniable: celebrity is a primary contemporary means to power, privilege, and mobility. Audiences recognize this when they seek brushes with it and when they fantasize about the freedom of fame and its riches and about the distinction of popularity and attention. They recognize it when they assert their own power to tear down the star. They recognize it when they seek to watch and be a part of the media spectacle. They recognize it when they speak admiringly of the celebrity's capacity to achieve, maintain, and manage a public image: if fame is power, the capacity to achieve it is an even greater one.

People in diverse industries have recognized the power of celebrity. The logic and nascent production arrangements of entertainment celebrity have spread rapidly, taking hold in arenas beyond entertainment: fashion, architecture, grass-roots social movements, literature, art, medicine, academia, and especially in electoral politics.[1] This much is obvious, even trite, but bears repeating: one does not need to travel farther than the supermarket to pick up on the coincidence of entertainment and political celebrity.

The July 20, 1992, *People* cover story, for instance, features presidential candidate Bill Clinton, his wife Hillary, and their daughter Chelsea in their backyard in Little Rock. (See figure 8.) The article offers talk about "tag-team parenting, their bruising run for the White House and staying in love," talk about "friends, family, faith—and pierced ears." Mixed in with Bill's and Hillary's thoughts on issues such as race relations and public service are the personal tidbits usually offered on celebrities. Chelsea (first names only here) plays for a dentist-sponsored softball team called the Molar Rollers, and her dad sometimes embarrasses her by yelling too loud and jumping up and down. Bill recently took Chelsea to her first R-rated movie, *Lethal Weapon 3*. The family "relaxes by playing pinochle and other card games with Chelsea or taking her to the mall." If his house caught fire, the record album Bill would save would be Judy Collins's *Colors of the Day*. When Hillary introduced herself to Bill at Yale and asked his name, he "was so surprised that he forgot his name." Bill proposed marriage by buying a "prairie bungalow with beamed ceilings and a bay window" that Hillary had admired in passing. The photos are all home shots: in the living room, outside in the hammock, Hillary playing softball.[2]

The magazine story, an "exclusive," bears a remarkable resemblance to the Clinton video produced for the Democratic National Convention by television sitcom producers Harry Thomason and Linda Bloodworth-Thomason. The video is a *People* story set to sentimental music. The story of the name forgetting introduction to Hillary is here, along with Chelsea's description of her father's embarrassing softball cheering. Bill Clinton talks about his small-town roots, and Hillary Clinton tells how baby Bill's mother tacked playing cards on the drapes to teach him to read. Later, over shots of a jet in the sunset, Bill lets on that "sometimes, late at night on the campaign plane, I look out the window and think how far I am from that little town in Arkansas, yet [shots of small town] in many ways I know that all I am or ever will be came from there." Bill tells the nameless, invisible interviewer how amazing it was to be present for his daughter's birth; Chelsea recalls Bill speaking in a funny voice when as a little girl she would squeeze his nose. Bill and his mother, in cross-cutting interview snippets, tell the story of Bill's confrontation with the drunken stepfather ("Don't you ever, ever lay a hand on my mother again"), who replaced Bill's biological father, a car-accident victim. Later, over snippets from Clinton home videos, Bill describes the "sadness in me that I never heard the sound of my father's voice or felt his hand around mine."

Beyond the get-to-know-them video, the entire 1992 Democratic convention—like most electoral campaigns—was unapologetically scripted.

Figure 8. Politician as celebrity: "What album would he save
if his house caught fire?" The Clintons on the cover of *People*,
1992. "PEOPLE" Weekly is a registered trademark of Time,
Inc., used with permission.

At the Republican National Convention twenty years prior, the revelation of such tight control was scandalous, a CNN commentator points out. This time, the Democrats not only scripted it, they distributed the script openly. "We all have got a copy of the script," he tells viewers. "They're packaging a very slick show for television." The packagers are continually pointed out: the "image managers," the spokespeople, the "spin doctors." Indeed, like entertainment television audiences, convention audiences become performers. The delegates, CNN reports, "know they're props in the show, that they're really set decorations. They're wearing the funny hats, they're applauding when they're supposed to applaud, because they want to make sure it goes smoothly."[3] Spectators impersonate themselves rather than respond naturally.

In San Francisco's Mission District two weeks later, there is little to distinguish Clinton's appearance from a movie premiere. Crowd members are perched in trees, on telephone poles, on each other's shoulders, on tiptoes. The candidate's speech turns out to be quick and stale, five minutes of rehearsed stump rhetoric, performed by both candidate ("Are you ready to take your country back?") and supporters (loud cheers), not only for each other but for the cameras. But the crowd is satisfied, concerned not with substance but with a glimpse of the original being whose name and image they have seen on television and magazines and newspapers. "Now he is standing under that pole with the flag on it," tall people report to their shorter neighbors. "Now he is shaking people's hands." This is the primary level of the experience: to see in person the model for the hologram, to get an unmediated look at the original object, however distant, and report back to friends.[4] Spectators are charged as much by a glimpse of the face as by the spoken words, the policies presented, the leadership qualities.

The territory is familiar. The "politics of personality," commonly opposed to the "politics of substance," has become institutionalized in contemporary American politics. "Political manipulation and its cynicism are as American as apple pie," writes an analyst recently; they go back to the early republic but have intensified in recent years.[5] The production setting in which political figures come to public attention mimics, and sometimes borrows techniques directly from, entertainment celebrity. Ronald Reagan epitomized the borrowing: the actor as president and the president as actor.[6] Like entertainers, politicians are coached, handled, wardrobed, made up, carefully lit. Publicity practitioners have a central role, often building a conventional celebrity sell, inviting citizens to get to know the family just a bit. Intimacy is offered and identification fostered through accounts of personal traumas or idiosyncrasies or stories. Political figures read scripts often written by others, have questions often answered for them by others, are pitched as much on personality as on ability. They perform "as themselves" in public appearances and, more recently, on talk shows and MTV.

As in entertainment, commercial news reporters are heavily dependent on their sources and thus are professionally constrained from seriously crossing them. Like entertainment reporters, they often do not successfully resist the attempts of interested parties to replace them as information gatekeepers.[7] Reporting (the *People* story) and controlled promotion (the convention video) are often indistinguishable. Indeed, the professional and commercial conflicts are resolved in political personality texts much like they are in celebrity discourse: through the intimacy-stirring circulation of the personal details of love and pain and leisure, through gossip, through the cynic-flattering focus on image making and image management themselves, through the pragmatic mix of "man" and "myth," and the continual promise to sort out one from the other, to reveal the real person behind the image.

Yet, as Joshua Meyrowitz has pointed out, "because politics is a dramatic ritual, it is ultimately impossible to separate the thread of reality from the thread of performance."[8] Increasingly, politics is spoken in the middle-range language of semifiction. Take as an example a campaign sound bite from vice-presidential candidate Al Gore: "George Bush and Dan Quayle trying to use oil re-refining as a photo opportunity is like Bonnie and Clyde going back to the scene of the crime wanting a free toaster."[9] Even out of context, the quote rings rehearsed; but Gore was speaking from the same makeshift stage at the same oil recycling plant where Bush had appeared weeks earlier. The battle is eerie and typical: this is my photo opportunity, Gore says, my image, my symbol, my sales pitch. Self-conscious performance is taken for granted. Candidates not only attempt to point out a mismatch between image and policy; they charge each other with poor self-symbolizing, the inability to properly choose and control their own personas. Political leaders are more than ever explicit about being at once themselves and not themselves, like happy men and women testifying on detergent commercials, at once real people and advertisements for themselves.

All of this is regrettable. A concern for the vitality and depth of political life lies behind the complaints that opened this book, that a celebrity culture is a debased one, an "idiot culture."[10] Critics have warned that these practices pose dangers to informed participation in decisions that matter, that democratic choices require authentic voices. There is reason for alarm. Entertainment celebrity is an imperialist phenomenon, moving into new arenas and making them over in its own image.

Some comfort can be taken from the fact that the takeover is never complete, and the conquering armies, as we have seen, are wracked with internal conflict. Although explicit comparisons to other arenas have been beyond the scope of this study, entertainment-celebrity production suggests characteristics that may make certain domains less conducive to celebrity logic: a heavier dependence on a display of skills that cannot be easily mimicked or manufactured, a lesser dependence on the visual, an institutional autonomy from the mass media. These characteristics can be nurtured, the places where "the electronic ensemble does not penetrate" (local cultures, for example) can be protected.[11]

Politics, however, is not one of these places.[12] The picture of entertainment celebrity presented here has been continually revised to include its complexities and conflicts, a landscape that depicts much of the terrain of public life to come. It is a strange world, one in which "the oppositions that traditionally organized both social life and social critique, oppositions between surface and depth, the authentic and the inauthentic, the imaginary and the real, the signifier and the signified, seem to have broken down."[13] It is a cynical world as well, one in which people are commodified for financial or ideological profit.

Horror and dismay at the "celebrification" process are appropriate, if tired, responses. Shock and surprise are not. The entertainment-celebrity model takes over because it is a rational one, one that meets professional and commercial needs. The blurring of fact and fiction is not a conspiracy but a practicality; the uncoupling of merit and notoriety, hardly new or complete but certainly very advanced, is the result of the routine pursuit of profit.[14] That entertainment celebrity colonizes arenas beyond it is predictable. A society so heavily dependent on mediated information invites attempts to control that mediation; a society in which so many bits of information compete for attention invites attempts to encapsulate, dramatize, emotionalize. The spread of rationalized celebrity culture is perhaps inevitable, especially in the political arena, where consumption (in this case, votes) is so similarly affected by attention. However much one might wish it all away, however much one might want to keep celebrity logic out of the political realm, however much one might want to do away with television and its demands, there is no question of turning back. This is our situation.

Refusal, Withdrawal, Gullibility, Amusement

As politics adopts celebrity-industry practices, it also adopts its seams and its familiar cues. George Bush, for example, was reported to flub his answers when questions at a photo opportunity were asked out of order, when the prepared script was not followed.[15] Citizens continually encounter the stuff of politics as celebrity, both directly and through commentary: the botched lines, the handlers, the gossip, the coaches, the makeup artists, the *People* covers, the interview strategies, the talk-show appearances, the personal-life stories, the photo opportunities. The audience for politics is converted into an audience for celebrity. If we consider the positions thus triggered, the situation seems bleaker still.

At one extreme is the traditional believer. This position deflects reasoned evaluations of policy in favor of fantasy or personal-identification relationships and is plainly vulnerable to political manipulation. The believing watcher reads, moreover, a partially real text as realistic: the politician is what he says he is, seeing is believing, tough talk means a tough candidate. This undeniably gullible position has always been a threat to informed participation in public life; a dupe is a dupe. The believer position is now likely more rare, however, given the visibility of publicity-oriented activities. There is too much one must not see.

The citizen reading through the postmodern lens, at the other extreme, believes there is nothing much to see beyond publicity, "no there there." He or she is entirely cynical; exposing manipulative activities only feeds the cynicism. Political figures simply join others to be deconstructed. This is perhaps the most insidious of positions for democracy: it negates the possibility for authenticity and thus maintains the status quo; producing "the paradox of a people who fancy themselves tough but are in practice passive,"[16] it "is a form of legitimation through disbelief," a "mocking attitude that is in fact the opposite of critical."[17] All is performed. Political participation and the search for authentic voices are seen as ludicrous endeavors. A postmodern engagement in political celebrity is fundamentally disengaged from politics.

This position in pure form, we have seen, is also very rare. Celebrity watchers typically form a wide middle between these two positions; they are both cynical and believing.[18] Indeed, this broad middle makes sense: celebrity speaks not in lies but in a different language of neither lies nor truth. Celebrity watchers in one common middle-ground interpretive position believe in some because they are incredulous about most; "no one believes in truth like a person surrounded by liars." Spotting evidence of manipulation is adopted as self-flattery: I can find my way to reality through the maze of images. Even when they do not quite believe, second-order believers settle on a truth of suspended disbelief, putting the "postmodern savviness about contrivance" to use in the search for "solid, reliable grounding," a "channel of truth," a "domain of the unretouchable."[19] As Todd Gitlin has pointed out, the urgency of the need to get beneath the surface "can lead us astray, as the cultural industry and its attendants learn to exploit our old-fashioned, linear, unhip longings. That the taste for truth persists in a society supersaturated with fluff doesn't mean that we are going to get a culture with historical depth."[20] As this position is triggered, authenticity does remain pursued and salient. Skepticism and publicity literacy do not disengage from celebrity politics; but neither do they protect from the dangers to informed democratic participation.

Perhaps the most daunting prospect of all comes from the large portion of celebrity watchers whose game playing is fed by the revelation of celebrity production. Given the familiar cues that politics operates like celebrity, audiences are offered the chance to play their favorite celebrity games. On the one hand, gossips hold onto a kernel of rebellion, taking a position of refusal, rejecting the myths and the reverence, playing games of diversion and group story telling. Similarly, detection game players are literate in the peculiar semifictional celebrity language, engaged by the recognition that authenticity is problematic. They take pleasure in the very activity of uncovering, undoubtedly a healthy process for a democracy.

On the other hand, neither game includes an *end-point*. That is one of the main requirements: the game is made possible and fun by the fact that none of it matters, that the outcome is inconsequential. To the degree that politics continues to be a realm that makes a lived difference, there is a tiny glimpse of hope, because the invitation to play a game with politics may be and often is rejected on the grounds that politics is not a game. But to the degree that the political arena is used by audiences for gossip and the amusing image–reality play (did Bill Clinton really sleep with Gennifer Flowers or is she a publicity-seeking liar? does the Bush's dog Millie have lupus?), one can recognize a severe alienation from the democratic process that is very difficult to change. If these games are fun, the political arena is indeed empty, *already* experienced as having no direct impact on lives, as a commercial-cultural realm in which neither truth nor consequences matter, a realm good for nothing but play.

Hope from a Parallel World

A person can call for the revelation of the workings of the celebrity-production system, hoping to build a populace educated in the mechanics of political illusion. A person can call for the reform of political journalism, hoping to make certain that the organizational structure pushes away from rather than toward that of entertainment celebrity. A person can call for the reform of political leadership management, hoping to restrict the activities of handlers and public-relations managers. These pleas are well intentioned and deserve continued discussion; but they are also, this study has shown, sociologically and politically naive. Promise springs not from the cries of critics for demystification or responsible journalism or political reform, but from the most unlikely of places, the place from which the dangers also spring: from the free-floating world of entertainment celebrity and its active, meaning-making audiences.

Consider two nostalgias. The first comes from a pair of writers criticizing "the unreality industry," echoing Daniel Boorstin.

We have killed off—literally, in some cases—the conditions that make it possible for heroes to emerge, to lead, to sustain, to nourish us. . . . [Society's] present idols (celebrities) no longer are worthy of the role and the title "heroes," let alone "gods," because the modern process of the deliberate manufacturing of pseudo-heroes is at complete variance with the one by which true heroes historically have arisen.[21]

The second comes from Norma, a 57-year-old retired secretary.

When I was younger, they were much more glamorous. It was so different. I miss that. Now they are all alike to me. Today almost anybody's a star. And they're all very unglamorous. They're not as big. They're not larger than life like they used to be. You know, MGM and those guys used to have the starlets dating, and they went out in furs for premieres. Those men realized that they were selling America a dream, and they made those people tow the line, and they made them disciplined, and lose weight and all that. Today you've got a bunch of very ordinary people. They're not that admirable.

The nostalgia of social criticism longs for "true heroes" and looks back to a time before celebrity manufacture and the divorce of fame from merit. In the name of democratic society, it longs for an aristocracy of the naturally deserving. The nostalgia of the glamour seeker craves the time when celebrity manufacture was more centralized and controlled, when artifice was done right. It rebels against the democratization of fame, craving an elite of the extraordinarily well manufactured. In their own ways each nostalgia also expresses profound ambivalence about power in public life: who should have it, on what basis? They bring out as well anxieties about the relationship of commercial publicity apparatus to power: who controls it, to what end?

The fame discourse contains and provokes such ambivalence. Contemporary celebrity is composed of a string of antinomies: public roles opposing private selves, artificial opposing natural, image opposing reality, ideal opposing typical, special opposing ordinary, hierarchy opposing equality. Texts simultaneously celebrate effort and achievement as the open democratic routes to success and hold up for admiration the celebrity elite, successful because of inborn, extraordinary qualities. They simultaneously point out that, through marketing and the commercial system, ordinary people can become famous and rich and that one must always be on the lookout for ordinary people trying to pose as deserving celebrities. They contain a concurrent promotion of and distaste for equality. They at once demonize and idolize the commercial production system.

The cultural critics and the retired secretary, the traditional believer and the cynical believer are each making arguments in a crucial cultural conversation. Indeed, the key to the celebrity industry's ability to sustain itself while revealing artificial manufacturing processes is its adapted openness to interpretation and commentary on the predicaments of life in a commercial culture: the critical strains between merit and hierarchy and equality, the difficulty of finding the real amidst the role playing, the new confrontation with media-based forms of power. When audiences play with celebrity, they are playing with the dilemmas of democratic power.

It is crucial that the conflicts that celebrity comprises remain salient in everyday discussion, especially as entertainment-celebrity logic becomes a fixture of American politics. In most territories, politics particularly, this conversation among citizens is hampered by fear, anger, frustration, anxiety, suspicion, alienation, depth of consequence. The ultimate danger is that the conversation will be given up, the questions run from, treated as resolved by others or as unresolvable.

The dilemmas that compose contemporary celebrity most often dissolve into interesting ironies: the uniquely normal star, the elite of the not necessarily deserving, the reality of the image, the democratization by inauthenticity, the fiction that is also truth. Hope emerges from a final paradox.

Celebrity is a world in which organizational and professional conflicts resolve in simulation, performance, mimicry, blurring; a world in which authenticity is deferred and superficial fragments circulate. Therein lie its dangers, but also its promise: to keep alive the conflict-ridden questions of power, role playing, equality, and authority, to dwell in a cultural conversation that is elsewhere distorted or given up, indeed to protect it through its superficiality and triviality. The very characteristics that sustain entertainment celebrity and make it dangerous to democracy also make it absolutely essential. The parallel world of entertainment celebrity, so strange and familiar, so superficial yet so deeply alluring, offers the most free space of all in which to have the conversation: a world much like our own, but a world where nothing really matters.

Theoretical and Methodological Notes

My work has been a source of humor among my friends for quite some time. When they catch me watching a talk show or fluffy entertainment news or reading a celebrity magazine they make comments that seem to me at once affectionately disdainful and envious. "Doing research again, huh," they say, or, "You really ought to stop working once in a while." The comments capture an element of this project that makes it both accessible and difficult: much of its subject matter is widely available simply by living in America. Nearly anyone can join in the discussion, leaving the scholar without the trump card of exclusive "expertise." Perhaps because of this wide accessibility, and also perhaps because popular-culture work is often shoddy or exhibits a self-seriousness that conflicts dramatically with the lightness of the subject matter, academics and intellectuals tend to treat studies of popular culture with disrespect.[1] The student of popular culture must arguably work harder to be taken seriously by both colleagues and nonacademic readers, and this can be very trying. I have attempted to welcome these challenges, imagining myself accountable to both sets of audiences.

The bigger challenge, though, comes from the subject matter itself. The study of celebrity, and popular amusement more generally, has many built-in frustrations. The topic is broad rather than deep and thus is difficult both to break down and to get inside. Celebrity producers tend to be packagers, habitually constructing realities, and thus are hard to break through to in interviews. Audiences are widespread and varied, tend to do their interpretive work in varied casual settings, and thus are hard to listen to naturally. How does one go about digging deeply into something that appears, and often turns out to be, so superficial? How does one research a phenomenon so broad? How does one break through the habit of carefully canned response? How does one witness and eavesdrop on dispersed audiences?

Like the detectives I found in the audience, I wanted to get inside the phenomenon. Moreover, I wanted to use entertainment celebrity to illuminate dynamics of commercial culture more generally, to treat it as a case study. I was at the outset certain that a comprehensive look must include the basic elements of mass cultural phenomena: cultural text, cultural producers, and audiences. This gave me a rough outline of an approach, of the pieces to investigate and bounce off one another.[2] It also led me directly into key tugs-of-war in the sociology of culture.

Between the Institutional and the Interpretive

The study stands near the center of a major argument in approaching the relationship between culture and society, a dispute that pits an institutional outlook against an interpretive one.[3] In an institutional approach, cultural forms are taken as socially determined products, and their own meanings are skipped over: cultural forms reveal aspects of social structure, stratification, or an organizational system.[4] In an interpretive approach, meaning is taken as stable but hidden, to be revealed by the analyst: cultural forms contain a society's "deep structure," ideological messages, the "code for creating and recreating society from encounter to encounter and generation to generation."[5]

As Wendy Griswold argues, neither approach satisfies. The first shows a "relative disregard for cultural objects themselves except insofar as they have been influenced by, and influence, socioeconomic structures and institutions," while the latter suffers from "being neither generalizable nor confirmable. . . . The structure or symbolic system of a cultural object expresses and perpetuates the mentality of a social group. How do we know what the mentality of the group is? We find it in the group's culture."[6]

Analysis of celebrities has recapitulated this setup, exhibiting a similar gap between the institutional and the interpretive. When textual analysts look at celebrity, many see stars as "the direct or indirect reflections of the needs, drives and dreams of American society."[7] Stars in general or specific stars are thus interpreted much like dreams. So, for example, Edgar Morin writes that

in the last analysis it is neither talent nor lack of talent, neither the cinematic industry nor its advertising, but the *need* for her that creates a star. It is the misery of need, the mean and anonymous life that wants to enlarge itself to the dimensions of life in the movies. The imaginary life of the screen is the product of this genuine need; the star is its projection.[8]

Others read stars for their ideological significance, not for what they reflect but for what they teach. As Richard Dyer puts it, "stars have a privileged position in the definition of social roles and types, and this must have real consequences in terms of how people believe they can and should behave."[9] To their credit, advocates of this position tend to take things further than either simply the reflection or reproduction of social meanings, looking at "how star images reconcile, mask, or expose ideological contradictions."[10] Nonetheless, the text is assumed either to reflect or impose meaning on the audience or to manage contradictory meanings for it.

On the other side are those, far fewer, who focus on the star system. Barry King, in his sophisticated analysis of "stardom as an occupation," argues for seeing celebrity as created not by "popular selection" but "out of the exigencies of controlling the production and marketing of films."[11] In these studies, textual meaning is bypassed; the crucial determining factors are organizational.

Griswold's general call is to find a "way of thinking about culture that allows for variability and potential autonomy on either side of the social structure/culture relationship." Bringing in the actual receivers of culture is a major first step in that direction, since it focuses attention on the *meaning that emerges from the interaction* of the text with those encountering it. "Those experiencing the cultural object," Griswold argues, "interact with the symbolic and formal properties of the object to produce meaning, the meaning for them, there, then."[12]

Bringing in celebrity-watching audiences turns assumptions into questions. What evidence is there for reflection? For a "misery of need"? By what means are text, audience, and producers connected? How do production-setting requirements affect the contours of the celebrity text, the meanings available to audiences? How do audiences themselves make sense of the range of meanings and contradictions within the celebrity discourse?

Between the Text and the Audience

Examining audience reception, however, triggers another, parallel tug-of-war over the relationship between audiences and texts. At one time audiences for mass culture were conceived by theorists as passive recipients of injected ideologies. People were thought to encounter mass cultural messages, commercially produced by powerful elites, in an atomized mass; texts were stronger than them and closed to interpretation, received hypodermically, cultural serum in the service of maintaining the social order. This perspective, articulated primarily by members of the Frankfurt school, focused attention on the powerful new media developed during the twentieth century and sought to unmask the use of culture as a tool of power against masses of people.[13]

The conception of the audience as helpless and passive has certainly remained in studies of contemporary culture. Indeed, as W. Russell Neuman has recently noted, a number of arguments still circulating add up to "a modern reformulation of mass society theory." Theorists have suggested, for example, that critical capacities are worn down by "the pervasive and irresistible flow of media messages," that mass media are increasingly "subtle and effective," that media communication is essentially of an "addictive and habitual character," that new media drawing on senses rather than thought are themselves the message.[14] Effects research, for example, which does not share the Frankfurt school concern with elite power, nonetheless also presumes a powerful, influential textual "stimulus" and a malleable, powerless "respondent." Similarly, in textual approaches—analyses to reveal underlying meaning structures, and content analyses—meanings tend to be conceived as fixed and singular. An analysis of the text's meaning is presumed to be what anyone encountering it "really" encounters: content equals effect.[15]

The perception of media and texts as all-powerful and audiences as passive recipients, however, has been challenged by both theory and research, particularly since the early 1980s. The "uses and gratifications" approach essentially eliminated the power of texts and their producers to impose meaning, allowing for "as many meanings (or gratifications) as there are viewers (or uses)."[16] A more recent set of challenges, pushed primarily in the work of Stuart Hall, David Morley, and the Birmingham school, avoids these extremes. These approaches, with which I identify this study, emphasize the "interaction between active audience and active media,"[17] the "structuring role of the text and the constructive role of the viewer in negotiating meaning."[18] Meanings are a site of struggle. Among other things, culture, as John Fiske puts it, "is a struggle for meanings as society is a struggle for power."[19]

This reformulation has several aspects. Texts, to begin with, do not clearly exert a uniform set of meanings closed to interpretation. Rather than directly causing effects, mass media work "ideologically to promote and prefer certain meanings of the world, to circulate some meanings rather than others, and to serve some social interests better than others."[20] When the notion that meaning is static and singular is given up, the communication process, the making of texts' meanings by both producers and audiences, becomes the focus. Discourse is conceived as a flow between linked elements: messages encoded by producers that are then decoded by receivers.[21] Both the activity of producing a meaningful message and of getting meaning from the message, in David Morley's words, are "problematic 'work.' "[22]

The encoding process of popular texts is especially problematic. Producers have an interest in creating both a "preferred reading" that resides "somewhere within the repertoire of the dominant ideologies"[23] and a range of readings that draw in a range of interpreting audiences (what Fiske calls the "polysemic necessity").[24] Drawing on Umberto Eco, Fiske describes television, for example, as "a state of tension between forces of *closure,* which attempt to close down its potential meanings in favor of its preferred ones, and forces of *openness,* which enable its variety of viewers to negotiate an appropriate variety of meanings."[25] Popular texts are neither wholly closed nor wholly open, containing multiple meanings but in a structured hierarchy with certain messages dominating.

The decoding process is similarly complex. Stuart Hall argues that "audiences, whose decodings will inevitably reflect their own material and social conditions, will not necessarily decode events within the same ideological structures as those in which they have been encoded."[26] Put simply, textual meaning and impact cannot simply be inferred from an analyst's reading; if a text is to have an impact, it is only through the meaning *to the reader or viewer* that it can do so. Analyses therefore center on "the style, manner and rules by which the audience incorporate, accommodate, alter or reject media reality."[27]

Empirical studies, drawing on reader-oriented theories, have demonstrated people's various and often conflicting interpretations of the same texts.[28] David Morley, for example, found a range of audience understandings of a British nonfiction television program, from "dominant" (accepting the preferred reading), "oppositional" (rejecting the preferred reading in favor of an alternative), to "negotiated" (partial acceptance) positions; Morley links the differences to "social position" (socioeconomic class) plus "particular discourse positions" (from involvements in particular subcultures or institutions).[29] Similarly, Tamar Liebes and Elihu Katz found viewers of different ethnic backgrounds, viewing American television's "Dallas," were quite literally seeing different stories, interpreting the program with very different degrees of "critical distance."[30] Janice Radway studied a group of readers of romance novels, arguably among the most overtly patriarchal forms, who managed to "select and construct romances in such a way that their stories are experienced as a reversal of the oppression and emotional abandonment suffered by women in real life." This group of readers operated "within the system of literary mass production *in its own interests*," managing to "resist, alter, and reappropriate the materials designed elsewhere for their purchase."[31]

Negotiating the tug-of-war led me to privilege neither audience, producer, nor text but to focus instead on the moments and mechanisms of linkage between producers, audiences, and texts. The negotiation suggested fruitful places for investigation: the activity of collective interpretation and the limitations set on meanings by the text; how audiences are taken into account in production activity; the gaps between the codes of senders and receivers of cultural meaning. The analysis zeroes in on meaning creation, both as "problematic" and as "work." The text is examined for contradictory celebrity story lines and narrative resolutions; the producers for their practical celebrity-seeking activities, the roots of their negotiations and compromises over the control of the celebrity image; the audiences for the everyday activities into which they build celebrities and lenses through which they interpret them.

The three major pieces are taken up, moreover, with an eye to their interaction. Rather than seeing social structure as determining culture (and examining only cultural institutions and their economic base), or seeing culture as self-determining (and interpreting texts only as artifacts) or, indeed, cultural meaning as completely undetermined (and studying only audience uses and interpretations), this model directs attention to the varying ways in which each constrains and affects the other—when and how institutional and interpretive approaches intersect. The book asks, for example, how production processes and interest-driven activities (and the economic structures that inform them) affect the range of encoded textual meanings; how the text itself manages in its narratives to negotiate questions raised by visible production activities; and how audience readings are affected by characteristics of the discourse and by the practical meaning-production activities of celebrity producers.

The Translation into Methodology

These are all issues of theory and analysis, of situating the study within the sociology of culture, of theoretical disputes informing my approach. The practical task of investigating celebrity was complicated by my commitment to covering each constituent part of the phenomenon. The techniques for best researching and analyzing one element were inappropriate for comprehending the others, and I pushed toward a decidedly pluralistic methodological stance. By not wedding myself to one research technique, I allowed myself opportunities to fill in and check out conclusions derived from the variety of methods.

Both data collection and interpretation followed the general outlines of qualitative research described by Anselm Strauss: less a linear process than a continual doubling back and forth between theory and data, between provisional categories of analysis, directed data collection, rough coding, memoing, and writing.[32] The analysis of texts, which came earliest, suggested questions and analytical categories for the studies of producers and audiences; the analysis was ongoing, based on the cumulative patterns and challenges emerging from new data collection. Here I want simply to make the specific methods clear, to show from where the data and their interpretations derive, both to allow more fair and informed evaluations of my arguments and to expose some of the strengths and weaknesses of each technique.

Researching the History and the Texts

For historical background, I relied on the strength of existing work. To get at the history and content of textual discourse, however, I needed to go to the texts themselves, but for practical purposes only to a selection of them. What I wanted to capture was the celebrity text broadly construed (thus I refer to it also as discourse): that is, what was being said, and what seemed to be the limits of what was spoken, in the major outlets available to mainstream readers and viewers of celebrity. I wanted to be able to find, describe, and analyze the current form and its contours and to highlight it especially through historical comparison.[33]

I did so in three major ways. The first two left me at the mercy of the selection criteria and skills of others. I used several compilations of original articles from popular magazines in earlier parts of the century: Amory and Bradlee's selections from *Vanity Fair,* Gelman's selections from *Photoplay,* and Levin's selections from other early fan magazines.[34] Second, I drew from the subject files of the Margaret Herrick Library of the Academy of Motion Picture Arts and Sciences in Los Angeles, which include a broad selection of articles from a wide variety of magazines and newspapers dating back to before the turn of the century. Finally, to be more certain that I was drawing from a range of periodicals and that the emerging patterns were not the result of the idiosyncratic selections of others, I conducted my own search. Depending primarily on the *Reader's Guide to Periodical Literature,* I tracked down articles through a standard subject search (fame, greatness, celebrity, stars, heroes, actors and actresses, publicity, press agents, gossip, and so forth).

I divided the clippings roughly by decade, reading through each set with particular questions in mind. How was a star's rise to fame explained? How frequently was the publicity system mentioned and what was said about it? I looked more generally for patterns that might not arise from these questions, for thematic repetitions of any sort and for contradictions or oddities. I then needed to relate these patterns historically, to make sense of the particular changes in the discourse. Thus emerged the first section: a historical analysis of this century's discourse on celebrity based on secondary research on the history of fame and of fame-seeking apparatuses, and on a first-hand survey of popular-magazine writings.

This sort of argument, although driven by patterns I saw emerging from the clippings themselves, leaves open the question of exactly what this range of meanings represents. Although I located the text in the context of the history of production, the implications of ownership and production practices were not firmly developed. Who is determining the possibilities and limits on the meanings that get generated, on the form the text takes, on the available choices for those confronting it? Moreover, my interpretation of the discourse, even if it was exactly on target, told me nothing about the meaning made by others, by those choosing to engage the text daily.

Researching Production

To answer the first set of questions, I began to establish contacts in the entertainment industry in Los Angeles in preparation for a research stay of several months (January to May 1991). On an exploratory trip, I conducted several interviews to nail down the types of people whose work I would need to understand: most centrally, journalists, editors, television producers, and bookers, who make decisions about celebrity-coverage content; and publicists, whose job it is to effect and affect coverage for their celebrity or aspiring clients. Others also affected the outcome of a celebrity text, and I would seek them out as well: aspirants themselves (whom I see as coauthors of the texts), agents, and managers. In addition, each professional type could be found at different levels in which some dynamics might differ. Thus I sought out those working on powerful national newspapers, magazines, and programs as well as on smaller, less powerful ones; those working in large agencies, those in smaller agencies, and those working independently; those handling major stars and those handling minor celebrities; those who primarily represented companies or studios and those who primarily represented individuals.

I chose to interview these people directly and, when possible, to supplement those interviews with observations of my subjects' behavior at work.[35] To find these interview subjects, I employed "snowball sampling," using initial contacts to make further contacts, with several different balls rolling at once to ensure some variety of social circles. I determined which "types" were missing and needed, and I asked interview subjects to recommend others who might fit those requirements: thus a journalist sent me to a studio publicist, who sent me to a television talent booker, who sent me to a personal publicist, who sent me to a manager, and so on.

Interviews generally lasted one to two hours and were conducted at the interviewee's workplace. Some interviews were held at a public meeting place, such as a café or restaurant, and a few, with informants located outside Los Angeles, were held over the telephone. I always began by offering the informant anonymity, to be more certain he or she would speak freely and openly. Granting anonymity, and distinguishing myself as an outsider rather than as someone to whom one must pitch a line, were particularly crucial given the idiosyncrasies of interviewing in this environment. These are typically people who are used to the interview format and tend to approach it strategically. I needed to, and to a large degree I believe succeeded in, make these conversations different, to break the interviewees' habits of providing carefully packaged answers. (I also checked the interviews against my observations of production activities in celebrity-based settings, enumerated below.)

With two exceptions, interviews were taped and later transcribed and their patterns compared and analyzed. While I used the following interview schedule as a rough guide, being sure to cover the same ground in each interview, I retained the informality of open-ended questioning and free-flowing conversation.[36]

Sample Interview Schedule

I. General background
   What do you do? How long have you been doing this? What did you do before?

II. Theories of celebrity

   A. Why do you think some people become celebrities while others don't? To what degree is it something about them? Do celebrities have something special about them? To what degree can anyone, regardless of talent, be made famous? How do you explain the people on "The Hollywood Squares," or Zsa Zsa Gabor, or Angelyne?

   B. Many people describe celebrity as an "industry." Do you think that's an accurate way to talk about it? If yes, how would you describe the celebrity industry? What do you think the characterization of it as an industry misses, if anything?

III. Daily work life

   A. How do you do what you do? What do you do day to day that gets or tries to get [other people/yourself] more recognition? Or what do you do day to day that makes use of celebrities?

   B. Who are you working with now, and how are you going about it?

   C. Who are the other people you deal with the most? Who are you playing to the most (journalists? audience? etc.)?

   D. What are the biggest problems you face in getting the job done?

   E. What do you look for to emphasize, to use as a point of interest, etc.?

      1. [Publicists, managers, performers:] Are you more concerned with getting publicity (any publicity is good publicity) or with promoting a particular image?

      2. [Journalists, producers, bookers:] How do you decide what warrants coverage? What are you looking for?

IV. Relationship to audience

   A. Do you have any direct contact with audiences? Indirect contact, through audience research?

   B. What do you think audiences are getting out of watching famous people? What do you think they're doing?

   C. Are there things you try to find out or wish you could find out about audiences in general or particular audiences?

   D. How much control do you think they have over who becomes famous?

V. Public awareness of production activities

   How much do you think people know about the celebrity industry as an industry? Would you want them to know more (imagine a massive public awareness campaign to educate on the "facts" of how people become famous)?

I took my own boredom (usually after three or four interviews with a person in the same professional position) as the first clue that I was reaching a plateau in the data-gathering process. I stopped interviewing after one or two more sessions, when my predictions about the content of conversations became accurate. A list of interviewees and their positions follows. To those who requested anonymity I have given pseudonyms (indicated by quotation marks) and avoided the specifics of their professional position.

Interview Subjects

- Michael Alexander, entertainment magazine writer (*People*)
- Angelyne, entertainment personality (Angelyne, Inc.)
- Marilyn Beck, syndicated newspaper and magazine entertainment columnist (self-employed; *TV Guide*)
- "Marc Beyer," television studio publicist
- "Renee Billings," television and film actress
- "Linda Brown," film studio production publicist
- Bill Bruns, television magazine bureau chief (*TV Guide*)
- Arlene Dayton, personal manager (Arlene Dayton, Inc.)
- Bob Dolce, national television talk-show talent coordinator ("The Tonight Show")

- "Jack Emilio," film production company publicist
- Bill Faith, public relations professor (University of Southern California)
- Patrick Goldstein, music and film newspaper writer (*Los Angeles Times*)
- "Amy Green," television network research director
- Pete Hammond, television entertainment program producer ("Entertainment Tonight")
- "Rob Hass," major agency talent agent
- Scott Hennig, assistant to entertainment personality Angelyne (Angelyne, Inc.)
- "Jordan Kamisky," personality publicist (self-employed)
- "Marla Keane," actress and assistant to personal manager
- Michael Levine, personality publicist (Levine/Schneider)
- Bob Lewine, former network executive (CBS, NBC, ABC) and former president of the Academy of Television Arts and Sciences
- "John Martin," newspaper film section editor
- Bob Merlis, music company publicist (Warner Brothers)
- "Stan Meyer," entertainment magazine bureau chief and writer
- "Mary Morgan," tabloid magazine gossip columnist
- "Jerome North," major agency personality publicist
- Nia Peeples, entertainer and television personality
- "Mark Peters," newspaper television section staff writer
- Fridell Pogodin, independent film publicist (Dennis Davidson Associates)
- "Susan Rice," local television broadcasting director
- "John Rider," entertainment magazine writer
- Marsha Robertson, film market coordinator and former unit publicist (Twentieth Century Fox)
- "Don Roca," local television talk-show producer and talent coordinator

- Henry Rogers, personality publicist (Rogers and Cowan)
- "Janine Rosenblat," independent film and personality publicist
- "Miriam Ross," entertainment magazine editor and writer
- Richard Rothenstein, cable network publicist (HBO)
- "Ann Sandberg," network morning-program producer and talent coordinator
- "Marty Schneider," entertainment magazine editor-in-chief
- Robin Smalley, television director ("Lifestyles of the Rich and Famous")
- Jim Smeal, photographer (Ron Galella, Inc.)
- David Spiro, talent agent and personal manager (self-employed)
- "Stuart Stein," newspaper television critic
- "Todd Stoutland," casting director
- "Sarah Tamikian," cable network publicist
- Barbara Tenney, local television director of research (KNBC)
- "Margaret Thompson," major agency talent agent
- David Viscott, radio and television call-in psychologist (KABC, KNBC)
- "Amanda Weber," independent personality publicist
- Michael Weithorn, television writer and producer (Twentieth Century Fox)
- Diana Widdom, film studio publicist (Paramount)
- Gene Yusem, personal manager (self-employed)
- Bill Zehme, entertainment magazine senior writer (*Rolling Stone*)

Researching Audiences

I was left with the question of how best to gain textured insight into audience interpretations of celebrity. I needed first to hear people talk about it, and I had specific topics I wanted to hear about. But I also knew that insight from discussion would not allow me to check people's words against their behaviors; or would it take me inside the experience of celebrity watching or assure me that the issues I wanted to discuss were salient for others. I thus turned to participant observation, in which people are encountered "in their own time and space, in their own everyday lives," and which allows not just "direct observation of how people act but also how they understand and experience those acts" and "enables us to juxtapose what people say they are up to against what they actually do."[37]

Access to a single setting was difficult to come by, and I chose to broaden the field to the celebrity-watching tourist circuit in Los Angeles (January to May 1991). Although denied the focus of a single case, I was able to observe the same populations in a broad range of settings and pick up on patterns. Because I sought out settings (listed below) peopled primarily by visitors, I was able to guard against the geographical bias of Los Angeles, an environment in which celebrities and the celebrity industry are fairly commonplace. At each event I recorded observations and immediately afterward wrote extensive field notes and analysis, which became increasingly focused the longer I was in the field.

Observation Settings

- "The Tonight Show" with Johnny Carson, Burbank (waiting line and taping)
- Grauman's Chinese Theater, Hollywood
- Hair at Riley's, beauty salon to the stars, Beverly Hills
- Golden Globe Awards, Beverly Hills (outside)
- *Sleeping with the Enemy* premiere screening, Los Angeles (outside)
- "The Arsenio Hall Show," Hollywood (waiting line)
- *The Josephine Baker Story* premiere screening, Santa Barbara (outside and inside)
- "Into the Night with Rick Dees," Hollywood (waiting line and taping)
- Joan Collins book-signing appearance, Century City
- "AM Los Angeles," Hollywood (preparation and taping)
- Starline tour of movie stars' homes, Hollywood, Beverly Hills, and Bel Air

- Sixty-third Annual Academy Awards, Los Angeles (outside)
- Hollywood Walk of Fame star dedication ceremony, Hollywood
- "Party Machine," Hollywood (taping)
- "Sunday in Paris" television pilot, Hollywood (waiting line)
- "Match Game," Hollywood (waiting line and taping)
- Ginger Rogers book-signing appearance, San Francisco

Although I now had data on people's celebrity-watching behaviors and had certainly overheard, engaged in, and noted numerous conversations, I still lacked interpretations or readings of the celebrity text that I might be able to relate to the participant-observation data. I had observed only people's public watching behaviors and responses, which were shaped by the fact that they were primarily in the context of tourism, not everyday life. I needed to come as close as possible to everyday conversation. Returning to the San Francisco Bay Area, I turned to constructed conversations.

William Gamson, drawing on David Morgan's review of the focus-group methodology, lays out important advantages of "peer group conversations" over individual interviews: in conversation with others, "people search for a common basis of discourse," allowing the researcher to "witness people in the process of constructing and negotiating *shared* meaning"; groups allow "the natural vocabulary in which people formulate meaning" to more readily emerge; and through the disputes and movements of discussion, "participants are forced to become more consciously aware of their perspective."[38] The phenomenon of celebrity watching seemed also to be a particularly social one, whose meanings typically developed in discussion.

Recruitment of focus-group participants, without the benefit of great financial resources, was hard going. I zeroed in on San Francisco and its outlying areas. I used several methods to interest unpaid volunteers: placing flyers on cars in shopping center parking lots, distributing them at public events, and posting them at sponsoring libraries; placing paid and unpaid advertisements in local newspapers and securing newspaper coverage from interested journalists (which brought the largest influx of participants); and approaching high school teachers to "borrow" their students for discussions. Each respondent was screened to be certain that they fit the minimum celebrity-watcher criteria (once-a-week watcher or reader of a daily celebrity-based program or column; once-a-month watcher or reader of weekly or monthly celebrity-based program or publication) and to eliminate fans with a singular rather than a general focus of interest. (Although I also tried to screen for educational level, race or ethnicity, and so forth, in order to arrange groups of specific types, it quickly became evident that managing such arrangements was impractical.) Each respondent was also asked if they had friends who might like to participate, and in several cases meetings of friendship groups were arranged.

Although these conversations in many ways mimicked focus groups, I also diverged from the market-research strategy in a variety of ways, primarily because informality was central. Groups were typically small, usually four or five people. Whenever possible, they were composed of acquaintances (to more closely approximate the makeup of typical discussions) and were conducted in a neutral or participant-friendly setting (a library, a participant's home, my home). Moreover, although I made it clear that I would facilitate the conversation when necessary, I told participants that I—a celebrity watcher myself—was genuinely interested in whatever might come up and urged them to talk and disagree freely. I assured them their last names would not be used in my writing.

Conversations typically began with a round-the-room sharing of names of favorite celebrities or of celebrity-encounter stories, often triggered by the pile of magazines that I threw down in the center of the group, and moved from there into other topic areas. As with the individual production interviews, I followed a rough schedule (below), covering the same ground but in an order dictated by conversational flow, and allowed, often encouraged, digressions.

Sample Discussion Schedule

   I. Introductions and celebrity-encounter experience or favorite celebrity

 II. Interest in celebrities

    A. Would you want to meet a famous person? If you could meet any famous person, who would it be? Why would you want to meet them?

    B. What would you want to ask them? When you read about them or hear about them, what is it that you want to find out? What kind of stuff tends to bore you and what tends to grab you?

    C. Do you think of these people as like you or different from you?

III. Reading and viewing habits

Do you just read about your favorites or will you read about pretty much anybody? When do you read about or watch celebrities the most? What kind of a time is it for you? Are you concentrating, or are you doing other things at the same time? Do you talk about it with friends?

IV. Theories about rise to and claims to celebrity

A. Do you think all celebrities deserve to be famous? If just some of them do, how do you tell the difference between the ones that deserve it and the ones that don't?

B. How do you think people got to where they are? Why are they famous? How do they get there? How much do other people have to do with it? If anyone, who else is involved? How do you think these people got on the covers of these magazines? How much do we have to do with it?

Discussions typically lasted between an hour and an hour and a half and were tape recorded and later transcribed and analyzed. After each session ended, participants were asked to complete a one-page information sheet. The results are compiled below, giving a rough picture of the diversity of groups. (The only information reported that was not gleaned from these questionnaires is sexual orientation.)

Participant Composition (Group Types)

Total number of groups	16
Female only	7
Male only	3
Mixed gender	6
Urbanite only	7
Suburbanite only	9
People of color only	3
White only	6
Mixed race	7
Youth only	4
Adult only (mixed ages)	12

Higher educated only	4
High school educated only	0
High school students only	4
Mixed educational backgrounds	8
Gay male only	2
Mixed/undeclared sexual orientation	14

Participant Composition (Individuals)

Total participants	73
Male	28
Female	45
White	44
African-American	9
Latino	13
Asian-American	2
Other race/undeclared race	5
Urban dweller	33
Suburban dweller	40
No higher education	15
Higher education	36
High school student	20
Educational background unknown	2
Under 18 years old	20
18–30 years old	15
31–45 years old	27
46–60 years old	10
Over 60 years old	1
Openly gay	12
Self-reported working class	5
Self-reported lower-middle class	11
Self-reported middle class	27
Self-reported upper-middle class	21
Self-reported upper class	1
Class not reported	8

Self-reported religious	35
Self-reported nonreligious	34
Religiosity not reported	4
Student	25
Office worker/secretary/receptionist	10
Salesperson	7
Administrator	6
Teacher	4
Homemaker	3
Bank employee; restaurant/bar worker; self-employed; social service worker; occupation unknown	2 each
Accountant; actor; artist; community worker; flight attendant; landscape architect; legal worker; mail clerk; mortgage broker; real estate appraiser; researcher; unemployed; writer	1 each

The composition of the groups is not intended to establish a claim about representative sampling; the means of collecting volunteers were too unsystematic and the numbers too small for that. A study on a more scientific model might, examining larger portions of the audience and keeping certain variables constant, take up interesting questions that I could not. What is the relationship between social location (class, gender, race, sexual identity, and so forth) to variations in interpretation? What is the relationship between the type of response and the type of celebrity figure (actor, rapper, game-show host)? Although my analysis could not systematically answer these questions, it does derive from a wide range of participant backgrounds. The interpretive strategies found in this study cross many of the boundaries of social location.

Notes

Introduction

1. Michael Danahy, "Blonde Ambition," *Los Angeles,* October 1987, p. 59.
2. "Here's a New Way to Fame," *People,* June 22, 1987, p. 73.
3. Scott Hennig, interview with author, April 11, 1991.
4. Angelyne, quoted in Danahy, "Blonde Ambition," p. 60.
5. Angelyne, quoted in Charles Marowitz, "The Angel of Publicity," *Los Angeles Herald Examiner,* September 24, 1989, p. E9.
6. Ibid., p. E1.
7. Ibid.
8. Hugo Maisnick, quoted in Danahy, "Blonde Ambition," p. 62; p. 61.
9. "Here's a New Way to Fame," p. 73.
10. See Laura Mulvey, "Visual Pleasure and Narrative Cinema," *Screen* 16, no. 3 (Autumn 1975): pp. 6–18; and John Berger, *Ways of Seeing* (London: British Broadcasting Corporation, 1972).
11. "Mary Hart's Voice Triggers Seizures," *San Francisco Chronicle,* July 11, 1991, p. A3.
12. See Richard Dyer, *Stars* (London: British Film Institute, 1979); Charles Affron, *Star Acting: Gish, Garbo, Davis* (New York: Dutton, 1977); and Edgar Morin, *The Stars* (New York: Grove Press, 1960).
13. See C. Wright Mills, *The Power Elite* (London: Oxford University Press, 1956).
14. See Francesco Alberoni, "The Powerless 'Elite': Theory and Sociological Research on the Phenomenon of the Stars," in Denis McQuail, ed., *Sociology of Mass Communications* (Harmondsworth, England: Penguin Books, 1972).
15. See Richard Schickel, *Intimate Strangers: The Culture of Celebrity* (New York: Fromm International, 1985).
16. See Patrick Brantlinger, *Bread and Circuses: Theories of Mass Culture as Social Decay* (New York: Cornell University Press, 1985), and Michael Schudson, "Delectable Materialism: Were the Critics of Consumer Culture Wrong All Along?" *American Prospect* 1, no. 5 (Spring 1991): pp. 26–35.

17. Michael Parenti, *Make-Believe Media: The Politics of Entertainment* (New York: St. Martin's Press, 1992), p. 181.

18. Schudson, "Delectable Materialism," p. 30.

19. Neil Postman, *Amusing Ourselves to Death: Public Discourse in the Age of Show Business* (New York: Penguin Books, 1985), p. 141.

20. Stuart Ewen, *All Consuming Images: The Politics of Style in Contemporary Culture* (New York: Basic Books, 1989), pp. 264, 248, 266.

21. See Theodor Adorno and Max Horkheimer, "The Culture Industry: Enlightenment as Mass Deception," in James Curran, Michael Gurevitch, and Janet Woolacott, eds., *Mass Communication and Society* (Beverly Hills: Sage Publications, 1977); and Brantlinger, *Bread and Circuses,* chap. 7.

22. Parenti, *Make-Believe Media,* p. 181.

23. Ian Mitroff and Warren Bennis, *The Unreality Industry: The Deliberate Manufacturing of Falsehood and What It Is Doing to Our Lives* (New York: Carol Publishing Group, 1989), p. xi; p. 10.

24. Jean Baudrillard, "Simulacra and Simulations," in Mark Poster, ed., *Jean Baudrillard: Selected Writings* (Stanford: Stanford University Press, 1988), p. 167. See also Fredric Jameson, "Postmodernism and Consumer Society," in Hal Foster, ed., *The Anti-Aesthetic: Essays on Postmodern Culture* (Port Townsend, Wash.: Bay Press, 1983).

25. Mark Poster, "Introduction," in Poster, ed., *Jean Baudrillard: Selected Writings,* pp. 5–6.

26. Ewen, *All Consuming Images,* p. 271.

27. Postman, *Amusing Ourselves to Death,* pp. 160–61.

28. Parenti, *Make-Believe Media,* p. 213; p. 12 (emphasis added).

29. See William J. Goode, *The Celebration of Heroes: Prestige as a Social Control System* (Berkeley: University of California Press, 1978); Mills, *The Power Elite,* p. 71; p. 74.

30. James Monaco, *Celebrity* (New York: Delta, 1978), p. 6.

31. Daniel J. Boorstin, *The Image: A Guide to Pseudo-Events in America* (New York: Harper and Row, 1961), p. 57.

32. Ibid., p. 47; p. 240.

33. John Lahr, "Notes on Fame," *Harper's,* January 1978, pp. 77–80.

34. Barbara Goldsmith, "The Meaning of Celebrity," *New York Times Magazine,* December 4, 1983, pp. 75, 76, 120.

35. Monaco, *Celebrity,* pp. 5–6, 8.

36. Schudson, "Delectable Materialism," p. 33.

37. Andrew Sullivan, "Buying and Nothingness," *New Republic,* May 8, 1989, pp. 39–40.

38. Schudson, "Delectable Materialism," p. 33.

39. Sullivan, "Buying and Nothingness," p. 40.

Chapter 1. The Great and the Gifted

1. "The Final Fling," in Martin Levin, ed., *Hollywood and the Great Fan Magazines* (New York: Arbor House, 1970), p. 39.

2. Edith Efron, "How to Manufacture a Celebrity," *TV Guide,* August 11, 1967, p. 16.

3. "How Fleet It Is!" *People,* December 28, 1987–January 4, 1988, p. 88.

4. Leo Braudy, *The Frenzy of Renown: Fame and Its History* (New York: Oxford University Press, 1986), p. 32. I draw very heavily in the early parts of this chapter from Braudy's book, which deserves to be encountered in full form. See also the excellent historical discussion in Charles L. Ponce de Leon, "Idols and Icons: Representations of Celebrity in American Culture, 1850–1940," (Ph.D. diss., Rutgers University, 1992), chap. 1.

5. Braudy, *The Frenzy of Renown,* pp. 81–89.

6. Ibid., p. 56 (see pp. 55–114); pp. 117, 152 (see pp. 150–92); p. 121; p. 28.

7. Ibid., p. 207.

8. Ibid., pp. 267–68; p. 317.

9. Ibid., p. 229.

10. Ponce de Leon, "Idols and Icons," p. 12. In this discussion, Ponce de Leon draws on C. B. Macpherson, *The Political Theory of Possessive Individualism* (New York: Oxford University Press, 1962), and Jean-Christophe Agnew, *Worlds Apart: The Market and the Theater in Anglo-American Thought, 1550–1750* (New York: Cambridge University Press, 1986).

11. Ponce de Leon, "Idols and Icons," p. 16.

12. Ibid., p. 13.

13. Braudy, *The Frenzy of Renown,* pp. 371–72; pp. 392–93.

14. Barry Schwartz, *George Washington: The Making of an American Symbol* (New York: Free Press, 1987), p. 6; p. 102.

15. Parson Weems, quoted in Schwartz, *George Washington,* p. 181.

16. Neil Postman, *Amusing Ourselves to Death: Public Discourse in the Age of Show Business* (New York: Penguin Books, 1985), p. 65.

17. See Michael Schudson, *Discovering the News: A Social History of American Newspapers* (New York: Basic Books, 1978).

18. Ponce de Leon, "Idols and Icons," p. 20.

19. Richard Schickel, *Intimate Strangers: The Culture of Celebrity* (New York: Fromm International, 1985), p. 40; see also Braudy, *The Frenzy of Renown,* pp. 508–9; and Schudson, *Discovering the News, passim.*

20. Braudy, *The Frenzy of Renown,* p. 495.

21. Oliver Wendell Holmes, quoted in Stuart Ewen, *All Consuming Images: The Politics of Style in Contemporary Culture* (New York: Basic Books, 1989), p. 25. I am indebted in this piece of the argument to Ewen's insightful discussion of Holmes's article "The Stereoscope and the Stereograph," in Beaumont Newhall, ed., *Photography: Essays and Images* (New York: Museum of Modern Art, 1980). Holmes's article appeared originally in *Atlantic Monthly,* June 1859, pp. 738–48.

22. Braudy, *The Frenzy of Renown,* p. 497.

23. Candice Jacobson Fuhrman, *Publicity Stunt!* (San Francisco: Chronicle Books, 1989), p. 14.

24. Carl Bode, "Introduction," in P. T. Barnum, *Struggles and Triumphs* (Harmondsworth, England: Penguin Books, 1981), p. 12. My discussion of

Barnum is drawn primarily from Braudy's discussion of Barnum (*The Frenzy of Renown,* pp. 498–506) and from Neil Harris, *Humbug: The Art of P. T. Barnum* (Boston: Little, Brown and Co., 1973).

25. Bode, "Introduction," p. 13; p. 15.

26. Barnum, *Struggles and Triumphs,* p. 103.

27. Ticket seller quoted in Robert C. Toll, *On with the Show: The First Century of Show Business in America* (New York: Oxford University Press, 1976), p. 26.

28. Bode, "Introduction," p. 23.

29. Braudy, *The Frenzy of Renown,* p. 381.

30. Harris, *Humbug,* p. 79; p. 75.

31. Schudson, *Discovering the News,* p. 133. See also Alex Carey, "Reshaping the Truth: Pragmatists and Propagandists in America," in Donald Lazare, ed., *American Media and Mass Culture* (Berkeley: University of California Press, 1987).

32. Ivy Lee, quoted in Marvin N. Olasky, *Corporate Public Relations: A New Historical Perspective* (Hillsdale, N.J.: Lawrence Erlbaum Associates, 1987), p. 49.

33. Edward Bernays, quoted in Schudson, *Discovering the News,* p. 138.

34. Schudson, *Discovering the News,* p. 140.

35. See Richard Wightman Fox and T. J. Jackson Lears, eds., *The Culture of Consumption: Critical Essays in American History, 1880–1980* (New York: Pantheon, 1983).

36. Lary May, *Screening Out the Past: The Birth of Mass Culture and the Motion Picture Industry* (New York: Oxford University Press, 1980), pp. 29–30, 201–2.

37. This early marketing plan was essentially "preindustrial"; the division of labor, writes Robert Allen, came not from the industry but within the vaudeville presentation itself. Production, distribution, and exhibition were collapsed into the operator, "who, with his projector, became the self-contained vaudeville act" (Robert Allen, quoted in introduction to Tino Balio, ed., *The American Film Industry* [Madison: University of Wisconsin Press, 1985], p. 8). See also Robert Allen, "The Movies in Vaudeville: Historical Context of the Movies as Popular Entertainment," in ibid.

38. Tino Balio, "A Novelty Spawns Small Businesses, 1894–1908," ibid., p. 19.

39. May, *Screening Out the Past,* p. 35.

40. Alexander Walker, *Stardom: The Hollywood Phenomenon* (New York: Stein and Day, 1970), p. 29.

41. Ibid.

42. May, *Screening Out the Past,* pp. 99–100.

43. Walker, *Stardom,* pp. 29–30.

44. Balio, "A Novelty Spawns Small Businesses," *The American Film Industry,* p. 21.

45. See Janet Staiger, "Seeing Stars," in Christine Gledhill, ed., *Stardom: Industry of Desire* (London: Routledge, 1991).

46. Tino Balio, "Struggles for Control, 1908–1930," in Balio, ed., *The American Film Industry*, pp. 108–13.

47. Ibid., p. 111.

48. Ibid., p. 114.

49. Cathy Klaprat, "The Star as Market Strategy: Bette Davis in Another Light," in Balio, ed., *The American Film Industry*, pp. 351–54. I am indebted to Klaprat's article for this piece of the history.

50. Richard deCordova, *Picture Personalities: The Emergence of the Star System in America* (Urbana: University of Illinois Press, 1990), p. 140. Indeed, as deCordova describes it, the emergence of the star system "involved a strict regulation of the *type* of knowledge produced about the actor." DeCordova traces three transformations: from an early discourse on acting (1907–9), in which films were differentiated at the level of performances; to the development of the picture personality (1909–14), in which players' names began to be circulated and differentiation operated at the level of "the personality of the player as it was depicted in film"; and finally to the star (beginning around 1914), in which "the question of the player's existence outside his/her work in films entered discourse." Again, the regulation of knowledge at each of these points amounted to industry attempts to differentiate the film product. See deCordova's *Picture Personalities* and "The Emergence of the Star System in America," in Christine Gledhill, ed., *Stardom*.

51. The early star system was aided in its development by innovations in the use of film as a medium. In particular, the close-up, brought into film by D. W. Griffith around 1908, allowed the face to take over the screen. The close-up provided the star system with two critical characteristics. The focus on the face, with signs of emotion greatly magnified, established a sense of intimacy between audience and stranger-performer. And, by "isolating and concentrating the player's looks and personality, sometimes unconnected with his or her abilities," it provided a means of establishing a performer's "unique" personality (Walker, *Stardom*, p. 21). The apparent revelation by the close-up of the "unmediated personality of the individual," Bela Balazs has pointed out, and the consequent "*belief* in the 'capturing' of the 'unique' 'person' of a performer" is essential for the star phenomenon (quoted in Richard Dyer, *Stars* [London: British Film Institute, 1979], p. 17). The coming of sound in the late 1920s further shortened the psychological distance between performer and audience and further increased the apparent uniqueness and "realness" of the apprehended performer. "What seemed to be their last significant secret, their tones of voice," writes Richard Schickel, "was now revealed—or so it seemed" (*Intimate Strangers*, p. 99). No longer pantomimed emotion, performance was less stylized; with voices, performers were less unlike the audiences.

52. For descriptions of film industry organization, see Balio, ed., *The American Film Industry*, and Hortense Powdermaker, *Hollywood the Dream Factory* (Boston: Little, Brown and Co., 1950).

53. Edgar Morin, *The Stars* (New York: Grove Press, 1960), p. 59.

54. Robert C. Allen and Douglas Gomery, *Film History: Theory and Practice* (New York: Alfred A. Knopf, 1985), pp. 175–76.

55. Henry Rogers, interview with author, February 10, 1991. Unless otherwise noted, subsequent quotations are also taken from author interviews.

56. Walker, *Stardom,* pp. 51–52.

57. Cathy Klaprat, for example, traces Bette Davis's early career, in which she made five movies, "each one an experiment to determine the correct narrative match" ("The Star as Market Strategy," p. 355).

58. May, *Screening Out the Past,* pp. 156–58.

59. Klaprat, "The Star as Market Strategy," p. 366. For more on the importance of photographs—they were "sent out by the thousands, factory inscribed; they appeared endlessly in magazines; they decorated the advertisements which persuaded women to use Lux soap because nine out of ten Hollywood stars did, or served as a ready-made model, pinned up by a mirror, as women plucked or thickened their eyebrows, painted their lips into a Cupid's bow or a Joan Crawford letter box"—see John Russell Taylor, "The Image Makers," *American Film,* July–August 1976, pp. 23–24.

60. Klaprat, "The Star as Market Strategy," p. 360. Establishing a "real-life" image also allowed another common practice: "off casting," or playing against type. The flip side of matching offscreen and onscreen personas, this strategy "provided the variation to sustain audience interest, but also served to enhance the image of the star as a great performer" (pp. 372–75).

61. Hedda Hopper and James Brough, *The Whole Truth and Nothing But* (Garden City, N.Y.: Doubleday and Co., 1963), p. 264.

62. Schickel, *Intimate Strangers,* pp. 113, 111.

63. See Richard deCordova, *Picture Personalities,* pp. 117–51. See also Kenneth Anger, *Hollywood Babylon* (New York: Delta, 1975).

64. Tino Balio, "A Mature Oligopoly, 1930–1948," in Balio, ed., *The American Film Industry,* p. 266.

65. Louella Parsons, backed by the Hearst newspaper empire, "could wield power like Catherine of Russia," wrote rival Hopper, giving stars the silent treatment if they crossed her, able to "get any story she wanted front-paged in the Los Angeles *Examiner* and all other Hearst papers, none of them accustomed to making much distinction between real news and flagrant publicity" (Hopper and Brough, *The Whole Truth,* pp. 60–61).

66. Braudy, *The Frenzy of Renown,* p. 551.

67. Emil Ludwig, "What Makes a Man Stand Out from the Crowd?" *American Magazine,* May 1930, pp. 15, 164.

68. See Cleveland Amory and Frederic Bradlee, eds., *Vanity Fair: Selections from America's Most Memorable Magazine* (New York: Viking Press, 1960).

69. Leo Lowenthal, "The Triumph of Mass Idols," in *Literature, Popular Culture, and Society* (Palo Alto, Calif.: Pacific Books, 1968), p. 115.

70. May, *Screening Out the Past,* pp. 145–46, 166, 190.

71. See Levin, ed., *Hollywood and the Great Fan Magazines,* and Barbara Gelman, ed., *Photoplay Treasury* (New York: Bonanza Books, 1972).

72. Morin, *The Stars,* p. 90.

73. Quoted in Lowenthal, "The Triumph of Mass Idols," p. 123.

74. Schickel, *Intimate Strangers,* pp. 99, 100.

75. "The New Hollywood," *Life*, November 4, 1940, pp. 65–67 (emphasis added).

76. Ben Maddox, "What about Clark Gable Now?" in Levin, ed., *Hollywood and the Great Fan Magazines*, p. 174.

77. Schickel, *Intimate Strangers*, pp. 100–101.

78. Ben Maddox, "The One Star Who Has No Enemies," in Levin, ed., *Hollywood and the Great Fan Magazines*, p. 25.

79. Joan Crawford, "The Story of a Dancing Girl," in Gelman, ed., *Photoplay Treasury*, p. 88.

80. "What Should I Do? Your Problems Answered by Bette Davis," in Gelman, ed., *Photoplay Treasury*, pp. 264–65.

81. Warren Susman argues that the shift in vocabulary reflected a shift from the "culture of character" of a producer-capitalist republic to a "culture of personality" consistent with consumer capitalism. The stress on heroes with traits of "social significance and moral quality"—captured in key words such as "citizenship, duty, democracy, work, building, golden deeds, outdoor life, conquest, honor, reputation, morals, manners, integrity, and above all, manhood"—was giving way to a culture in which personality was neither good nor bad but "fascinating, stunning, attractive, magnetic, glowing, masterful, creative, dominant, forceful." As the consistent advice-manual definition put it (linking, significantly, personality to celebrity), "Personality is the quality of being Somebody." Susman ties this change in modal types to the change in the culture they are bearing: "character" provides a model of self-mastery and self development fitting to the needs of the early producer-capitalist republic, "personality" a model fitting a consumer "culture of abundance." See Susman, *Culture as History* (New York: Pantheon, 1984), pp. 273–77.

82. Don Eddy, "Hollywood Spies on You," *American Magazine*, July 1940, p. 162.

83. Sonia Lee, "Jean Harlow: From Extra to Star," in Levin, ed., *Hollywood and the Great Fan Magazines*, pp. 43–44.

84. Morin, *The Stars*, p. 51.

85. Alfred Cohn, "What Every Girl Wants to Know," in Gelman, ed., *Photoplay Treasury*, p. 33.

86. Maddox, "What about Clark Gable Now?" p. 174.

87. Eddy, "Hollywood Spies on You," p. 25.

88. Caroline Somers Hoyt, "It's Ruby's Turn Now!" in Levin, ed., *Hollywood and the Great Fan Magazines*, p. 51.

89. Peter Joel, "The First True Story of Garbo's Childhood," in Levin, ed., *Hollywood and the Great Fan Magazines*, pp. 172–73.

90. Lowenthal, "The Triumph of Mass Idols," pp. 124–25 (emphasis added).

91. Edna Ferber, "They Earn Their Millions," *Collier's*, December 4, 1920, p. 7.

92. "Starlets Are World's Most Envied of Girls," *Life*, January 29, 1940, p. 37 (emphasis added).

93. Arthur Lockwood, "Press Agent Tells All," *American Mercury*, February 1940, p. 180.

94. Michael Costello, "They Pronounce It Pre-meer," *Reader's Digest,* February 1941, p. 88.

95. Frank Ward O'Malley, "Hot off the Press Agent," *Saturday Evening Post,* June 25, 1921, p. 56.

96. Walter Lippmann, "Blazing Publicity: Why We Know So Much about 'Peaches' Browning, Valentino, Lindbergh, and Queen Marie," in Amory and Bradlee, eds., *Vanity Fair,* p. 121.

97. "On the Public's Beach," in Amory and Bradlee, eds., *Vanity Fair,* p. 229.

98. Faith Service, "So You'd Like to Be a Star: Myrna Loy Shows You What Is Back of Hollywood's Glamor Front," in Levin, ed., *Hollywood and the Great Fan Magazines,* p. 142.

99. Robert Taylor, "Why Did I Slip?" in Levin, ed., *Hollywood and the Great Fan Magazines,* p. 203.

100. Service, "So You'd Like to Be a Star," p. 214 (emphasis added).

101. William Boehnel, "Dietrich Is Still Selling Glamour," in Levin, ed., *Hollywood and the Great Fan Magazines,* p. 218.

102. "Fame," *Nation,* October 28, 1931, p. 450.

103. "Celebrity Unlimited," *American Mercury,* February 1944, pp. 204–5.

104. Barry King, "Stardom as an Occupation," in Paul Kerr, ed., *The Hollywood Film Industry* (London: Routledge and Kegan Paul, 1986), p. 174.

105. "Starlets Are World's Most Envied of Girls," pp. 37–39.

Chapter 2. The Name and the Product

1. Tino Balio, "Retrenchment, Reappraisal, and Reorganization, 1948–," in Tino Balio, ed., *The American Film Industry* (Madison: University of Wisconsin Press, 1985), p. 402.

2. Ibid., p. 401.

3. Ibid., pp. 418–19. Balio also points out that agents, working on commission, were out to exact the best terms for the package, thus boosting production costs, "so that mostly surefire projects were favored."

4. Ibid., p. 419; pp. 422–23.

5. Barry King, "Stardom as an Occupation," in Paul Kerr, ed., *The Hollywood Film Industry* (London: Routledge and Kegan Paul, 1986), pp. 169–70.

6. Jeff Blyskal and Marie Blyskal, *PR: How the Public Relations Industry Writes the News* (New York: William Morrow and Co., 1985), p. 27; p. 30.

7. Andrew Sullivan, "Buying and Nothingness," *New Republic,* May 8, 1989, p. 37.

8. Through its close association with advertising, public relations has become increasingly rationalized through the use of market research to "discern and monitor existing public opinion," to "find which target publics need to be influenced," to "single out the most appropriate media vehicles to carry the PR message," to "keep track of what and how many PR messages the target public has been exposed to," and to "learn what effect the PR has had on altering opinion and whether additional PR is needed" (Blyskal and Blyskal, *PR,* p. 89). In the world

of television, this trend is well captured by "Performer Q," a rating service offered since the early 1970s by a company called Marketing Evaluations: ranking some 500 celebrities according to a survey of American families, it provides subscribers with "a demographic road map" for each celebrity, breaking down his or her audience appeal by sex, age, income, education, and occupation (Rowland Barber, "Just a Little List," *TV Guide,* August 10, 1974, pp. 4–5).

9. Blyskal and Blyskal, *PR,* p. 48.

10. Ibid., pp. 99–102.

11. "Introducing . . . ," *People,* March 4, 1974, p. 2.

12. "The People Perplex," *Newsweek,* June 6, 1977, p. 89.

13. Richard Stolley, quoted in "The People Perplex," p. 90. On the expansion of celebrity into previously untapped fields, see Deyan Sudjic, *Cult Heroes* (New York: W. W. Norton and Co., 1989).

14. Stanley Rothman and Robert Lerner, "Television and the Communications Revolution," *Society* 26, no. 1 (November/December 1988): p. 65.

15. Richard Schickel, *Intimate Strangers: The Culture of Celebrity* (New York: Fromm International, 1985), p. 13.

16. As David Kehr points out, the "principle of repetition" that established film stars is intensified through television: "instead of seeing your favorite star two or three times a year in a similar part, you can now see him/her/it fifty-two times a year in an identical part." See Kehr, "A Star Is Made," *Film Comment,* January–February 1979, p. 10.

17. As a medium that makes particularly frequent use of the close-up, television not only encourages a sense of intimacy but "invites us to read character into the face, to formulate, from the lines and wrinkles therein, an impression easily mistaken for a detailed, knowledgeable portrait of the star." Rather than an individuated, recognizable physical setting, the talk-show set, "that nowhere that is anywhere and everywhere," further increases the possibilities for an emotional link with celebrities by allowing viewers to "relocate them anywhere that suits our purposes." See Schickel, *Intimate Strangers,* pp. 13–16.

18. Karen Thomas, "An Aura Can Be Honed but Not Created," *USA Today,* January 4, 1991, pp. D1–2.

19. Schickel, *Intimate Strangers,* p. 103.

20. "Does TV Drama Need a Star System?" *TV Guide,* October 30, 1953, p. 6.

21. "For the Stars, the Postman Always Rings *More* than Twice," *TV Guide,* December 29, 1956, p. 6.

22. Dick Hobson, "The 10 Percenter," *TV Guide,* December 28, 1968, p. 6 (emphasis added).

23. "Television's Biggest Struggle: The Battle of Billings," *TV Guide,* October 4, 1958, p. 21.

24. Elaine Kendall, "Success (?) Secret of the Starmakers," *New York Times Magazine,* September 30, 1962, pp. 37–40.

25. Edith Efron, "How to Manufacture a Celebrity," *TV Guide,* August 11, 1967, pp. 16–19.

26. Press agent, quoted in Dick Hobson, "The Hollywood Flack," *TV Guide,* April 12, 1969, p. 10 (emphasis added).

27. Cleveland Amory, "Who Killed Hollywood Society?" *TV Guide,* November 25, 1967, p. 33.

28. "The Stuff That Stars Are Made Of," *TV Guide,* January 5, 1957, pp. 8–9.

29. "How to Make It in Hollywood." Transcript 128 of "Geraldo," March 17, 1988, pp. 3–4.

30. Thomas Morgan, "Gentlemen of the Pressure," *TV Guide,* October 19, 1963, pp. 8–9; October 26, 1963, p. 22.

31. Robert de Roos, "Hollywood's Mother Hen," *TV Guide,* November 4, 1961, pp. 28–29.

32. Joseph N. Bell, "Canonizing the Superficial," *Saturday Review,* October 8, 1966, p. 115.

33. Peter Bart, "Well, What's an Interview For?" *New York Times,* March 27, 1966, p. X13.

34. Ellen Shaw, "Never Get Riled, Don't Knock Women, Chefs—and Bring Your Own Pillow," *TV Guide,* October 2, 1982, p. 56.

35. Lynn Hirschberg, "The Power of Hot," *Rolling Stone,* May 22, 1986, p. 28.

36. William A. Henry, "Pssst . . . Did You Hear About?" *Time,* March 5, 1990, pp. 46–51.

37. Jacob K. Javits, "You Can't Fool the Camera," *TV Guide,* October 1, 1960, p. 11.

38. Arlene Francis, "Just Be Yourself," *TV Guide,* September 3, 1960, p. 6.

39. Laura Rosetree, "Every Face Has a Secret," *Redbook,* April 1990, p. 54.

40. Similarly for the self as a public performer, as Arlene Francis demonstrates in her all-the-world's-a-television-screen article. In order to be successful, one's exterior must match one's interior, and the interior is what counts—"just be yourself," Francis suggests, and express "genuine charm," "that certain something," "your real self." Significantly, the most practical instructions she can give involve performing false charm as "limbering up exercises" until they become "second nature": putting on a strong handshake, looking interested, giving compliments, smiling as if expecting the best. The familiar "personality" as an explanation of success reappears, but more problematically. The idea that staging cannot make a person something they are not is asserted, mixed with the implication that what a person is in fact grows from staging. Whereas in earlier texts internal qualities would be *brought out* in public performance (star personality discovered), here it is implied that they will be *created in* performance; personality is represented as, at least possibly, artificially produced. See Francis, "Just Be Yourself," pp. 4–7.

41. "The Truth about Groucho's Ad Libs," *TV Guide,* March 19, 1954, pp. 5–6.

42. "Familiar Gestures," *TV Guide,* March 26, 1954.

43. Jay Martel, "Sweet Fifteen," *Rolling Stone,* May 21, 1987, p. 91. The

reference to Andy Warhol's claim that "in the future everyone will be world famous for fifteen minutes" began to be commonplace in the 1970s.

44. *Spy,* April 1989 (cover); June 1989 (cover); "The State of Celebrity 1990," *Spy* (January 1990), pp. 59–69.

45. Kendall, "Success (?) Secret of the Starmakers," p. 37.

46. "The People Perplex," p. 90.

47. Nora Ephron, "Famous First Words," *Esquire,* June 1989, p. 104.

48. "The Making of Billy Gable," *Life,* Spring 1989, p. 54.

49. Wayne Warga, "The Three Stages of Hollywood Stardom," *TV Guide,* October 9, 1982, pp. 4–5.

50. Cameron Stauth, "The Secrets of Hollywood's Casting Directors," *TV Guide,* April 2, 1988, p. 5.

51. Todd Gitlin, Review of *Rolling Stone: The Photographs, New York Times,* December 3, 1989, p. G14.

52. *Esquire* 111 (June 1989).

53. Gitlin, Review of *Rolling Stone.*

54. Tom Wolfe, quoted in Chuck Workman, "*Superstar: The Life and Times of Andy Warhol* (Marilyn Lewis Entertainment, Ltd., 1990).

55. Mark Crispin Miller, *Boxed In: The Culture of TV* (Evanston, Ill.: Northwestern University Press, 1988), p. 16; pp. 326–27; p. 331.

Chapter 3. Industrial-Strength Celebrity

1. Irving J. Rein, Philip Kotler, and Martin R. Stoller, *High Visibility* (New York: Dodd, Mead and Co., 1987), p. 6.

2. "How Stars Are Made." Transcript 02204 of "Donahue," pp. 3–4. Unless otherwise noted, quotations in this and subsequent chapters are taken from author interviews with industry workers, conducted from January to May 1991 in Los Angeles. Some workers are identified by actual name and some by pseudonym, since some interview subjects requested anonymity.

3. "Gene Schwam: The P.R. Role," *Hollywood Reporter,* 52nd Annual, December 1982, p. 106.

4. Rein, Kotler, and Stoller, *High Visibility,* p. 168; p. 70; p. 66.

5. Ibid., p. 71; pp. 206–34.

6. Ibid., p. 126; p. 147. As we've seen earlier, the power of managed storylines is a "discovery" that dates back much further than the 1970s and 1980s.

7. Ibid., pp. 282, 298, 262, 281.

8. Ibid., p. 234.

9. For the authors of *High Visibility,* what mess there is must simply be cleared away. Mystical beliefs in such things as "the natural," "charisma," and "the lucky break" must be shown to be industry "self-cloaking strategies" and replaced by rational, industrial counterparts. Characteristics that "cause aspirants to be perceived as talented" must be developed, polished, and selectively emphasized; charisma must be "programmed" through "a distillation of the classic behaviors and images associated with success" in a given sector (ibid., p. 8, 166, 181, 190).

I argue in a different direction: that mess and conflict are built into the structure of the celebrity industry.

Chapter 4. The Negotiated Celebration

1. Lisa Gubernick, quoted in Neal Koch, "The Hollywood Treatment," *Columbia Journalism Review* (January/February 1991): p. 31.

2. Oscar Gandy, *Beyond Agenda Setting* (Norwood, N.J.: Ablex Publishing, 1982).

3. Paul Hirsch, "Processing Fads and Fashions: An Organization-Set Analysis of Cultural Industry Systems," *American Journal of Sociology* 77 (1972): 640.

4. Moreover, says David Israel, a newspaper columnist turned television producer, the push to maintain good relationships is underlined by the lure of eventually becoming what you're reporting on: "Covering Hollywood is the only job where reporters aren't sure whether to pitch or catch. All those people who, while they're doing journalism, would like to think that they're being objective, many, in the back of their minds think, 'These guys buy screenplays; maybe I have a shot'" (quoted in Koch, "The Hollywood Treatment," p. 31).

5. Philip Elliott, "Media Organizations and Occupations: An Overview," in James Curran, Michael Gurevitch, and Janet Woolacott, eds., *Mass Communication and Society* (Beverly Hills: Sage Publications, 1977), p. 149.

6. This is often expressed through a cynical sense of humor. Patrick Goldstein will call his friend at Associated Press and pose as the publicist who can always be counted on to call with a quote from a celebrity client. "Mickey Rooney is deeply saddened," Goldstein will tell the other writer in his mock-sincere publicist's voice, "by the death of his very good friend." Their discomfort with their dependence on publicists comes through in ridicule.

7. See Eliot Freidson, "The Changing Nature of Professional Control," *Annual Review of Sociology* (1984).

8. This is not simply an implicit interest. In numerous cases, in fact, image-ownership and celebrity-as-commodity battles have found their way into the court system. Questions of individual versus corporate ownership of an image, and celebrity as financially valuable property to be divided upon divorce, for example, have been legally disputed. For an interesting treatment of these sorts of contests, see Jane Gaines, *Contested Culture: The Image, the Voice, and the Law* (Chapel Hill: University of North Carolina Press, 1991).

9. See Michael Cieply, "Hollywood's High-Powered Image Machine," *Los Angeles Times Magazine*, July 10, 1988; Jonathan Alter, "The Art of the Deals," *Newsweek*, January 9, 1989.

10. Kathie Berlin, quoted in Aimee Lee Ball, "The Starmakers," *New Woman*, November 1988, p. 123.

11. Yoffe, "E! Is for Entertainment," *Newsweek*, August 12, 1991, p. 58.

12. Elliott, "Media Organizations and Occupations," p. 148.

13. To think that commercial news organizations operate according to such traditional criteria is naive; what I am describing here is not exclusive to entertain-

ment news. The point is the distinctive degree to which criteria of "newsworthiness" and the pursuit and provision of "truth" simply do not circulate in these environments.

Chapter 5. Props, Cues, and Not Knowing

1. Todd Gitlin, *Inside Prime Time* (New York: Pantheon, 1983), p. 22.

2. In *Managing Public Relations* (New York: CBS College Publishing, 1984), James Grunig and Todd Hunt lay out four different models of public relations: "press agentry or publicity," in which the purpose is propaganda, communication is one-way, and truth inessential; "public information," in which the purpose is the dissemination of information, communication is still one-way, but truth is important; "two-way asymmetric," in which the purpose is scientific persuasion, and communication runs back and forth between parties but with imbalanced effects; and "two-way symmetric," in which the purpose is mutual understanding, and communication goes two ways, with balanced effects. Although the extent to which publics and organizations (particularly commercial ones) can be effectively linked in a balanced, mutually effecting communication deserves to be questioned, this outline helps to make sense of the celebrity industry by clarifying alternatives.

3. In this sense, celebrity production operates generally in what John Meyer and Brian Rowan call a "decoupled" or "loosely coupled" state. Conformity through inspection is not enforced, output quality is not closely monitored, the efficiency of various units is not evaluated, goals are not unified and coordinated. Meyer and Rowan suggest that "elements of structure are decoupled from activities and from each other" because "attempts to control and coordinate activities in institutionalized organizations lead to conflicts and loss of legitimacy." See John W. Meyer and Brian Rowan, "Insitutionalized Organizations: Formal Structure as Myth and Ceremony," in John W. Meyer and W. Richard Scott, eds., *Organizational Environments: Ritual and Rationality* (Beverly Hills: Sage Publications, 1983).

4. Herbert Gans, *Deciding What's News* (New York: Vintage Books, 1979), pp. 229–34. See also Gaye Tuchman, *Making News: A Study in the Construction of Reality* (New York: Free Press, 1978).

5. Gans, *Deciding What's News*, p. 232.

6. Television networks are a definite exception. They conduct extensive research—including minute-by-minute studies to see exactly when people are "bailing out"—to aid in keeping audience attention, and thus ratings, and thus advertising revenues. (Film studios also research audiences extensively, but primarily to aid in advertising and promotion.) "What's real to the viewer is what's real," says Barbara Tenney, a Los Angeles television-station director of research. "That's what we're delivering. Their perceptions are real, and we have to learn what their perceptions are." When focus groups commented on a talk-show host's hair style and skirt length, the host got a haircut and lengthened her skirts. Even such extensive research is used not to tease out patterns of audience interest (why do they like certain celebrities, for example, and not others?) but to tinker with

current products (do they like her hair?) or to select among possibilities (is this host more appealing than the other?).

7. The fact that celebrity-based outlets proclaim as trivial the information they are delivering relieves much of the tension. *People* is "an hour away from serious cares," says a *People* editor. "Fun. Prurient interest. R and R." The responsibility to amuse is a less demanding one than the responsibility to illuminate. After all, many of these journalists suggest, this is not something that really matters, like politics. The job is to "distract the world from its own mundane self," as *Rolling Stone*'s Bill Zehme says.

8. These textual phenomena should be familiar from the earlier discussion of celebrity texts. Here we see that they are not only resolutions of textual dilemmas but resolutions of professional ones as well.

Chapter 6. Hunting, Sporting, and the Willing Audience

1. Autograph hounds and fan-club devotees have long been staples of the celebrity scene. In 1991, *Newsweek* reported, there is "a fan club for everyone and everything," including Gumby, news reporter Arthur Kent, the ex-husband of Frank Sinatra's daughter, an Elvis impersonator, "nearly forgotten TV actor" Buddy Ebsen (Ned Zeman, "The Adoration of the Elvii," *Newsweek*, April 22, 1991, pp. 62–63). Singer Engelbert Humperdinck has 250 fan clubs. Some are even loosely federated into the National Association of Fan Clubs (NAFC), formed in 1977 to "upgrade the standards of fan-clubbing," to "strive for recognition and respect as worthwhile organizations," to "inform the public of what fan clubs are all about," and to "act as sounding board for complaints from fans who feel they have been cheated as a fan club." Here the attempt is to distinguish fan clubs from the swooning-girl stereotype. "Contrary to what a lot of people think, fan clubs are *not* made up of 'star struck' teenagers," NAFC President Blanche Trinajstick writes (National Association of Fan Clubs, Information Sheet, 1991). "There *are* some young people in fan clubs, of course, but most of the people involved are mature, and dedicated fans who are willing to put in a lot of time, energy and money to support the career of an admired celebrity who they believe in." Neither the star-struck nor the well-organized admiring fan is a baseless stereotype, then. I'm suggesting, however, that they are widely exaggerated and misapplied notions of the celebrity-watching audience.

2. See John Berger, *Ways of Seeing* (London: British Broadcasting System, 1972), pp. 132–33. See also Leo Braudy, *The Frenzy of Renown: Fame and Its History* (New York: Oxford University Press, 1986), p. 590: "If you cannot get fame yourself, then you can become a fan, gathering reflected glory by carefully monitoring the rise and fall of those more avid for the absolute prizes. . . . Fandom mediates the disparity between the aspirations fostered by the culture and the relatively small increments of personal status possible in a mass society."

3. Andrew Tudor, for one, has argued that these processes are "the basic psychological machinery through which most people relate to film" (*Image and*

Influence: Studies in the Sociology of Film [New York: St. Martin's Press, 1974], p. 76). He classifies the audience–star relation according to the "range of consequences" (those limited to the specific context of watching and those with a more diffuse impact on aspects of a fan's life) and the "range of star–individual identification" (high or low) (p. 80). For someone who is involved more broadly in the lives of stars, he suggests two processes: imitation, for those with a lower level of identification, and projection, in which "the 'real world' becomes constituted in terms derived from the 'star world' " (p. 83), for those with a high level of identification. For Tudor, however, the process of watching is conceived as an entirely individual one, and the explanation of involvement is thus entirely psychological. This picture, I am arguing, is challenged by the observational data.

4. Peter Schrag, "Heeere's Johnny!" in James Monaco, ed., *Celebrity* (New York: Delta, 1978), p. 54.

5. Richard Dyer, "*A Star Is Born* and the Construction of Authenticity," in Christine Gledhill, ed. *Stardom: Industry of Desire* (London: Routledge, 1991), p. 135.

6. Ibid., p. 135.

7. John J. MacAloon, "Olympic Games and the Theory of Spectacle in Modern Societies," in John J. MacAloon, ed., *Rite, Drama, Festival, Spectacle: Rehearsals toward a Theory of Cultural Performance* (Philadelphia: Institute for the Study of Human Issues, 1981), p. 272.

8. For a classic and intelligent example of critical wisdom on this point, see John Lahr, "Notes on Fame," *Harper's*, January 1978, pp. 77–80.

Chapter 7. Can't Beat the Real Thing

1. William J. Goode, *The Celebration of Heroes: Prestige as a Social Control System* (Berkeley: University of California Press, 1978), p. 7.

2. Ibid., p. 235.

3. Francesco Alberoni, "The Powerless 'Elite': Theory and Sociological Research on the Phenomenon of the Stars," in Denis McQuail, ed., *Sociology of Mass Communications* (Harmondsworth, England: Penguin Books, 1972), p. 90.

4. Joshua Meyrowitz, *No Sense of Place: The Impact of Electronic Media on Social Behavior* (New York: Oxford University Press, 1985), p. 169; p. 48; p. 270; p. 47; pp. 65–66.

5. Richard Dyer, "*A Star Is Born* and the Construction of Authenticity," in Christine Gledhill, ed., *Stardom: Industry of Desire* (London: Routledge, 1991), p. 135; p. 136; p. 137; p. 137.

6. Although a number of groups met in homogeneous groupings, because of resource restrictions the majority of groups mixed ages, genders, races and ethnicities, and levels of education. Two caveats should be kept in mind. First, although it's significant that the differences tend to bleed across sociodemographic categories, the description and analysis presented here is entirely of middle-class people. Second, the patterns discerned cannot provide more than hints at the link between different "decoding positions" and specific social locations or identities.

The link I will emphasize is that between different understandings of celebrity and the different activities into which they feed.

7. Michael Billig has recently produced an interesting study of British "common-sense talk about royalty," with questions and findings that overlap with my study. See Billig, *Talking of the Royal Family* (London: Routledge, 1992).

8. Dyer, "*A Star Is Born,*" p. 136.

9. Billig found a similar "cynical consciousness, whose patterns match what is often called 'postmodernism' " in his discussions of British royals (*Talking of the Royal Family,* p. 23). And, similarly, he found that "mockery and cynicism do not lead to a rebellious republicanism," that "the cynical consciousness might expose the images as images, but the exposure was part of the show," that "the royal conjurers are to continue performing before an audience, which claims to see through the tricks but which sympathizes with the performers on that very account" (p. 203).

10. Madonna represents "a kind of postmodern feminist image that builds on, or combines, elements of the 'new' woman," writes Ann E. Kaplan, for example, in *Rocking Around the Clock: Music Television, Postmodernism, and Consumer Culture* (New York: Methuen, 1987), p. 130. For a criticism of such work, see Daniel Harris, "Blonde Ambitions: The Rise of Madonna Studies," *Harper's,* August 1992.

11. Todd Gitlin, "Postmodernism: Roots and Politics," in Ian Angus and Sut Jhally, eds., *Cultural Politics in Contemporary America* (New York: Routledge, 1989), p. 350.

12. A version of this sometimes appears in the postmodern-style discussions, as well: celebrities are those performers who work hard at and are driven to manipulate their own images, to control their own artificial creations.

13. In this case, rather than believing in authenticity, audiences often settle for a self-consciously "as if" approach similar to the semifictional reading discussed later, and their position is more gamelike than the activities of traditional believers.

14. Jean Baudrillard, "Simulacra and Simulations," in Mark Poster, ed., *Jean Baudrillard: Selected Writings* (Stanford: Stanford University Press, 1988), p. 177.

15. Meyrowitz, *No Sense of Place,* p. 303.

Chapter 8. Believing Games

1. Donald Horton and R. Richard Wohl, "Mass Communication and Para-Social Interaction: Observations on Intimacy at a Distance," *Psychiatry* 19, no. 3 (August 1956): p. 217; p. 216.

2. Michael Schudson, *Advertising: The Uneasy Persuasion* (New York: Basic Books, 1984), p. 214.

3. Patricia Meyer Spacks, *Gossip* (New York: Alfred A. Knopf, 1985), pp. 5–6; pp. 21–22; p. 15.

4. Michael Sorkin, "Faking It," in Todd Gitlin, ed., *Watching Television* (New York: Pantheon Books, 1986), p. 173.

5. Michael Parenti, *Make-Believe Media: The Politics of Entertainment* (New York: St. Martin's Press, 1992), pp. 11–12.

6. John Fiske, *Television Culture* (London: Routledge, 1987), p. 239.

7. On the "producerly" stance, see ibid., p. 95; p. 239.

8. Johan Huizinga, *Homo Ludens: A Study of the Play Element in Culture* (Boston: Beacon Press, 1956), p. 13; Clifford Geertz, "Deep Play: Notes on the Balinese Cockfight," in Clifford Geertz, *The Interpretation of Cultures* (New York: Basic Books, 1973), p. 443; Francesco Alberoni, "The Powerless 'Elite': Theory and Sociological Research on the Phenomenon of the Stars," in Denis McQuail, ed., *Sociology of Mass Communications* (Harmondsworth, England: Penguin Books, 1972), p. 75.

9. Geertz, "Deep Play," p. 448.

Conclusion

1. See, for example, Jeff Blyskal and Marie Blyskal, *PR: How the Public Relations Industry Writes the News* (New York: William Morrow and Co., 1985); Deyan Sudjic, *Cult Heroes* (New York: W. W. Norton and Co., 1989). On the impact of celebrity on social movements, see Todd Gitlin, *The Whole World Is Watching: Mass Media in the Making and Unmaking of the New Left* (Berkeley: University of California Press, 1980), chap. 5.

2. Landon Y. Jones, "Road Warriors," *People*, July 20, 1992, pp. 68–79.

3. CNN coverage of the Democratic National Convention, July 15, 1992.

4. "If, as Walter Benjamin has argued, mechanical reproduction results in the loss of the aura of the real object, then the star system might be seen as a peculiar attempt to replace it," writes Richard deCordova (*Picture Personalities: The Emergence of the Star System in America* [Urbana: University of Illinois Press, 1990], p. 146). "That replacement is never fully achieved, however. In effect, the dialectic of presence and absence remains." See also Walter Benjamin, "The Work of Art in the Age of Mechanical Reproduction," in Walter Benjamin, *Illuminations* (New York: Schocken, 1968).

5. Jeffrey Goldfarb, *The Cynical Society: The Culture of Politics and the Politics of Culture in American Life* (Chicago: University of Chicago Press, 1991), p. 10. Goldfarb offers a fascinating account of the historical and cultural roots of cynical political practices and beliefs. See also Kathleen Hall Jamieson, *Packaging the Presidency: A History and Criticism of Presidential Campaign Advertising* (New York: Oxford University Press, 1984).

6. See, for example, Michael Rogin, *Ronald Reagan, the Movie, and Other Episodes in Political Demonology* (Berkeley: University of California Press, 1987).

7. See, for example, Mark Hertsgaard, *On Bended Knee: The Press and the Reagan Presidency* (New York: Farrar Straus Giroux, 1988); and Leon Sigal, *Reporters and Officials: The Organization and Politics of Newsmaking* (Lexington, Mass.: D. C. Heath, 1973).

8. Joshua Meyrowitz, *No Sense of Place: The Impact of Electronic Media on Social Behavior* (New York: Oxford University Press, 1985), p. 277.

9. "Gore's Speech at Bay Plant Challenged," *San Francisco Chronicle*, August 4, 1992, p. A1, A10.

10. Carl Bernstein, "The Idiot Culture," *San Francisco Chronicle*, July 26, 1992, This World section, pp. 7–11.

11. Todd Gitlin, "On Being Sound-Bitten: Reflections on Truth, Impression, and Belief in a Time of Media Saturation," *Boston Review*, December 1991, p. 17.

12. Even in politics, it is important to notice, the dominance of personality politics does not mean that democratic institutions are eliminated. "Though our political life is strikingly imprecise and emotional rather than rational, it still is democratic," Jeffrey Goldfarb cautions (*The Cynical Society*, p. 7). "A fog of cynicism surrounds American politics, but they are still animated by fully institutionalized democratic norms and traditions."

13. Rogin, *Ronald Reagan and Other Episodes*, p. 9. See also Stuart Ewen, *All Consuming Images: The Politics of Style in Contemporary Culture* (New York: Basic Books, 1989).

14. Recall that the uncoupling of merit and renown did not begin in this century: visibility has always been one means to social and political gain, there have always been attempts to gain it by appearing to have the valued qualities. Recall also that the celebrity-production system does not push uniformly toward separating celebrity and merit: some organizations must emphasize the celebrity's work, while others emphasize the celebrity's person. Yet with the industrialization of the means to recognition, that uncoupling has become widespread and fully institutionalized.

15. "Bush Is Overheard Asking If He Gave 'Proper Answer,' " *San Francisco Chronicle*, November 27, 1991, p. D6.

16. Richard Sennett, "The Decline of Public Discourse," *Contemporary Sociology* 21 (1992): p. 16.

17. Goldfarb, *The Cynical Society*, p. 1; p. 22. Goldfarb effectively argues, along the same lines I am pursuing here, that cynicism is often confused "with democratic deliberation and political wisdom" (p. 2).

18. W. Russell Neuman argues that about 75 percent of the American population falls in a "great middle stratum" of political sophistication. As opposed to a small apolitical group (about 20 percent) and an even smaller activist stratum (about 5 percent), the middle group "are marginally attentive to politics and mildly cynical about the behavior of politicians, but they accept the duty to vote, and they do so with fair regularity." They "can communicate political ideas, but they are hunt-and-peck typists" (*The Paradox of Mass Politics* [Cambridge, Mass.: Harvard University Press, 1986], pp. 171–72).

19. Gitlin, "On Being Sound-Bitten," p. 16.

20. Ibid., p. 17.

21. Ian Mitroff and Warren Bennis, *The Unreality Industry: The Deliberate Manufacturing of Falsehood and What It Is Doing to Our Lives* (New York: Carol Publishing Group, 1989), p. 49. The historical claim, we saw early on, is overstated.

Appendix

1. On popular-culture studies, see Michael Schudson, "The New Validation of Popular Culture: Sense and Sentimentality in Academia," in Robert Avery and David Eason, eds., *Critical Perspectives on Media and Society* (New York: Guilford Press, 1991). On the relationship between intellectuals and popular culture, see Andrew Ross, *No Respect: Intellectuals and Popular Culture* (New York: Routledge, 1989).

2. Examining entertainment celebrity alone was already biting off a lot, and comparative research on celebrity in other domains (or, for that matter, in other countries) was necessarily excluded. Such comparisons are by far the most fruitful area for future research on celebrity.

3. See Wendy Griswold, "The Fabrication of Meaning: Literary Interpretation in the United States, Great Britain, and the West Indies," *American Journal of Sociology* 92 (1987): pp. 1079–82. Others have analyzed the field in different, parallel ways. See, for example, Richard Peterson, "Revitalizing the Culture Concept," *Annual Review of Sociology* 5 (1979): pp. 137–66, and Paul Hirsch, "Social Science Approaches to Popular Culture," *Journal of Popular Culture* 11 (1977): pp. 401–13.

4. On social structure, see Raymond Williams, "Base and Superstructure in Marxist Cultural Theory," *New Left Review* 82 (November–December 1973): pp. 3–16. On stratification, see, for example, Pierre Bourdieu, *Distinction: A Social Critique of the Judgement of Taste* (Cambridge, Mass.: Harvard University Press, 1984). On organizational system, see, for example, Paul Hirsch, "Processing Fads and Fashions: An Organization-Set Analysis of Cultural Industry Systems," *American Journal of Sociology* 77 (1972): pp. 639–59; Cynthia White and Harrison White, "Institutional Change in the French Painting World," in R. N. Wilson, ed., *The Arts in Society* (Englewood Cliffs, N.J.: Prentice-Hall, 1964); and Muriel Cantor, *The Hollywood TV Producer* (New Brunswick, N.J.: Transaction Books, 1988).

5. On deep structure, see, for example, Clifford Geertz, *The Interpretation of Cultures* (New York: Basic Books, 1973); and Will Wright, *Sixguns and Society: A Structural Analysis of the Western* (Berkeley: University of California Press, 1975). On ideological messages, see, for example, Tania Modleski, ed., *Studies in Entertainment: Critical Approaches to Mass Culture* (Bloomington: Indiana University Press, 1986); and Ariel Dorfman, *The Empire's Old Clothes: What the Lone Ranger, Babar, and Other Innocent Heroes Do to Our Minds* (New York: Pantheon, 1983). The quotation is from Peterson, "Revitalizing the Culture Concept," p. 143.

6. Griswold, "The Fabrication of Meaning," pp. 1080–81.

7. Alexander Walker, *Stardom: The Hollywood Phenomenon* (New York: Stein and Day, 1970), p. 13.

8. Edgar Morin, *The Stars* (New York: Grove Press, 1960), p. 98.

9. Richard Dyer, *Stars* (London: British Film Institute, 1979), p. 8.

10. Christine Gledhill, "Introduction," in Christine Gledhill, ed., *Stardom: Industry of Desire* (London: Routledge, 1991), p. xiv.

11. Barry King, "Stardom as an Occupation," in Paul Kerr, ed., *The Holly-wood Film Industry* (London: Routledge and Kegan Paul, 1986), p. 155. See also Cathy Klaprat, "The Star as Market Strategy: Bette Davis in Another Light," in Tino Balio, ed., *The American Film Industry* (Madison: University of Wisconsin Press, 1985); and Hortense Powdermaker, *Hollywood the Dream Factory* (Boston: Little, Brown and Co., 1950).

12. Griswold, "The Fabrication of Meaning," pp. 1080–81; p. 1081.

13. The classic statement of this position is Theodor Adorno and Max Hork-heimer, "The Culture Industry: Enlightenment as Mass Deception," in James Curran, Michael Gurevitch, and Janet Woolacott, eds., *Mass Communication and Society* (Beverly Hills: Sage Publications, 1977).

14. W. Russell Neuman, *The Future of the Mass Audience* (Cambridge: Cambridge University Press, 1991), p. 81. Neuman goes on to demonstrate that none of these claims have been borne out by social science research. Individuals attend to the media selectively and with attention that varies by mood, time of day, medium, and other simultaneous activities; make different uses of the media; have modest recall of media content and are even more modestly affected in behavior; and show no evidence of being more heavily persuaded, informed, or emotionally aroused by visual media than others. See pp. 86–97.

15. There are a number of helpful overviews of approaches to audiences in the fields of mass communications, social psychology, and sociology. See, for example, Elihu Katz, "Communications Research since Lazarsfeld," *Public Opinion Quarterly* 51 (1987): pp. 25–45; Sonia M. Livingstone, *Making Sense of Television: The Psychology of Audience Interpretation* (Oxford: Pergamon Press, 1990), chaps. 1–2; and David Morley, *The "Nationwide" Audience* (London: British Film Institute, 1980), chaps. 1–3.

16. Livingstone, *Making Sense of Television*, p. 21.

17. Neuman, *The Future of the Mass Audience,* p. 89.

18. Livingstone, *Making Sense of Television*, p. 21.

19. John Fiske, *Television Culture* (London: Routledge, 1987), p. 20.

20. Ibid., p. 20.

21. See Stuart Hall, "Culture, the Media, and the 'Ideological Effect,' " in Curran, Gurevitch, and Woolacott, eds., *Mass Communication and Society;* and Morley, *The "Nationwide" Audience.*

22. Morley, *The "Nationwide" Audience,* p. 13.

23. Hall, "Culture, the Media, and the 'Ideological Effect,' " p. 343.

24. John Fiske, "Television: Polysemy and Popularity," *Critical Studies in Mass Communication* (1986): p. 392.

25. Fiske, *Television Culture,* p. 84. On Umberto Eco, see his *The Role of the Reader: Explorations in the Semiotics of Texts* (Bloomington: Indiana University Press, 1979). Sonia Livingstone cautions against conflating the notion of openness with that of indeterminacy. Closed texts, she points out, "are more indeterminate because of their inability to control or anticipate social conditions of reading, while the breadth of vision and demanding nature of the open texts makes unexploited interpretative resources and hence unanticipated reading far less likely" (*Making Sense of Television,* pp. 41–42). Closed texts are produced to favor a

particular reading, in which case a divergent reading is an aberrant one; open texts are produced to ensure multiple readings, in which case divergent readings may "indicate communicative success on the part of the text" (p. 42).

26. Hall, "Culture, the Media, and the 'Ideological Effect,' " p. 344.

27. Fred Fejes, "Critical Mass Communications Research and Media Effects: The Problem of the Disappearing Audience," *Mass Communications Review Yearbook* 5 (1985): p. 520.

28. See Jane Tompkins, "Introduction," in Jane Tompkins, ed., *Reader-Response Criticism* (Baltimore: Johns Hopkins University Press, 1980); W. Iser, "The Reading Process: A Phenomenological Approach," in Tompkins, ed., *Reader-Response Criticism;* H. R. Jauss, *Towards an Aesthetic of Reception* (Minneapolis: University of Minnesota Press, 1982).

29. Morley, *The "Nationwide" Audience.* Morley borrows this overall framework (dominant, negotiated, oppositional) from Frank Parkin, *Class Inequality and Political Order* (London: Paladin, 1973). For more on subcultural dynamics, see Dick Hebdige, *Subculture: The Meaning of Style* (London: Methuen, 1986).

30. Elihu Katz and Tamar Liebes, "Decoding Dallas," in Horace Newcomb, ed., *Television: The Critical View* (New York: Oxford University Press, 1987); and Tamar Liebes and Elihu Katz, *The Export of Meaning: Cross-Cultural Readings of Dallas* (New York: Oxford University Press, 1990). For a comparative study with similar findings, in this case of "readings" of Madonna's music videos by different American groups, see Jane D. Brown and Laurie Schulze, "The Effects of Race, Gender, and Fandom on Audience Interpretations of Madonna's Music Videos," *Journal of Communication* 40, no. 2 (Spring 1990): pp. 88–102.

31. Janice Radway, *Reading the Romance: Women, Patriarchy, and Popular Literature* (Chapel Hill: University of North Carolina Press, 1984), pp. 55, 16–17. See also the findings of Wendy Griswold in "The Fabrication of Meaning."

32. See Anselm L. Strauss, *Qualitative Analysis for Social Scientists* (Cambridge: Cambridge University Press, 1987).

33. I use the term "celebrity text" broadly, to connote a single interpretable landscape that is in fact "intertextual," composed from various sorts of texts (formal performances, media coverage, biographical and autobiographical writings). See Richard deCordova, "The Emergence of the Star System in America," in Gledhill, ed., *Stardom.* This treatment of cultural forms is a common one in cultural studies: cultural forms as composed of discrete artifacts but forming a larger unit (formula, genre, and so forth) whose meaning cannot be gleaned from any single work. See, for example, the essays in Modleski, ed., *Studies in Entertainment;* and John G. Cawelti, *Adventure, Mystery, and Romance: Formula Stories as Art and Popular Culture* (Chicago: University of Chicago Press, 1976).

34. Cleveland Amory and Frederic Bradlee, eds., *Vanity Fair: Selections from America's Most Memorable Magazine* (New York: Viking Press, 1960); Barbara Gelman, ed., *Photoplay Treasury* (New York: Bonanza Books, 1972); and Martin Levin, ed., *Hollywood and the Great Fan Magazines* (New York: Arbor House, 1970).

35. I was told early on that access to observation of these people at work would be difficult to achieve. That, coupled with the fact that I needed to under-

stand a broad range of players, that no single setting would provide what I needed, ruled out the otherwise promising method of participant observation in the production system.

36. See Elliot Mishler, *Research Interviewing: Context and Narrative* (Cambridge, Mass.: Harvard University Press, 1986).

37. Michael Burawoy, "Introduction," in Burawoy, et al., *Ethnography Unbound: Power and Resistance in the Modern Metropolis* (Berkeley: University of California Press, 1991), p. 2. Burawoy takes this further, arguing that participant observation is "the paradigmatic way of studying the social world" by highlighting and combining understanding and explanation, the hermeneutic and the scientific dimensions of social science (pp. 3–5). For more on the technique itself, see John Lofland and Lyn Lofland, *Analyzing Social Settings* (Belmont, Calif.: Wadsworth, 1984); and Leonard Schatzman and Anselm Strauss, *Field Research: Strategies for a Natural Sociology* (Englewood Cliffs, N.J.: Prentice-Hall, 1973).

38. William A. Gamson, *Talking Politics* (Cambridge: Cambridge University Press, 1992), pp. 191–94. On focus-group methodology, see David L. Morgan, *Focus Groups as Qualitative Research* (Newbury Park, Calif.: Sage Publications, 1988).

Works Cited

Adorno, Theodor, and Max Horkheimer. "The Culture Industry: Enlightenment as Mass Deception." In *Mass Communication and Society,* edited by James Curran, Michael Gurevitch, and Janet Woolacott. Beverly Hills: Sage Publications, 1977.

Affron, Charles. *Star Acting: Gish, Garbo, Davis.* New York: Dutton, 1977.

Agnew, Jean-Christophe. *Worlds Apart: The Market and the Theater in Anglo-American Thought, 1550–1750.* New York: Cambridge University Press, 1986.

Alberoni, Francesco. "The Powerless 'Elite': Theory and Sociological Research on the Phenomenon of the Stars." In *Sociology of Mass Communications,* edited by Denis McQuail. Harmondsworth, England: Penguin Books, 1972.

Allen, Robert C. "The Movies in Vaudeville: Historical Context of the Movies as Popular Entertainment." In *The American Film Industry,* rev. ed., edited by Tino Balio. Madison: University of Wisconsin Press, 1985.

Allen, Robert C., and Douglas Gomery. *Film History: Theory and Practice.* New York: Alfred A. Knopf, 1985.

Alter, Jonathan. "The Art of the Deals." *Newsweek,* January 9, 1989, pp. 58–59.

Amory, Cleveland. "Who Killed Hollywood Society?" *TV Guide,* October 28, 1967, pp. 4–8; November 4, 1967, pp. 29–32; November 11, 1967, pp. 27–32; November 18, 1967, pp. 26–40; November 25, 1967, pp. 32–36.

Amory, Cleveland, and Frederic Bradlee, eds. *Vanity Fair: Selections from America's Most Memorable Magazine.* New York: Viking Press, 1960.

Anger, Kenneth. *Hollywood Babylon.* New York: Delta, 1975.

Balio, Tino, ed. *The American Film Industry,* rev. ed. Madison: University of Wisconsin Press, 1985.

Ball, Aimee Lee. "The Starmakers." *New Woman,* November 1988, pp. 121–24.

Barber, Rowland. "Just a Little List." *TV Guide,* August 10, 1974, pp. 4–8.

Barnum, P. T. *Struggles and Triumphs.* Edited by Carl Bode. Harmondsworth, England: Penguin Books, 1981.

Bart, Peter. "Well, What's an Interview For?" *New York Times,* March 27, 1966, p. X13.

Baudrillard, Jean. "Simulacra and Simulations." In *Jean Baudrillard: Selected Writings,* edited by Mark Poster. Stanford: Stanford University Press, 1988.

Bell, Joseph N. "Canonizing the Superficial." *Saturday Review,* October 8, 1966, p. 115.

Benjamin, Walter. "The Work of Art in the Age of Mechanical Reproduction." In *Illuminations.* New York: Schocken, 1968.

Berger, John. *Ways of Seeing.* London: British Broadcasting System, 1972.

Bernays, Edward L. "The Engineering of Consent." *Annals of the American Political and Social Science Association* 250 (March 1947): pp. 113–20.

———. "Manipulating Public Opinion: The Why and the How." *American Journal of Sociology* 33 (1928): pp. 958–71.

———. *Public Relations.* Norman: University of Oklahoma Press, 1952.

Bernstein, Carl. "The Idiot Culture." *San Francisco Chronicle,* July 26, 1992, This World section, pp. 7–11.

Billig, Michael. *Talking of the Royal Family.* London: Routledge, 1992.

Blyskal, Jeff, and Marie Blyskal. *PR: How the Public Relations Industry Writes the News.* New York: William Morrow and Co., 1985.

Bode, Carl. "Introduction" in P. T. Barnum, *Struggles and Triumphs.* Harmondsworth, England: Penguin Books, 1981.

Boehnel, William. "Dietrich Is Still Selling Glamour." In *Hollywood and the Great Fan Magazines,* edited by Martin Levin. New York: Arbor House, 1970.

Boorstin, Daniel J. *The Image: A Guide to Pseudo-Events in America.* New York: Harper and Row, 1961.

Bourdieu, Pierre. *Distinction: A Social Critique of the Judgement of Taste.* Cambridge, Mass.: Harvard University Press, 1984.

Brantlinger, Patrick. *Bread and Circuses: Theories of Mass Culture as Social Decay.* New York: Cornell University Press, 1985.

Braudy, Leo. *The Frenzy of Renown: Fame and Its History.* New York: Oxford University Press, 1986.

Brown, Jane, and Laurie Schulze. "The Effects of Race, Gender, and Fandom on Audience Interpretations of Madonna's Music Videos." *Journal of Communication* 40, no. 2 (Spring 1990): pp. 88–102.

Burawoy, Michael, Alice Burton, Ann Arnett Ferguson, Kathryn J. Fox, Joshua Gamson, Nadine Gartrell, Leslie Hurst, Charles Kurzman, Leslie Salzinger, Josepha Schiffman, and Shiori Ui. *Ethnography Unbound: Power and Resistance in the Modern Metropolis.* Berkeley: University of California Press, 1991.

"Bush Is Overheard Asking If He Gave 'Proper Answer.' " *San Francisco Chronicle,* November 27, 1991.

Cantor, Muriel. *The Hollywood TV Producer.* New Brunswick, N.J.: Transaction Books, 1988.

Carey, Alex. "Reshaping the Truth: Pragmatists and Propagandists in America." In *American Media and Mass Culture,* edited by Donald Lazare. Berkeley: University of California Press, 1987.

Cawelti, John G. *Adventure, Mystery, and Romance: Formula Stories as Art and Popular Culture.* Chicago: University of Chicago Press, 1976.

"Celebrity Unlimited." *American Mercury,* February 1944, pp. 204–5.

Cieply, Michael. "Hollywood's High-Powered Image Machine." *Los Angeles Times Magazine,* July 10, 1988.

Cohn, Alfred. "What Every Girl Wants to Know." In *Photoplay Treasury,* edited by Barbara Gelman. New York: Bonanza Books, 1972.

Costello, Michael. "They Pronounce It Pre-meer." *Reader's Digest,* February 1941, pp. 88–92.

Crawford, Joan. "The Story of a Dancing Girl." In *Photoplay Treasury,* edited by Barbara Gelman. New York: Bonanza Books, 1972.

Danahy, Michael. "Blonde Ambition." *Los Angeles,* October 1987, pp. 56–62.

deCordova, Richard. "The Emergence of the Star System in America." In *Stardom: Industry of Desire,* edited by Christine Gledhill. London: Routledge, 1991.

———. *Picture Personalities: The Emergence of the Star System in America.* Urbana: University of Illinois Press, 1990.

de Roos, Robert. "Hollywood's Mother Hen." *TV Guide,* November 4, 1961, pp. 28–30.

"Does TV Drama Need a Star System?" *TV Guide,* October 30, 1953, pp. 5–7.

Dorfman, Ariel. *The Empire's Old Clothes: What the Lone Ranger, Babar, and Other Innocent Heroes Do to Our Minds.* New York: Pantheon, 1983.

Dyer, Richard. "*A Star Is Born* and the Construction of Authenticity." In *Stardom: Industry of Desire,* edited by Christine Gledhill. London: Routledge, 1991.

———. *Stars.* London: British Film Institute, 1979.

Eco, Umberto. *The Role of the Reader: Explorations in the Semiotics of Texts.* Bloomington: Indiana University Press, 1979.

Eddy, Don. "Hollywood Spies on You." *American Magazine,* July 1940.

Efron, Edith. "How to Manufacture a Celebrity." *TV Guide,* August 11, 1967, pp. 16–19.

Elliott, Philip. "Media Organizations and Occupations: An Overview." In *Mass Communication and Society,* edited by James Curran, Michael Gurevitch, and Janet Woolacott. Beverly Hills: Sage Publications, 1977.

Ephron, Nora. "Famous First Words." *Esquire,* June 1989, pp. 103–5.

Ewen, Stuart. *All Consuming Images: The Politics of Style in Contemporary Culture.* New York: Basic Books, 1989.

"Fame." *Nation,* October 28, 1931, p. 450.

"Familiar Gestures." *TV Guide,* March 26, 1954.

Fejes, Fred. "Critical Mass Communications Research and Media Effects: The Problem of the Disappearing Audience." *Mass Communications Review Yearbook* 5 (1985): pp. 517–30.

Ferber, Edna. "They Earn Their Millions." *Collier's,* December 4, 1920, pp. 7–8.

"The Final Fling." In *Hollywood and the Great Fan Magazines,* edited by Martin Levin. New York: Arbor House, 1970.

Fiske, John. "Television: Polysemy and Popularity." *Critical Studies in Mass Communication* 3 (1986): pp. 391–408.

———. *Television Culture.* London: Routledge, 1987.

"For the Stars, the Postman Always Rings *More* than Twice." *TV Guide,* December 29, 1956, pp. 4–6.

Foster, Hal, ed. *The Anti-Aesthetic: Essays in Postmodern Culture.* Port Townsend, Wash.: Bay Press, 1983.

Fox, Richard Wightman, and T. J. Jackson Lears, eds. *The Culture of Consumption: Critical Essays in American History, 1880–1980.* New York: Pantheon, 1983.

Francis, Arlene. "Just Be Yourself." *TV Guide,* September 3, 1960, pp. 4–7.

Freidson, Eliot. "The Changing Nature of Professional Control." *Annual Review of Sociology* (1984): pp. 1–20.

Fuhrman, Candice Jacobson. *Publicity Stunt!* San Francisco: Chronicle Books, 1989.

Gaines, Jane. *Contested Culture: The Image, the Voice, and the Law.* Chapel Hill: University of North Carolina Press, 1991.

Gamson, William A. *Talking Politics.* Cambridge: Cambridge University Press, 1992.

Gandy, Oscar. *Beyond Agenda Setting.* Norwood, N.J.: Ablex Publishing, 1982.

Gans, Herbert J. *Deciding What's News.* New York: Vintage Books, 1979.

Geertz, Clifford. *The Interpretation of Cultures.* New York: Basic Books, 1973.

Gelman, Barbara, ed. *Photoplay Treasury.* New York: Bonanza Books, 1972.

"Gene Schwam: The P.R. Role." *Hollywood Reporter,* 52nd Annual, December 1982, pp. 104–5.

Gitlin, Todd. *Inside Prime Time.* New York: Pantheon, 1983.

———. "On Being Sound-Bitten: Reflections on Truth, Impression, and Belief in a Time of Media Saturation." *Boston Review,* December 1991, pp. 15–17.

———. "Postmodernism: Roots and Politics." In *Cultural Politics in Contemporary America,* edited by Ian Angus and Sut Jhally. New York: Routledge, 1989.

———. Review of *Rolling Stone: The Photographs. New York Times,* December 3, 1989, p. G14.

———. *The Whole World Is Watching: Mass Media in the Making and Unmaking of the New Left.* Berkeley: University of California Press, 1980.

Gledhill, Christine, ed. *Stardom: Industry of Desire.* London: Routledge, 1991.

Goffman, Erving. *The Presentation of Self in Everyday Life.* Garden City, N.Y.: Doubleday Anchor Books, 1959.

Goldfarb, Jeffrey. *The Cynical Society: The Culture of Politics and the Politics of Culture in American Life.* Chicago: University of Chicago Press, 1991.

Goldsmith, Barbara. "The Meaning of Celebrity." *New York Times Magazine,* December 4, 1983, pp. 75–83.

Goode, William J. *The Celebration of Heroes: Prestige as a Social Control System.* Berkeley: University of California Press, 1978.

"Gore's Speech at Bay Plant Challenged." *San Francisco Chronicle,* August 4, 1992, p. A1.

Gray, Spalding. "The Haul of Fame." *Rolling Stone,* May 21, 1987.

Greene, Theodore. *America's Heroes: The Changing Models of Success in American Magazines.* New York: Oxford University Press, 1970.

Griswold, Wendy. "The Fabrication of Meaning: Literary Interpretation in the United States, Great Britain, and the West Indies." *American Journal of Sociology* 92 (1987): pp. 1077–1117.

Grunig, James, and Todd Hunt. *Managing Public Relations.* New York: CBS College Publishing, 1984.

Hall, Stuart. "Culture, the Media, and the 'Ideological Effect.' " In *Mass Communication and Society,* edited by James Curran, Michael Gurevitch, and Janet Woolacott. Beverly Hills: Sage Publications, 1977.

Harris, Daniel. "Blonde Ambitions: The Rise of Madonna Studies." *Harper's,* August 1992, pp. 30–33.

Harris, Neil. *Humbug: The Art of P. T. Barnum.* Boston: Little, Brown and Co., 1973.

Hebdige, Dick. *Subculture: The Meaning of Style.* London: Methuen, 1986.

Henry, William A. "Pssst . . . Did You Hear About?" *Time,* March 5, 1990, pp. 46–51.

"Here's a New Way to Fame." *People,* June 22, 1987, p. 73.

Hertsgaard, Mark. *On Bended Knee: The Press and the Reagan Presidency.* New York: Farrar Straus Giroux, 1988.

Hirsch, Paul. "Processing Fads and Fashions: An Organization-Set Analysis of Cultural Industry Systems." *American Journal of Sociology* 77 (1972): pp. 639–59.

———. "Social Science Approaches to Popular Culture." *Journal of Popular Culture* 11 (1977): pp. 401–13.

Hirschberg, Lynn. "The Power of Hot." *Rolling Stone,* May 22, 1986, pp. 25–28.

Hobson, Dick. "The Hollywood Flack." *TV Guide,* April 12, 1969, pp. 6–11.

——— "The 10 Percenter." *TV Guide,* December 28, 1968, pp. 4–9.

Holmes, Oliver Wendell. "The Stereoscope and the Stereograph." *Atlantic Monthly,* June 1859, pp. 738–48.

Hopper, Hedda, and James Brough. *The Whole Truth and Nothing But.* Garden City, N.Y.: Doubleday and Co., 1963.

Horton, Donald, and R. Richard Wohl. "Mass Communication and Para-Social Interaction: Observations on Intimacy at a Distance." *Psychiatry* 19, no. 3 (August 1956): pp. 215–29.

"How Fleet It Is!" *People,* December 28, 1987–January 4, 1988, pp. 88–91.

"How Stars Are Made." Transcript 02204 of "Donahue," February 20, 1984. Cincinnati: Multimedia Entertainment, Inc.

"How To Make It in Hollywood." Transcript 128 of "Geraldo," March 17, 1988. New York: Investigative News Group, Inc.

Hoyt, Caroline Somers. "It's Ruby's Turn Now!" In *Hollywood and the Great Fan Magazines,* edited by Martin Levin. New York: Arbor House, 1970.

Huizinga, Johan. *Homo Ludens: A Study of the Play Element in Culture.* Boston: Beacon Press, 1956.

"Introducing . . ." *People,* March 4, 1974, p. 2.

Iser, W. "The Reading Process: A Phenomenological Approach." In *Reader-Response Criticism,* edited by Jane Tompkins. Baltimore: Johns Hopkins University Press, 1980.

Jameson, Fredric. "Postmodernism and Consumer Society." In *The Anti-Aesthetic: Essays on Postmodern Culture,* edited by Hal Foster. Port Townsend, Wash.: Bay Press, 1983.

Jamieson, Kathleen Hall. *Packaging the Presidency: A History and Criticism of Presidential Campaign Advertising.* New York: Oxford University Press, 1984.

Jauss, H. R. *Towards an Aesthetic of Reception.* Minneapolis: University of Minnesota Press, 1982.

Javits, Jacob K. "You Can't Fool the Camera." *TV Guide,* October 1, 1960, pp. 8–11.

Joel, Peter. "The First True Story of Garbo's Childhood." In *Hollywood and the Great Fan Magazines,* edited by Martin Levin. New York: Arbor House, 1970.

Jones, Landon Y. "Road Warriors." *People,* July 20, 1992, pp. 68–79.

Kaplan, Ann E. *Rocking Around the Clock: Music Television, Postmodernism, and Consumer Culture.* New York: Methuen, 1987.

Katz, Elihu. "Communications Research since Lazarsfeld." *Public Opinion Quarterly* 51 (1987): pp. 25–45.

Katz, Elihu, and Tamar Liebes. "Decoding Dallas." In *Television: The Critical View,* edited by Horace Newcomb. New York: Oxford University Press, 1987.

Kehr, David. "A Star Is Made." *Film Comment,* January–February 1979, pp. 8–12.

Kendall, Elaine. "Success (?) Secret of the Starmakers." *New York Times Magazine,* September 30, 1962, pp. 37–40.

King, Barry. "Stardom as an Occupation." In *The Hollywood Film Industry,* edited by Paul Kerr. London: Routledge and Kegan Paul, 1986.

Klaprat, Cathy. "The Star as Market Strategy: Bette Davis in Another Light." In *The American Film Industry,* rev. ed., edited by Tino Balio. Madison: University of Wisconsin Press, 1985.

Koch, Neal. "The Hollywood Treatment." *Columbia Journalism Review* (January/February 1991): pp. 25–31.

Lahr, John. "Notes on Fame." *Harper's,* January 1978, pp. 77–80.

Lee, Sonia. "Jean Harlow: From Extra to Star." In *Hollywood and the Great Fan Magazines,* edited by Martin Levin. New York: Arbor House, 1970.

Lemann, Nicholas. "Confidence Games." *The New Republic,* November 5, 1991, pp. 27–34.

Levin, Martin, ed. *Hollywood and the Great Fan Magazines.* New York: Arbor House, 1970.

Liebes, Tamar, and Elihu Katz. *The Export of Meaning: Cross-Cultural Readings of Dallas.* New York: Oxford University Press, 1990.

Lippmann, Walter. "Blazing Publicity: Why We Know So Much about 'Peaches' Browning, Valentino, Lindbergh and Queen Marie." In *Vanity Fair: Selections from America's Most Memorable Magazine,* edited by Cleveland Amory and Frederic Bradlee. New York: Viking Press, 1960.

Livingstone, Sonia M. *Making Sense of Television: The Psychology of Audience Interpretation.* Oxford: Pergamon Press, 1990.

Lockwood, Arthur. "Press Agent Tells All." *American Mercury,* February 1940, pp. 173–80.

Lofland, John, and Lyn Lofland. *Analyzing Social Settings.* Belmont, Calif.: Wadsworth, 1984.

Lowenthal, Leo. "The Triumph of Mass Idols." In *Literature, Popular Culture, and Society.* Palo Alto, Calif.: Pacific Books, 1968.

Ludwig, Emil. "What Makes a Man Stand Out from the Crowd?" *American Magazine,* May 1930, p. 15.

MacAloon, John J. "Olympic Games and the Theory of Spectacle in Modern Societies." In *Rite, Drama, Festival, Spectacle: Rehearsals toward a Theory of Cultural Performance.* Philadelphia: Institute for the Study of Human Issues, 1981.

Macpherson, C. B. *The Political Theory of Possessive Individualism.* New York: Oxford University Press, 1962.

Maddox, Ben. "The One Star Who Has No Enemies." In *Hollywood and the Great Fan Magazines,* edited by Martin Levin. New York: Arbor House, 1970.

————."What about Clark Gable Now?" In *Hollywood and the Great Fan Magazines,* edited by Martin Levin. New York: Arbor House, 1970.

"The Making of Billy Gable." *Life,* Spring 1989, pp. 53–54.

Marcus, Greil. *Lipstick Traces: A Secret History of the Twentieth Century.* Cambridge, Mass.: Harvard University Press, 1989.

Marowitz, Charles. "The Angel of Publicity." *Los Angeles Herald Examiner,* September 24, 1989, pp. E1, E9.

Martel, Jay. "Sweet Fifteen." *Rolling Stone,* May 21, 1987, p. 91.

"Mary Hart's Voice Triggers Seizures." *San Francisco Chronicle,* July 11, 1991, p. A3.

May, Lary. *Screening Out the Past: The Birth of Mass Culture and the Motion Picture Industry.* New York: Oxford University Press, 1980.

Meyer, John W., and Brian Rowan. "Institutionalized Organizations: Formal Structure as Myth and Ceremony." In *Organizational Environments: Ritual and Rationality,* edited by John W. Meyer and W. Richard Scott. Beverly Hills: Sage Publications, 1983.

Meyrowitz, Joshua. *No Sense of Place: The Impact of Electronic Media on Social Behavior.* New York: Oxford University Press, 1985.

Miller, Mark Crispin. *Boxed In: The Culture of TV.* Evanston, Ill.: Northwestern University Press, 1988.

Mills, C. Wright. *The Power Elite.* London: Oxford University Press, 1956.

Mishler, Elliot. *Research Interviewing: Context and Narrative.* Cambridge, Mass.: Harvard University Press, 1986.

Mitroff, Ian, and Warren Bennis. *The Unreality Industry: The Deliberate Manufacturing of Falsehood and What It Is Doing to Our Lives.* New York: Carol Publishing Group, 1989.

Modleski, Tania, ed. *Studies in Entertainment: Critical Approaches to Mass Culture.* Bloomington: Indiana University Press, 1986.

Monaco, James. *Celebrity.* New York: Delta, 1978.

Morgan, David L. *Focus Groups as Qualitative Research.* Newbury Park, Calif.: Sage Publications, 1988.

Morgan, Thomas. "Gentlemen of the Pressure." *TV Guide,* October 19, 1963, pp. 6–9; October 26, 1963, pp. 22–24; November 2, 1963, pp. 22–24.

Morin, Edgar. *The Stars.* New York: Grove Press, 1960.

Morley, David. *The "Nationwide" Audience*. London: British Film Institute, 1980.

Mulvey, Laura. "Visual Pleasure and Narrative Cinema." *Screen* 16, no. 3 (Autumn 1975): 6–18.

National Association of Fan Clubs. Information Sheet. 1991.

Neuman, W. Russell. *The Future of the Mass Audience*. Cambridge: Cambridge University Press, 1991.

———. *The Paradox of Mass Politics*. Cambridge, Mass.: Harvard University Press, 1986.

"The New Hollywood." *Life*, November 4, 1940, pp. 65–67.

Olasky, Marvin N. *Corporate Public Relations: A New Historical Perspective*. Hillsdale, N.J.: Lawrence Erlbaum Associates, 1987.

O'Malley, Frank Ward. "Hot off the Press Agent." *Saturday Evening Post*, June 25, 1921.

Parenti, Michael. *Make-Believe Media: The Politics of Entertainment*. New York: St. Martin's Press, 1992.

Parkin, Frank. *Class Inequality and Political Order*. London: Paladin, 1973.

"The People Perplex." *Newsweek*, June 6, 1977, pp. 89–90.

Peterson, Richard. "Revitalizing the Culture Concept." *Annual Review of Sociology* 5 (1979): pp. 137–66.

Ponce de Leon, Charles L. "Idols and Icons: Representations of Celebrity in American Culture, 1850–1940." Ph.D. diss., Rutgers University, 1992.

Poster, Mark, ed. *Jean Baudrillard: Selected Writings*. Stanford: Stanford University Press, 1988.

Postman, Neil. *Amusing Ourselves to Death: Public Discourse in the Age of Show Business*. New York: Penguin Books, 1985.

Powdermaker, Hortense. *Hollywood the Dream Factory*. Boston: Little, Brown and Co., 1950.

Radway, Janice. *Reading the Romance: Women, Patriarchy, and Popular Literature*. Chapel Hill: University of North Carolina Press, 1984.

Rein, Irving J., Philip Kotler, and Martin R. Stoller. *High Visibility*. New York: Dodd, Mead and Co., 1987.

Rogin, Michael. *Ronald Reagan, the Movie, and Other Episodes in Political Demonology*. Berkeley: University of California Press, 1987.

Rosetree, Laura. "Every Face Has a Secret." *Redbook*, April 1990, pp. 54–55.

Ross, Andrew. *No Respect: Intellectuals and Popular Culture*. New York: Routledge, 1989.

Rothman, Stanley, and Robert Lerner. "Television and the Communications Revolution." *Society* 26, no. 1 (November/December 1988): 64–70.

Schatzman, Leonard, and Anselm Strauss. *Field Research: Strategies for a Natural Sociology*. Englewood Cliffs, N.J.: Prentice-Hall, 1973.

Schickel, Richard. *Intimate Strangers: The Culture of Celebrity*. New York: Fromm International, 1985.

Schiller, Herbert. *The Mind Managers*. Boston: Beacon Press, 1973.

Schrag, Peter. "Heeere's Johnny!" In *Celebrity*, edited by James Monaco. New York: Delta, 1978.

Schudson, Michael. *Advertising: The Uneasy Persuasion.* New York: Basic Books, 1984.

———. "Delectable Materialism: Were the Critics of Consumer Culture Wrong All Along?" *American Prospect* 1, no. 5 (Spring 1991): pp. 26–35.

———. *Discovering the News: A Social History of American Newspapers.* New York: Basic Books, 1978.

———. "The New Validation of Popular Culture: Sense and Sentimentality in Academia." In *Critical Perspectives on Media and Society,* edited by Robert Avery and David Eason. New York: Guilford Press, 1991.

Schwartz, Barry. *George Washington: The Making of an American Symbol.* New York: The Free Press, 1987.

Sennett, Richard. "The Decline of Public Discourse." *Contemporary Sociology* 21 (1992): pp. 15–17.

Service, Faith. "So You'd Like to Be a Star: Myrna Loy Shows You What Is Back of Hollywood's Glamor Front." In *Hollywood and the Great Fan Magazines,* edited by Martin Levin. New York: Arbor House, 1970.

Shaw, Ellen. "Never Get Riled, Don't Knock Women, Chefs—and Bring Your Own Pillow." *TV Guide,* October 2, 1982, pp. 56–60.

Sigal, Leon. *Reporters and Officials: The Organization and Politics of Newsmaking.* Lexington, Mass.: D. C. Heath, 1973.

Sorkin, Michael. "Faking It." In *Watching Television,* edited by Todd Gitlin. New York: Pantheon Books, 1986.

Spacks, Patricia Meyer. *Gossip.* New York: Alfred A. Knopf, 1985.

Staiger, Janet. "Seeing Stars." In *Stardom: Industry of Desire,* edited by Christine Gledhill. London: Routledge, 1991.

"Starlets Are World's Most Envied of Girls." *Life,* January 29, 1940, pp. 37–39.

"The State of Celebrity 1990." *Spy,* January 1990, pp. 59–69.

Stauth, Cameron. "The Secrets of Hollywood's Casting Directors." *TV Guide,* April 2, 1988, pp. 2–6.

Strauss, Anselm. *Qualitative Analysis for Social Scientists.* Cambridge: Cambridge University Press, 1987.

"The Stuff That Stars Are Made Of." *TV Guide,* January 5, 1957, pp. 8–11.

Sudjic, Deyan. *Cult Heroes.* New York: W. W. Norton and Co., 1989.

Sullivan, Andrew. "Buying and Nothingness." *New Republic,* May 8, 1989, pp. 37–41.

Susman, Warren. *Culture as History.* New York: Pantheon, 1984.

Taylor, John Russell. "The Image Makers." *American Film,* July-August 1976, pp. 23–26.

Taylor, Robert. "Why Did I Slip?" In *Hollywood and the Great Fan Magazines,* edited by Martin Levin. New York: Arbor House, 1970.

"Television's Biggest Struggle: The Battle of Billings." *TV Guide,* October 4, 1958, pp. 21–23.

Thomas, Karen. "An Aura Can Be Honed but Not Created." *USA Today,* January 4, 1991, pp. D1–2.

Toll, Robert C. *On with the Show: The First Century of Show Business in America.* New York: Oxford University Press, 1976.

Tompkins, Jane, ed. *Reader-Response Criticism.* Baltimore: Johns Hopkins University Press, 1980.

"The Truth about Groucho's Ad Libs." *TV Guide,* March 19, 1954, pp. 5–7.

Tuchman, Gaye. *Making News: A Study in the Construction of Reality.* New York: Free Press, 1978.

Tudor, Andrew. *Image and Influence: Studies in the Sociology of Film.* New York: St. Martin's Press, 1974.

Walker, Alexander. *Stardom: The Hollywood Phenomenon.* New York: Stein and Day, 1970.

Warga, Wayne. "The Three Stages of Hollywood Stardom." *TV Guide,* October 9, 1982, pp. 4–10.

"What Should I do? Your Problems Answered by Bette Davis." In *Photoplay Treasury,* edited by Barbara Gelman. New York: Bonanza Books, 1972.

White, Cynthia, and Harrison White. "Institutional Change in the French Painting World." In *The Arts in Society,* edited by R. N. Wilson. Englewood Cliffs, N.J.: Prentice-Hall, 1964.

Williams, Raymond. "Base and Superstructure in Marxist Cultural Theory." *New Left Review* 82 (November–December 1973): pp. 3–16.

Workman, Chuck. *Superstar: The Life and Times of Andy Warhol.* Marilyn Lewis Entertainment, Ltd., 1990.

Wright, Will. *Sixguns and Society: A Structural Analysis of the Western.* Berkeley: University of California Press, 1975.

Yoffe, Emily. "E! Is for Entertainment—Twenty-Four Hours a Day." *Newsweek,* August 12, 1991, p. 58.

Zeman, Ned. "The Adoration of the Elvii." *Newsweek,* April 22, 1991, pp. 62–63.

Index

Compositor: Maryland Composition
Text: 10/13 Sabon
Display: Sabon
Printer: Maple-Vail Book Mfg. Group
Binder: Maple-Vail Book Mfg. Group